World Hunger
and
Moral Obligation

World Hunger
and
Moral Obligation

EDITED BY

WILLIAM AIKEN
Chatham College

HUGH LA FOLLETTE
University of Alabama in Birmingham

PRENTICE-HALL, INC., ENGLEWOOD CLIFFS, NEW JERSEY 07632

Library of Congress Cataloging in Publication Data

Main entry under title:

World hunger and moral obligation.

    Bibliography: p.
     1. Food supply—Addresses, essays, lectures.
2. Food relief—Moral and religious aspects—Addresses,
essays, lectures. I. Aiken, William (date)
II. LaFollette, Hugh (date)
HD9000.6.W62   179   76-56381
ISBN 0-13-967968-5
ISBN 0-13-967950-2 pbk.

PRENTICE-HALL INTERNATIONAL, INC., *London*
PRENTICE-HALL OF AUSTRALIA PTY. LIMITED, *Sydney*
PRENTICE-HALL OF CANADA, LTD., *Toronto*
PRENTICE-HALL OF INDIA PRIVATE LIMITED, *New Delhi*
PRENTICE-HALL OF JAPAN, INC., *Tokyo*
PRENTICE-HALL OF SOUTHEAST ASIA PTE. LTD., *Singapore*

CONTENTS

v

PREFACE

Many people in the world cannot get enough to eat; at least ten thousand a day die from starvation. Those of us who live in affluent nations could do something about this situation. This volume of essays examines the question: What *ought* we to do about world hunger? Although it does not provide a final answer, it should stimulate others to consider the *moral* aspects of this problem.

We do not want to profit from other people's misery, nor do we want to give the impression that philosophical discussion alone can solve moral problems. So we intend to donate whatever money we receive from the sale of this book to famine relief. In addition, many of the contributors to this volume have instructed us to donate their honorariums. As you read this book, we hope you will not forget that in moral problems, thinking and action are inseparable.

This book is designed to engage the reader—to encourage reflection and intellectual involvement. We have asked many questions, both in the introduction and in the editors' paragraphs before each essay, to stimulate your thinking. There are no easy answers and no automatic solutions. As you read these essays, you must decide for yourself what *ought* to be done about world hunger.

World Hunger
and
Moral Obligation

INTRODUCTION

Widespread world hunger is a reality. At least 10,000 people die of starvation every day; as many as two billion more are malnourished. This hunger —real hunger—is not something one "feels" before a leisurely steak dinner. Nor is it the stomach pangs we sometimes experience while on a diet. For many people, hunger is not a passing discomfort; it is an ever-present reality. One-fourth of the world's population is caught in this cycle of hunger, sickness, and death. Hunger continues day after day, year after year; all too often death is the only release from suffering. Yet, a portion of the world's population—those in more affluent nations—seem unfamiliar with its reality, unaware of its scope, and unconcerned by its destructiveness. But it is there, nonetheless.

What is the reaction of those in affluent nations to widespread hunger? Actually, most of them don't react at all, for hunger is not something they personally confront, even though the presence of intercontinental communication has begun broadcasting its reality. They see it on the news, but they don't grasp its actuality; it seems too far away. Only a few have asked: "What do I think about world hunger?"

What *do* I think about world hunger? Or maybe it would be better to ask: "What should I think about it?" Well, we might think about the agricultural innovations which are necessary to produce sufficient food to feed the world, or we might discuss the political benefits of helping (or failing to help) malnourished or starving people. These may well be interesting, even important, questions. But they are not our primary question. Our question—the question raised in this book—is a moral one: What moral responsibility do affluent nations (or those people in them) have to the starving masses? Hunger is present; there's no doubt about that. But what is the moral response to it?

This question does not generate an easy response; that is why it is a moral *problem*. There are numerous sincere opinions about what the moral response should be. This immediately brings us to an important consideration: Why do we regard this as a moral question at all? There certainly

1

are other ways to look at it. Why not presume it is *merely* a prudential question—one which is decided not by reference to moral considerations, but rather by ascertaining how providing needed food assistance would benefit an individual giver, a nation, a civilization, or the species? To answer this we need to know how to identify a moral question, which is a difficult task.[1] However, it seems clear to us (the editors) that, since this issue could (and in some sense already does) affect everyone in the world, if anything is a moral question, world hunger is. The contributors to this volume agree. Most begin with the assumption that it is a moral question (Frankena, in "Moral Philosophy and World Hunger," discusses the issue in some detail). They obviously think, as do we, that it is an only-too-reasonable assumption to make; it is difficult to imagine how one could suppose otherwise.

Of course, even if we decide that world hunger is a moral concern—one that should be evaluated on the criteria of morality rather than (solely) on grounds of self-interest—we have still not made it very far. For even if we know the issue should be considered on moral grounds, we do not know whether anyone is morally required to *do* anything to ease the world hunger problem.[2] It may be that although it would be good to feed the starving, it is, nonetheless, not something anyone is morally required to do. On this view, helping the starving would be an act of charity and, therefore, a good thing to do; it might even make the agent a better person.

Other thinkers, of course, might disagree with the claim that helping the starving—at least some of them—is good at all. Joseph Fletcher and Garrett Hardin argue, for example, that we are morally required *not* to feed (at least some of) the starving—it would be wrong to feed them.[3] The consequences of indiscriminate feeding, they say, would be disastrous. Hardin claims it would ultimately threaten the human species; Fletcher argues it would damage recipient nations. Both contend it would greatly increase human misery. Thus, they conclude, one should not feed (all) the starving.

There seem to be three major alternative positions an individual can take assuming (as we are) that this is a moral question. One can claim that: 1) well-off people should feed the starving, it would be wrong not to feed them; 2) it would be good to help, although it is not morally required; or

---

[1]See G. Wallace and A. D. M. Walker, eds., *The Definition of Morality* (London: Methuen and Co. Ltd., 1970).

[2]Throughout this introductory essay, we will speak loosely of individuals being 'morally required,' 'having a duty,' or 'having an obligation,' as meaning that an individual is required by moral rules (whether ideal or actual) to assist the hungry. The distinguishing feature of such duties is that an individual is morally required to act even if he does not want, on grounds of self-interest, to do so. However, we are purposively varying use of these terms to familiarize the reader with the range of expressions utilized by the essayists in this book.

[3]Fletcher's essay, "Give If It Helps But Not If It Hurts," and Hardin's, "Lifeboat Ethics: The Case Against Helping the Poor," are included in this volume.

3) everyone is morally required *not* to feed the hungry masses, it would be wrong to do so. All moral opinion on this question would be roughly categorizable into one of these general positions, although there would also be certain hybrid views. Thus, one might hold, as does John Arthur in "Rights and the Duty to Bring Aid," that well-off people are morally required to help the starving in some circumstances; however, since the individuals in affluent nations *also* have rights (e.g., rights over their property), their decision to give assistance would, in many other circumstances, go beyond what is morally required of them. In at least these cases, assistance would be best described as 'charity.'

There is another important point we should make here. We will be intentionally ambiguous in our use of 'duty.' At times, we will speak of the duty of individuals; at other times, of the duty of nations. We will try to be noncommital between the two. For there is a whole nexus of questions which need to be asked, and simply to talk in one way or the other would be to shut off important debate prematurely. We need to know: Who can be said to have this duty, nations, or individuals? Can nations be considered moral entities at all? Is it even possible for nations to have duties, or is this merely an elliptical way of saying that individuals who reside in that nation have certain duties? Are nations *and* individuals morally required to relieve world hunger? And if we decide that individuals do have a duty to act, we would want to know how they are to meet this obligation. Do they, as Singer argues in "Famine, Affluence, and Morality," primarily satisfy this duty through individual donations to food distribution agencies? Or should they rather, as Narveson suggests in "Morality and Starvation," spend their time and money influencing governments to use their massive financial resources to attack the world hunger problem? Or should individual efforts be concentrated on curtailing population growth as a long-range remedy to the problem? Before this problem can be solved, we need to discover the answers to these questions.

Of course, even if we decide that someone does have a duty, and we can identify who does, we still need to know: Who is to be assisted? Should every hungry (starving) person be fed, or only those who reside in "friendly" nations? In other words, should food be used as a political tool —a good which is sent to "friendly" countries yet is purposively withheld from others? This is an important practical question, for the stance of affluent nations has usually been to aid primarily, if not solely, its allies. However, as Frankena suggests, such action appeals more to prudential motives than to moral ones. Hence, the position seems to be roughly equivalent to—and thus requires the same verdict as—the purely prudential arguments discussed earlier.

There are, in addition, other very important questions generated from an issue crucial to the world hunger debate. The issue: the long-range effects of feeding (all) the hungry. In particular, will massive food aid to all starving people have disastrous consequences? Will it, for example, increase the world population so much that it would be impossible, in the future, to feed everyone? If so, argue Hardin and Fletcher, then food relief will only increase human misery in the future; consequently, assistance should be entirely withheld, or at most, only selectively given. To give indiscriminately, they claim, would be wrong.

It should be immediately apparent that this is the main—and probably the only—basis upon which someone could argue that it would be wrong to feed the starving. If these futuristic projections are mistaken, then food assistance to the hungry would be at least permissible, possibly even required. So a careful study of these projections is imperative.

Now, what is actually claimed by these Neo-Malthusian thinkers? Fletcher and Hardin begin with the contention that many countries have outstripped their "carrying capacity," that is, in these countries population has exceeded productivity. They are not—nor can they be—self-sufficient. Thus, feeding the people in these countries will merely increase population even further beyond the land's carrying capacity. This, of course, will ultimately lead to massive starvation in these countries—starvation which could not be curtailed by food assistance. Hence, the long-range effects of food assistance will be increased human misery in these countries; future generations, or even the human species, may be endangered. Consequently, they say, assistance should not be (indiscriminately) given; to do so would be wrong.

This is a position which must be taken very seriously. There are, however, several pointed questions which anyone holding this position must answer, the most obvious question being: Does anyone have reason to accept these futuristic projections? For example, have many (any) countries really exceeded their carrying capacity? Are there clearly identifiable population trends which indicate major worldwide population growth? Are these trends irreversible? Hardin and Fletcher obviously think the answer to these questions is yes. Other essayists disagree. A number of them (Rachels,[4] Singer, and Narveson) argue that immediate food assistance, coupled with developmental assistance (particularly for improved food production) could contain and even eradicate widespread hunger. There are even explicit disagreements about the "ecological" status of particular countries. Fletcher, for example, argues that India has already exceeded its carrying capacity. Rachels concludes just the opposite: he thinks India's population is clearly controllable and that India is potentially productive enough to support its population.

Most of the essayists do feel, however, that assistance, at least to those countries with chronic food shortages, must be coupled with population

---

[4]"Vegetarianism and 'The Other Weight Problem,' " included in this volume.

control measures. Otherwise, they say, the Neo-Malthusian projections *will* come true. Hence, birth control and groceries should be an inseparable tandem in a package deal to these countries. If such coercion is necessary to insure that these projections do not come true, then coercion must be utilized. To reject such coercive measures, says Narveson, would be mere hypocrisy.

Neo-Malthusians (and many moral philosophers) do suppose that the truth of these futuristic projections would justify the claim that those in affluent nations ought not to help the starving masses. But Watson, in "Reason and Morality in a World of Limited Food," rejects this contention. The highest moral principle is equity, he claims, and this principle dictates equal sharing of food resources even if such sharing would leave everyone malnourished. The survival of the species is irrelevant in moral debate. The species (or a nation) is not the sort of thing that can have rights: it is not a moral agent. Thus, he argues, the principle of equity stands. The hungry must be fed.

Yet, even for those who escape the grip of Watson's stringent version of the principle of equity, there are still more questions. Suppose that the Neo-Malthusian projections are correct: feeding the starving will ultimately lead to massive worldwide starvation (or, if presently starving people were given enough food to survive, the givers would die of starvation). Further suppose that Slote's claims, in "The Morality of Wealth," are correct: that in at least most cases the affluent nations became affluent— gained their wealth—by commissively wronging the very nations which are now racked with starvation. Can affluent nations keep their goods and let the people in the less-well off countries die (or remain malnourished) even though those affluent nations are at least partially responsible for the poor countries' plight?

Actually, the last question leads to a more general question about this view. Again, let us assume that the Neo-Malthusian projections are correct: some people are going to die of starvation, but feeding the hungry will increase population in those starving countries and, thus, will increase human misery even more. Each nation, so the argument goes, is a lifeboat;[5] but not all lifeboats are adequately supplied. Hence, some people will have to die. The presumption made by Neo-Malthusian thinkers—in fact, by many philosophers—is that those on the well-equipped lifeboats (the ones in affluent nations) are the ones who must live. They have the goods, so they should survive. But why this presumption? For if their projections are correct, the world would be in a situation of extreme scarcity, rather than moderate scarcity or moderate abundance. Some philosophers have suggested that under such circumstances principles of justice disappear. If

---

[5]Garrett Hardin suggests this metaphor; however, Onora O'Neill, in her essay "Lifeboat Earth" (included in this volume) calls the whole globe a lifeboat.

they do disappear, morality is no longer a basis for action; mere self-preservation becomes the acceptable guideline for behavior. But should moral considerations be surrendered? If not, we should ask: Can those who find themselves on the well-equipped lifeboat justifiably assume that they, and they alone, morally deserve to live?

In our examination of this view that affluent nations should not assist the starving people, we have uncovered several serious questions. This does not mean, however, that the other general positions mentioned earlier are exempt from criticism; they are not—as we shall see.

Some philosophers have argued that affluent nations are morally required to assist those who are starving. But how could an individual decide that he is morally *required* to help a starving person? What would be the basis for such a duty? The authors in this volume who contend that some individuals (or nations) do have such a duty use very different methods in attempting to establish that duty. They also recommend (prescribe) different duties.

Several of them appeal to general moral principles and then argue, from those principles, to particular prescriptions. Watson, for example, adopts the principle of equity and argues that adherence to that principle requires equal sharing of food—even if that sharing ultimately leads to the death of the human species. Although such sharing seems irrational, it is, he claims, required by morality.

Peter Singer also begins his argument from a general principle—a principle which he thinks everyone will accept: persons are morally required to prevent something bad from happening if they can do so without sacrificing anything of "comparable moral significance." He then argues that the truth of this principle is sufficient to establish a stringent duty to feed the hungry. People in affluent nations are morally required to give so much that such giving would radically change their lifestyles. They might even be required to give, he claims, up to the point of marginal utility—that is, up to the point where additional giving would result in as much suffering for them as it would prevent.

Although Singer's prescription is not as strong as Watson's, many find it far too severe. John Arthur, for example, argues that Singer's position is inadequate since it gives insufficient weight to the rights of the affluent. Yet, he also concludes that affluent people sometimes have a duty, founded on the principle of benevolence, to assist others in at least some situations. They are not, however, required to help—although it would be nice to— in cases where the cost to them (the affluent) would be "substantial."

Michael Slote also argues that those in affluent nations are sometimes morally required to assist those in impoverished countries, but his method is noticeably different. He arrives at his conclusion dialectically; that is, he tries to defeat two arguments which allegedly justify retention of personal and national wealth. He begins by setting out these arguments in their most cogent form and, after analyzing them, concludes that although these arguments might be applicable in the abstract, in reality they rarely (if ever) justify refusal to help the starving.

Aiken ("The Right to Be Saved from Starvation") and O'Neill take a different tack. Whereas the other authors are primarily concerned with the moral obligations of people in affluent nations, they emphasize the rights of malnourished peoples against those in affluent nations. Consequently, providing needed food assistance is not just something which affluent nations can choose to do or even are (merely?) required to do; it is something *owed* to those who are starving.[6]

As we have seen, essayists differ in the methods they use to establish a moral duty to aid the starving. But they *do* agree that there is a duty. However, there are some important questions which must be answered by all those who argue that affluent nations (or those in them) are morally required to aid the starving. They must show, for example, that the Neo-Malthusian projections are mistaken—that the situation is not as gloomy as supposed; or that *even if* the projections are plausible, the conclusion (that we ought not to help) does not follow from them. Unless doubt can be thrown on these projections or their irrelevance demonstrated, assertions about individuals' duties remain in the abstract; that is, people would actually have the duties only if the facts (about population projections and their relevance to this debate) were different. In addition, they must also explain why those people who have the goods—and who allegedly have rights to those goods—are morally required to give them up. The goods which are to be used to feed the malnourished are not unowned; they are owned by people who have worked to acquire them. Why must they give up the fruits of their labor for the benefit of others? Furthermore, how can an individual have a duty to someone he doesn't even know? Why should he be held morally responsible to alleviate suffering he neither created, intended, nor desired?

As we have seen, there are difficulties with this position. We also observed problems with the Neo-Malthusian alternative. This might suggest to some readers that neither of these two options is correct. Rather than suppose we are required to assist or to refrain from assisting, we might hold a third alternative: that assisting is not something we either must or must not do. Instead, it is an action which is morally permissible. That is, although assistance might be desirable—even good—it certainly is not required. Helping the malnourished is an option of the well-fed; it is an act of charity.

[6]For one view on the importance of rights in moral discourse, see Joel Feinberg, "The Nature and Value of Rights," *The Journal of Value Inquiry*, IV (1970), 243–57.

This position, in the hands of some of its proponents, appears to merge with the duty position. Yet even though they may be difficult to separate, they are distinct. Narveson suggests several ways to distinguish them. For instance, if one has a duty, he may be required to act even in cases where he does not want to.

This "middle of the road" position, however, like the others, is vulnerable to attack. In fact, both alternatives we have examined would challenge it. Those who argue against giving aid would object to assistance whether given out of charity or duty. Food assistance given out of charity, the Neo-Malthusians say, would have the same bad consequences as that given out of duty, since both would ultimately cause overpopulation with a subsequent increase in human misery. Hence, those adopting this third view, like those who claim some people are obligated to help the starving, would have to show that the futuristic projections were either mistaken or irrelevant.

This 'charity' position is also subject to objections from those who think affluent nations are required to assist malnourished peoples. Why, for example, is something this important relegated to charity? Given the human tendency toward self-interest, is there any realistic hope that massive world hunger can be stopped with charity alone? A proponent of the duty position might also note that those holding the charity position assume that personal property rights are extensive, if not unlimited. But why, one might ask, should anyone suppose that individuals have rights to nonnecessary goods (e.g., a second luxury car) even when others will die unless they acquire food purchased with the money used to buy these goods? Suppose that at least one million people could be saved and hundreds of millions could gain increased health if each affluent nation would give two percent of its gross national product for the alleviation of hunger. If this supposition is true (as it seems to be), would retention of wealth be justified? Or one might also ask: "Do those who now have the goods in their possession have moral rights over those goods?" Did they, for example, acquire those goods, directly or indirectly, because of commissive wrongdoings, thereby forfeiting their justified claim of right?

Hence, we see that those who favor this position also must deal with some tough questions. In fact, all three major positions must confront difficult questions. That should be a sure sign of a tough moral problem: there are divergent opinions—each with certain plausibility, each with certain weaknesses. In short, there are no apparent, clear-cut solutions. Only with careful thought and careful argument can we hope to find an acceptable one.

Each of the three general positions examined so far has, at least in the form in which we have examined it, primarily emphasized questions of distributive justice. Some people have goods—more than they need;

others don't have enough. Consequently, if the problem is to be (should be) remedied, these goods must be redistributed. For this reason, much of the world hunger debate centers around distribution. Some people (e.g., Watson) believe that goods should be redistributed; others (e.g., Hardin) argue they should not be. Still others might suggest that although it would be good to have a voluntary redistribution, it is not something which the "haves" must do for the "have-nots."

Howard Richards, however, in "Productive Justice," wants to (at least partly) challenge the centrality of distributive questions for this debate. Although distribution is important, he argues, it is not the only, and maybe not even the most important, question. There are other considerations—considerations of productive justice—which are essential to the issue of world hunger. If requirements of productive justice were satisfied, the world hunger problem would not be as severe.

James Rachels raises another concern relevant to the world hunger problem. He argues that the need for additional food to feed the starving requires that individuals decrease or eliminate meat from their diets. For meat, he argues, is a very inefficient source of protein. Feed-lot animals, particularly beef cattle, eat large amounts of human-consumable protein; yet, only a small portion of it is returned to humans in meat form. As much as 85% of the usable protein is lost in the production of meat. This lost protein, he argues, could be distributed to starving people; it could go a long way toward solving the world food shortage. Hence, he concludes, individuals in more affluent nations should slow down or cease their meat consumption. Vegetarianism is relevant to both productive justice and distributive justice.

CHALLENGE TO THE READER

We have now briefly introduced the problem of world hunger by offering a few conceptual tools for dissecting this knotty problem and by surveying some of the various responses to it. However, we cannot tell you what to believe or what to do. It is up to you, the reader, to ponder this problem and to make a personal decision, however tentative, about it. For it is a crucial problem which demands your attention. Keep these general questions in mind as you read the following essays. Also notice the suggestions and questions prior to each entry.

1. Who has the burden of proof in this debate? Must the individual who says: "We ought to act" show why we ought to do so? Must the person who advocates inaction (or action only if one desires to act) justify his or her position?

2.   Persons who are starving need food to stay alive. Is this need sufficient to indicate that the starving person has a right to be fed or that others have a duty to feed him (assuming these are different)? If mere need is not sufficient, what other criteria, if any, must one use to establish that some individuals are morally required to feed the starving?

3.   Suppose those in affluent nations do have a general duty to feed the hungry of the world. How strong is this duty? Is this duty sometimes overridden by conflicting moral claims? How strong must these competing claims be to override need? Is, for example, an individual justified in giving his children piano lessons rather than sending the money, which would be used to finance those lessons, to feed the poor?

4.   Property ownership is an issue relevant to all three general positions canvassed. Food resources (land, farm equipment, etc.) are presently owned, i.e., legal rules give rights over these goods to particular individuals. Hence, any goods sent to the starving masses must come from those who presently own them. How strong are these property rights? How much moral weight must be given them?

5.   What are the consequences of feeding the poor? Will it threaten the survival of the species? Or will it simply make the (Western) world a less pleasant place in which to live (e.g.. will we have to rely more on mass transit and less on the private automobile)? How bad must the consequence be before one is excused from meeting the alleged general duty to feed the hungry?

6.   If one ought to help the hungry, exactly how should one help? Should one make individual monetary contributions, lobby for (or support lobbyists who work for) national assistance to under-developed countries, work for increased production of needed food-stuffs, disseminate information on birth control, become a vege-tarian, or some combination of all of these? Or if one ought *not* to help the hungry, should one work against food aid organizations?

GARRETT HARDIN

Hardin argues against giving away food. Affluent nations, like well stocked lifeboats, should insure their own survival by retaining a safety factor of surplus, by preserving their environment for future generations, by protecting their life style against the poor who want handouts, and by keeping out others who might "swamp the boat."

1. Hardin says that "pure justice" is incompatible with survival. Does our survival override all concerns of justice?

2. He maintains that future generations have a claim against us. Watson disagrees. Do we have a moral responsibility to them?

3. If rich nations have contributed to the impoverishment of poor ones (as O'Neill and Slote imply), are Hardin's arguments weakened?

4. Notice that Hardin, unlike Fletcher, implies that not even developmental assistance should be given.

Garrett Hardin is Professor of Biology at the University of California, Santa Barbara. He has written numerous articles on the issue of world hunger.

Lifeboat Ethics:
The Case Against Helping the Poor

Environmentalists use the metaphor of the earth as a "spaceship" in trying to persuade countries, industries and people to stop wasting and polluting our natural resources. Since we all share life on this planet, they argue, no single person or institution has the right to destroy, waste, or use more than a fair share of its resources.

But does everyone on earth have an equal right to an equal share of its resources? The spaceship metaphor can be dangerous when used by misguided idealists to justify suicidal policies for sharing our resources through uncontrolled immigration and foreign aid. In their enthusiastic but unrealistic generosity, they confuse the ethics of a spaceship with those of a lifeboat.

A true spaceship would have to be under the control of a captain, since no ship could possibly survive if its course were determined by committee. Spaceship Earth certainly has no captain; the United Nations is merely a toothless tiger, with little power to enforce any policy upon its bickering members.

If we divide the world crudely into rich nations and poor nations, two thirds of them are desperately poor, and only one third comparatively rich, with the United States the wealthiest of all. Metaphorically each rich nation can be seen as a lifeboat full of comparatively rich people. In the ocean outside each lifeboat swim the poor of the world, who would like to get in, or at least to share some of the wealth. What should the lifeboat passengers do?

First, we must recognize the limited capacity of any lifeboat. For example, a nation's land has a limited capacity to support a population and as the current energy crisis has shown us, in some ways we have already exceeded the carrying capacity of our land.

Adrift in a Moral Sea

So here we sit, say fifty people in our lifeboat. To be generous, let us assume it has room for ten more, making a total capacity of sixty. Suppose the fifty of us in the lifeboat see 100 others swimming in the water outside, begging for admission to our boat or for handouts. We have several options: we may be tempted to try to live by the Christian ideal of being "our brother's keeper," or by the Marxist ideal of "to each according to his needs." Since the needs of all in the water are the same, and since they can all be seen as "our brothers," we could take them all into our boat, making a total of 150 in a boat designed for sixty. The boat swamps, everyone drowns. Complete justice, complete catastrophe.

Since the boat has an unused excess capacity of ten more passengers, we could admit just ten more to it. But which ten do we let in? How do we choose? Do we pick the best ten, the neediest ten, "first come, first served"? And what do we say to the ninety we exclude? If we do let an extra ten into our lifeboat, we will have lost our "safety factor," an engineering principle of critical importance. For example, if we don't leave room for excess capacity as a safety factor in our country's agriculture, a new plant disease or a bad change in the weather could have disastrous consequences.

Suppose we decide to preserve our small safety factor and admit no more to the lifeboat. Our survival is then possible, although we shall have to be constantly on guard against boarding parties.

While this last solution clearly offers the only means of our survival, it is morally abhorrent to many people. Some say they feel guilty about their good luck. My reply is simple: "Get out and yield your place to others." This may solve the problem of the guilt-ridden person's conscience, but it does not change the ethics of the lifeboat. The needy person to whom the guilt-ridden person yields his place will not himself feel guilty about his good luck. If he did, he would not climb aboard. The net result of conscience-stricken people giving up their unjustly held seats is the elimination of that sort of conscience from the lifeboat.

This is the basic metaphor within which we must work out our solutions. Let us now enrich the image, step by step, with substantive additions from the real world, a world that must solve real and pressing problems of overpopulation and hunger.

The harsh ethics of the lifeboat become even harsher when we consider the reproductive differences between the rich nations and the poor nations. The people inside the lifeboats are doubling in numbers every eighty-seven years; those swimming around outside are doubling, on the average, every thirty-five years, more than twice as fast as the rich. And since the world's resources are dwindling, the difference in prosperity between the rich and the poor can only increase.

As of 1973, the U.S had a population of 210 million people, who were increasing by 0.8 percent per year. Outside our lifeboat, let us imagine another 210 million people, (say the combined populations of Colombia, Ecuador, Venezuela, Morocco, Pakistan, Thailand and the Philippines) who are increasing at a rate of 3.3 percent per year. Put differently, the doubling time for this aggregate population is twenty-one years, compared to eighty-seven years for the U.S.

Multiplying the Rich and the Poor

Now suppose the U.S. agreed to pool its resources with those seven countries, with everyone receiving an equal share. Initially the ratio of Americans to non-Americans in this model would be one-to-one. But consider what the ratio would be after eighty-seven years, by which time the Americans would have doubled to a population of 420 million. By then, doubling every twenty-one years, the other group would have swollen to 354 billion. Each American would have to share the available resources with more than eight people.

But, one could argue, this discussion assumes that current population trends will continue, and they may not. Quite so. Most likely the rate of population increase will decline much faster in the U.S. than it will in the other countries, and there does not seem to be much we can do about it. In sharing with "each according to his needs," we must recognize that needs are determined by population size, which is determined by the rate of reproduction, which at present is regarded as a sovereign right of every nation, poor or not. This being so, the philanthropic load created by the sharing ethic of the spaceship can only increase.

The Tragedy of the Commons

The fundamental error of spaceship ethics, and the sharing it requires, is that it leads to what I call "the tragedy of the commons." Under a system of private property, the men who own property recognize their responsibility to care for it, for if they don't they will eventually suffer. A farmer, for instance, will allow no more cattle in a pasture than its carrying capacity justifies. If he overloads it, erosion sets in, weeds take over, and he loses the use of the pasture.

If a pasture becomes a commons open to all, the right of each to use it may not be matched by a corresponding responsibility to protect it. Asking everyone to use it with discretion will hardly do, for the considerate herdsman who refrains from overloading the commons suffers more than a selfish one who says his needs are greater. If everyone would restrain himself, all would be well; but it takes only one less than everyone to ruin a system of voluntary restraint. In a crowded world of less than perfect human beings, mutual ruin is inevitable if there are no controls. This is the tragedy of the commons.

One of the major tasks of education today should be the creation of such an acute awareness of the dangers of the commons that people will recognize its many varieties. For example, the air and water have become polluted because they are treated as commons. Further growth in the population or per-capita conversion of natural resources into pollutants will only make the problem worse. The same holds true for the fish of the oceans. Fishing fleets have nearly disappeared in many parts of the world, technological improvements in the art of fishing are hastening the day of complete ruin. Only the replacement of the system of the commons with a responsible system of control will save the land, air, water and oceanic fisheries.

The World Food Bank

In recent years there has been a push to create a new commons called a World Food Bank, an international depository of food reserves to which nations would contribute according to their abilities and from which they would draw according to their needs. This humanitarian proposal has received support from many liberal international groups, and from such prominent citizens as Margaret Mead, U.N. Secretary General Kurt Waldheim, and Senators Edward Kennedy and George McGovern.

A world food bank appeals powerfully to our humanitarian impulses. But before we rush ahead with such a plan, let us recognize where the greatest political push comes from, lest we be disillusioned later. Our experience with the "Food for Peace program," or Public Law 480, gives us the answer. This program moved billions of dollars worth of U.S. surplus grain to food-short, population-long countries during the past two decades. But when P.L. 480 first became law, a headline in the business magazine *Forbes* revealed the real power behind it: "Feeding the World's Hungry Millions: How It Will Mean Billions for U.S. Business."

And indeed it did. In the years 1960 to 1970, U.S. taxpayers spent a total of $7.9 billion on the Food for Peace program. Between 1948 and 1970, they also paid an additional $50 billion for other economic-aid programs, some of which went for food and food-producing machinery and technology. Though all U.S. taxpayers were forced to contribute to the cost of P.L. 480, certain special interest groups gained handsomely under the program. Farmers did not have to contribute the grain; the Government, or rather the taxpayers, bought it from them at full market prices. The increased demand raised prices of farm products generally. The manufacturers of farm machinery, fertilizers and pesticides benefited by the farmers' extra efforts to grow more food. Grain elevators profited from storing the surplus until it could be shipped. Railroads made money hauling it to ports, and shipping lines profited from carrying it overseas. The implementation of P.L. 480 required the creation of a vast Government bureaucracy, which then acquired its own vested interest in continuing the program regardless of its merits.

Extracting Dollars

Those who proposed and defended the Food for Peace program in public rarely mentioned its importance to any of these special interests. The public emphasis was always on its humanitarian effects. The combination of silent selfish interests and highly vocal humanitarian apologists made a powerful and successful lobby for extracting money from taxpayers. We can expect the same lobby to push now for the creation of a World Food Bank.

However great the potential benefit to selfish interests, it should not be a decisive argument against a truly humanitarian program. We must ask if such a program would actually do more good than harm, not only momentarily but also in the long run. Those who propose the food bank usually refer to a current "emergency" or "crisis" in terms of world food supply. But what is an emergency? Although they may be infrequent and sudden, everyone knows that emergencies will occur from time to time. A well-run family, company, organization or country prepares for the likelihood of accidents and emergencies. It expects them, it budgets for them, it saves for them.

Learning the Hard Way

What happens if some organizations or countries budget for accidents and others do not? If each country is solely responsible for its own well-being, poorly managed ones will suffer. But they can learn from experience. They may mend their ways, and learn to budget for infrequent but certain emergencies. For example, the weather varies from year to year, and periodic crop failures are certain. A wise and competent government saves out of the production of the good years in anticipation of bad years to come. Joseph taught this policy to Pharaoh in Egypt more than 2,000 years ago. Yet the great majority of the governments in the world today do not follow such a policy. They lack either the wisdom or the competence, or both. Should those nations that do manage to put something aside be forced to come to the rescue each time an emergency occurs among the poor nations?

"But it isn't their fault!" some kindhearted liberals argue. "How can we blame the poor people who are caught in an emergency? Why must they suffer for the sins of their governments?" The concept of blame is simply not relevant here. The real question is, what are the operational consequences of establishing a world food bank? If it is open to every country every time a need develops, slovenly rulers will not be motivated to take Joseph's advice. Someone will always come to their aid. Some countries will deposit food in the world food bank, and others will withdraw it. There will be almost no overlap. As a result of such solutions to food shortage emergencies, the poor countries will not learn to mend their ways, and will suffer progressively greater emergencies as their populations grow.

Population Control the Crude Way

On the average, poor countries undergo a 2.5 percent increase in population each year; rich countries, about 0.8 percent. Only rich countries have anything in the way of food reserves set aside, and even they do not have as much as they should. Poor countries have none. If poor countries received no food from the outside, the rate of their population growth would be periodically checked by crop failures and famines. But if they can always draw on a world food bank in time of need, their population can continue to grow unchecked, and so will their "need" for aid. In the short run, a world food bank may diminish that need, but in the long run it actually increases the need without limit.

Without some system of worldwide food sharing, the proportion of people in the rich and poor nations might eventually stabilize. The overpopulated poor countries would decrease in numbers, while the rich countries that had room for more people would increase. But with a well-meaning system of sharing, such as a world food bank, the growth differential between the rich and the poor countries will not only persist, it will increase. Because of the higher rate of population growth in the poor countries of the world, 88 percent of today's children are born poor, and only 12 percent rich. Year by year the ratio becomes worse, as the fast-reproducing poor outnumber the slow-reproducing rich.

A world food bank is thus a commons in disguise. People will have more motivation to draw from it than to add to any common store. The less provident and less able will multiply at the expense of the abler and more provident, bringing eventual ruin upon all who share in the commons. Besides, any system of "sharing" that amounts to foreign aid from the rich nations to the poor nations will carry the taint of charity, which will contribute little to the world peace so devoutly desired by those who support the idea of a world food bank.

As past U.S. foreign-aid programs have amply and depressingly demonstrated, international charity frequently inspires mistrust and antagonism rather than gratitude on the part of the recipient nation.

Chinese Fish and Miracle Rice

The modern approach to foreign aid stresses the export of technology and advice, rather than money and food. As an ancient Chinese proverb goes: "Give a man a fish and he will eat for a day; teach him how to fish and he will eat for the rest of his days." Acting on this advice, the Rockefeller and Ford Foundations have financed a number of programs for improving agriculture in the hungry nations. Known as the "Green Revolution," these programs have led to the development of "miracle rice" and "miracle wheat," new strains that offer bigger harvests and greater resistance to crop damage. Norman Borlaug, the Nobel Prize winning agronomist who, supported by the Rockefeller Foundation, developed "miracle wheat," is one of the most prominent advocates of a world food bank.

Whether or not the Green Revolution can increase food production as much as its champions claim is a debatable but possibly irrelevant point. Those who support this well-intended humanitarian effort should first consider some of the fundamentals of human ecology. Ironically, one man who did was the late Alan Gregg, a vice president of the Rockefeller Foundation. Two decades ago he expressed strong doubts about the wisdom of such attempts to increase food production. He likened the growth and spread of humanity over the surface of the earth to the spread of cancer in the human body, remarking that "cancerous growths demand food; but, as far as I know, they have never been cured by getting it."

Overloading the Environment

Every human born constitutes a draft on all aspects of the environment: food, air, water, forests, beaches, wildlife, scenery and solitude. Food can, perhaps, be significantly increased to meet a growing demand. But what about clean beaches, unspoiled forests, and solitude? If we satisfy a growing population's need for food, we necessarily decrease its per capita supply of the other resources needed by men.

India, for example, now has a population of 600 million, which increases by 15 million each year. This population already puts a huge load on a relatively impoverished environment. The country's forests are now only a small fraction of what they were three centuries ago, and floods and erosion continually destroy the insufficient farmland that remains. Every one of the 15 million new lives added to India's population puts an additional burden on the environment, and increases the economic and social costs of crowding. However humanitarian our intent, every Indian life saved through medical or nutritional assistance from abroad diminishes the quality of life for those who remain, and for subsequent generations. If rich countries make it possible, through foreign aid, for 600 million Indians to swell to 1.2 billion in a mere twenty-eight years, as their current growth rate threatens, will future generations of Indians thank us for hastening the destruction of their environment? Will our good intentions be sufficient excuse for the consequences of our actions?

My final example of a commons in action is one for which the public has the least desire for rational discussion—immigration. Anyone who publicly questions the wisdom of current U.S. immigration policy is promptly charged with bigotry, prejudice, ethnocentrism, chauvinism, isolationism or selfishness. Rather than encounter such accusations, one would rather talk about other matters, leaving immigration policy to wallow in the crosscurrents of special interests that take no account of the good of the whole, or the interests of posterity.

Perhaps we still feel guilty about things we said in the past. Two generations ago the popular press frequently referred to Dagos, Wops, Polacks,

Chinks and Krauts, in articles about how America was being "overrun" by foreigners of supposedly inferior genetic stock. But because the implied inferiority of foreigners was used then as justification for keeping them out, people now assume that restrictive policies could only be based on such misguided notions. There are other grounds.

A Nation of Immigrants

Just consider the numbers involved. Our Government acknowledges a net inflow of 400,000 immigrants a year. While we have no hard data on the extent of illegal entries, educated guesses put the figure at about 600,000 a year. Since the natural increase (excess of births over deaths) of the resident population now runs about 1.7 million per year, the yearly gain from immigration amounts to at least 19 percent of the total annual increase, and may be as much as 37 percent if we include the estimate for illegal immigrants. Considering the growing use of birth-control devices, the potential effect of educational campaigns by such organizations as Planned Parenthood Federation of America and Zero Population Growth, and the influence of inflation and the housing shortage, the fertility rate of American women may decline so much that immigration could account for all the yearly increase in population. Should we not at least ask if that is what we want?

For the sake of those who worry about whether the "quality" of the average immigrant compares favorably with the quality of the average resident, let us assume that immigrants and nativeborn citizens are of exactly equal quality, however one defines that term. We will focus here only on quantity; and since our conclusions will depend on nothing else, all charges of bigotry and chauvinism become irrelevant.

Immigration vs. Food Supply

World food banks *move food to the people,* hastening the exhaustion of the environment of the poor countries. Unrestricted immigration, on the other hand, *moves people to the food,* thus speeding up the destruction of the environment of the rich countries. We can easily understand why poor people should want to make this latter transfer, but why should rich hosts encourage it?

As in the case of foreign-aid programs, immigration receives support from selfish interests and humanitarian impulses. The primary selfish interest in unimpeded immigration is the desire of employers for cheap labor, particularly in industries and trades that offer degrading work. In the past, one wave of foreigners after another was brought into the U.S. to work at wretched jobs for wretched wages. In recent years the Cubans, Puerto Ricans and Mexicans have had this dubious honor. The interests of the employers of cheap labor mesh well with the guilty silence of the country's

liberal intelligentsia. White Anglo-Saxon Protestants are particularly reluctant to call for a closing of the doors to immigration for fear of being
called bigots.

But not all countries have such reluctant leadership. Most educated
Hawaiians, for example, are keenly aware of the limits of their environment, particularly in terms of population growth. There is only so much
room on the islands, and the islanders know it. To Hawaiians, immigrants
from the other forty-nine states present as great a threat as those from
other nations. At a recent meeting of Hawaiian government officials in
Honolulu, I had the ironic delight of hearing a speaker, who like most of
his audience was of Japanese ancestry, ask how the country might practically and constitutionally close its doors to further immigration. One
member of the audience countered: "How can we shut the doors now? We
have many friends and relatives in Japan that we'd like to bring here some
day so that they can enjoy Hawaii too." The Japanese-American speaker
smiled sympathetically and answered: "Yes, but we have children now,
and someday we'll have grandchildren too. We can bring more people here
from Japan only by giving away some of the land that we hope to pass on
to our grandchildren some day. What right do we have to do that?"

At this point, I can hear U.S. liberals asking: "How can you justify
slamming the door once you're inside? You say that immigrants should be
kept out. But aren't we all immigrants, or the descendents of immigrants?
If we insist on staying, must we not admit all others?" Our craving for
intellectual order leads us to seek and prefer symmetrical rules and morals:
a single rule for me and everybody else; the same rule yesterday, today,
and tomorrow. Justice, we feel, should not change with time and place.

We Americans of non-Indian ancestry can look upon ourselves as the
descendants of thieves who are guilty morally, if not legally, of stealing
this land from its Indian owners. Should we then give back the land to the
now living American descendants of those Indians? However morally or
logically sound this proposal may be, I, for one, am unwilling to live by
it and I know no one else who is. Besides, the logical consequence would
be absurd. Suppose that, intoxicated with a sense of pure justice, we
should decide to turn our land over to the Indians. Since all our wealth has
also been derived from the land, wouldn't we be morally obliged to give
that back to the Indians too?

Pure Justice vs. Reality

Clearly, the concept of pure justice produces an infinite regression to
absurdity. Centuries ago, wise men invented statutes of limitations to
justify the rejection of such pure justice, in the interest of preventing
continual disorder. The law zealously defends property rights, but only

relatively recent property rights. Drawing a line after an arbitrary time has elapsed may be unjust, but the alternatives are worse.

We are all the descendants of thieves, and the world's resources are inequitably distributed. But we must begin the journey to tomorrow from the point where we are today. We cannot remake the past. We cannot safely divide the wealth equitably among all peoples so long as people reproduce at different rates. To do so would guarantee that our grandchildren, and everyone else's grandchildren, would have only a ruined world to inhabit.

To be generous with one's own possessions is quite different from being generous with those of posterity. We should call this point to the attention of those who, from a commendable love of justice and equality, would institute a system of the commons, either in the form of a world food bank, or of unrestricted immigration. We must convince them if we wish to save at least some parts of the world from environmental ruin.

Without a true world government to control reproduction and the use of available resources, the sharing ethic of the spaceship is impossible. For the foreseeable future, our survival demands that we govern our actions by the ethics of a lifeboat, harsh though they may be. Posterity will be satisfied with nothing less.

PETER SINGER

Singer proposes what he considers an uncontroversial moral principle: if it is in our power to prevent something bad from happening, without thereby sacrificing anything of comparable moral importance, we ought, morally, to do it. Adherence to this principle would substantially alter the lifestyle of the affluent.

> **1.** *Why do we have a duty to prevent something bad from happening to others if we are not responsible for its occurrence?*
>
> **2.** *Arthur argues that Singer's criterion of "comparable moral importance" is inadequate. Is it?*
>
> **3.** *Are we, as Singer implies, obligated to contribute up to the point of marginal utility?*
>
> **4.** *Notice Singer's postscript. Does it alter the position presented in his essay?*

Peter Singer is Senior Lecturer in Philosophy at La Trobe University (Australia). He is the author of Democracy and Disobedience *and* Animal Liberation.

Famine, Affluence, and Morality

As I write this, in November 1971, people are dying in East Bengal from lack of food, shelter, and medical care. The suffering and death that are occurring there now are not inevitable, not unavoidable in any fatalistic sense of the term. Constant poverty, a cyclone, and a civil war have turned

"Famine, Affluence, and Morality," by Peter Singer, *Philosophy and Public Affairs*, I, no. 3 (1972): pp. 229–243. Reprinted by permission of Princeton University Press.

at least nine million people into destitute refugees; nevertheless, it is not beyond the capacity of the richer nations to give enough assistance to reduce any further suffering to very small proportions. The decisions and actions of human beings can prevent this kind of suffering. Unfortunately, human beings have not made the necessary decisions. At the individual level, people have, with very few exceptions, not responded to the situation in any significant way. Generally speaking, people have not given large sums to relief funds; they have not written to their parliamentary representatives demanding increased government assistance; they have not demonstrated in the streets, held symbolic fasts, or done anything else directed toward providing the refugees with the means to satisfy their essential needs. At the government level, no government has given the sort of massive aid that would enable the refugees to survive for more than a few days. Britain, for instance, has given rather more than most countries. It has, to date, given £14,750,000. For comparative purposes, Britain's share of the nonrecoverable development costs of the Anglo-French Concorde project is already in excess of £275,000,000, and on present estimates will reach £440,000,000. The implication is that the British government values a supersonic transport more than thirty times as highly as it values the lives of the nine million refugees. Australia is another country which, on a per capita basis, is well up in the "aid to Bengal" table. Australia's aid, however, amounts to less than one-twelfth of the cost of Sydney's new opera house. The total amount given, from all sources, now stands at about £65,000,000. The estimated cost of keeping the refugees alive for one year is £464,000,000. Most of the refugees have now been in the camps for more than six months. The World Bank has said that India needs a minimum of £300,000,000 in assistance from other countries before the end of the year. It seems obvious that assistance on this scale will not be forthcoming. India will be forced to choose between letting the refugees starve or diverting funds from her own development program, which will mean that more of her own people will starve in the future.[1]

These are the essential facts about the present situation in Bengal. So far as it concerns us here, there is nothing unique about this situation except its magnitude. The Bengal emergency is just the latest and most acute of a series of major emergencies in various parts of the world, arising both from natural and from man-made causes. There are also many parts of the world in which people die from malnutrition and lack of food independent of any special emergency. I take Bengal as my example only because it is the present concern, and because the size of the problem has ensured that

---

[1]There was also a third possibility: that India would go to war to enable the refugees to return to their lands. Since I wrote this paper, India has taken this way out. The situation is no longer that described above, but this does not affect my argument, as the next paragraph indicates.

it has been given adequate publicity. Neither individuals nor governments can claim to be unaware of what is happening there.

What are the moral implications of a situation like this? In what follows, I shall argue that the way people in relatively affluent countries react to a situation like that in Bengal cannot be justified; indeed, the whole way we look at moral issues—our moral conceptual scheme—needs to be altered, and with it, the way of life that has come to be taken for granted in our society.

In arguing for this conclusion I will not, of course, claim to be morally neutral. I shall, however, try to argue for the moral position that I take, so that anyone who accepts certain assumptions, to be made explicit, will, I hope, accept my conclusion.

I begin with the assumption that suffering and death from lack of food, shelter, and medical care are bad. I think most people will agree about this, although one may reach the same view by different routes. I shall not argue for this view. People can hold all sorts of eccentric positions, and perhaps from some of them it would not follow that death by starvation is in itself bad. It is difficult, perhaps impossible, to refute such positions, and so for brevity I will henceforth take this assumption as accepted. Those who disagree need read no further.

My next point is this: if it is in our power to prevent something bad from happening, without thereby sacrificing anything of comparable moral importance, we ought, morally, to do it. By "without sacrificing anything of comparable moral importance" I mean without causing anything else comparably bad to happen, or doing something that is wrong in itself, or failing to promote some moral good, comparable in significance to the bad thing that we can prevent. This principle seems almost as uncontroversial as the last one. It requires us only to prevent what is bad, and not to promote what is good, and it requires this of us only when we can do it without sacrificing anything that is, from the moral point of view, comparably important. I could even, as far as the application of my argument to the Bengal emergency is concerned, qualify the point so as to make it: if it is in our power to prevent something very bad from happening, without thereby sacrificing anything morally significant, we ought, morally, to do it. An application of this principle would be as follows: if I am walking past a shallow pond and see a child drowning in it, I ought to wade in and pull the child out. This will mean getting my clothes muddy, but this is insignificant, while the death of the child would presumably be a very bad thing.

The uncontroversial appearance of the principle just stated is deceptive. If it were acted upon, even in its qualified form, our lives, our society, and our world would be fundamentally changed. For the principle takes, firstly, no account of proximity or distance. It makes no moral difference whether the person I can help is a neighbor's child ten yards from me or a Bengali whose name I shall never know, ten thousand miles away. Secondly, the principle makes no distinction between cases in which I am the only person who could possibly do anything and cases in which I am just one among millions in the same position.

I do not think I need to say much in defense of the refusal to take proximity and distance into account. The fact that a person is physically near to us, so that we have personal contact with him, may make it more likely that we *shall* assist him, but this does not show that we *ought* to help him rather than another who happens to be further away. If we accept any principle of impartiality, universalizability, equality, or whatever, we cannot discriminate against someone merely because he is far away from us (or we are far away from him). Admittedly, it is possible that we are in a better position to judge what needs to be done to help a person near to us than one far away, and perhaps also to provide the assistance we judge to be necessary. If this were the case, it would be a reason for helping those near to us first. This may once have been a justification for being more concerned with the poor in one's town than with famine victims in India. Unfortunately for those who like to keep their moral responsibilities limited, instant communication and swift transportation have changed the situation. From the moral point of view, the development of the world into a "global village" has made an important, though still unrecognized, difference to our moral situation. Expert observers and supervisors, sent out by famine relief organizations or permanently stationed in famine-prone areas, can direct our aid to a refugee in Bengal almost as effectively as we could get it to someone in our own block. There would seem, therefore, to be no possible justification for discriminating on geographical grounds.

There may be a greater need to defend the second implication of my principle—that the fact that there are millions of other people in the same position, in respect to the Bengali refugees, as I am, does not make the situation significantly different from a situation in which I am the only person who can prevent something very bad from occurring. Again, of course, I admit that there is a psychological difference between the cases; one feels less guilty about doing nothing if one can point to others, similarly placed, who have also done nothing. Yet this can make no real difference to our moral obligations.[2] Should I consider that I am less obliged to pull the drowning child out of the pond if on looking around

[2] In view of the special sense philosophers often give to the term, I should say that I use "obligation" simply as the abstract noun derived from "ought," so that "I have an obligation to" means no more, and no less, than "I ought to." This usage is in accordance with the definition of "ought" given by the *Shorter Oxford English Dictionary*: "the general verb to express duty or obligation." I do not think any issue of substance hangs on the way the term is used; sentences in which I use "obligation" could all be rewritten, although somewhat clumsily, as sentences in which a clause containing "ought" replaces the term "obligation."

I see other people, no further away than I am, who have also noticed the child but are doing nothing? One has only to ask this question to see the absurdity of the view that numbers lessen obligation. It is a view that is an ideal excuse for inactivity; unfortunately most of the major evils— poverty, overpopulation, pollution—are problems in which everyone is almost equally involved.

The view that numbers do make a difference can be made plausible if stated in this way: if everyone in circumstances like mine gave £5 to the Bengal Relief Fund, there would be enough to provide food, shelter, and medical care for the refugees; there is no reason why I should give more than anyone else in the same circumstances as I am; therefore I have no obligation to give more than £5. Each premise in this argument is true, and the argument looks sound. It may convince us, unless we notice that it is based on a hypothetical premise, although the conclusion is not stated hypothetically. The argument would be sound if the conclusion were: if everyone in circumstances like mine were to give £5, I would have no obligation to give more than £5. If the conclusion were so stated, however, it would be obvious that the argument has no bearing on a situation in which it is not the case that everyone else gives £5. This, of course, is the actual situation. It is more or less certain that not everyone in circumstances like mine will give £5. So there will not be enough to provide the needed food, shelter, and medical care. Therefore by giving more than £5 I will prevent more suffering than I would if I gave just £5.

It might be thought that this argument has an absurd consequence. Since the situation appears to be that very few people are likely to give substantial amounts, it follows that I and everyone else in similar circumstances ought to give as much as possible, that is, at least up to the point at which by giving more one would begin to cause serious suffering for oneself and one's dependents—perhaps even beyond this point to the point of marginal utility, at which by giving more one would cause oneself and one's dependents as much suffering as one would prevent in Bengal. If everyone does this, however, there will be more than can be used for the benefit of the refugees, and some of the sacrifice will have been unnecessary. Thus, if everyone does what he ought to do, the result will not be as good as it would be if everyone did a little less than he ought to do, or if only some do all that they ought to do.

The paradox here arises only if we assume that the actions in question —sending money to the relief funds—are performed more or less simultaneously, and are also unexpected. For if it is to be expected that everyone is going to contribute something, then clearly each is not obliged to give as much as he would have been obliged to had others not been giving too. And if everyone is not acting more or less simultaneously, then those giving later will know how much more is needed, and will have no obligation to give more than is necessary to reach this amount. To say this is not to deny the principle that people in the same circumstances have the same obligations, but to point out that the fact that others have given, or may be expected to give, is a relevant circumstance: those giving after it has become known that many others are giving and those giving before are not in the same circumstances. So the seemingly absurd consequence of the principle I have put forward can occur only if people are in error about the actual circumstances—that is, if they think they are giving when others are not, but in fact they are giving when others are. The result of everyone doing what he really ought to do cannot be worse than the result of everyone doing less than he ought to do, although the result of everyone doing what he reasonably believes he ought to do could be.

If my argument so far has been sound, neither our distance from a preventable evil nor the number of other people who, in respect to that evil, are in the same situation as we are, lessens our obligation to mitigate or prevent that evil. I shall therefore take as established the principle I asserted earlier. As I have already said, I need to assert it only in its qualified form: if it is in our power to prevent something very bad from happening, without thereby sacrificing anything else morally significant, we ought, morally, to do it.

The outcome of this argument is that our traditional moral categories are upset. The traditional distinction between duty and charity cannot be drawn, or at least, not in the place we normally draw it. Giving money to the Bengal Relief Fund is regarded as an act of charity in our society. The bodies which collect money are known as "charities." These organizations see themselves in this way—if you send them a check, you will be thanked for your "generosity." Because giving money is regarded as an act of charity, it is not thought that there is anything wrong with not giving. The charitable man may be praised, but the man who is not charitable is not condemned. People do not feel in any way ashamed or guilty about spending money on new clothes or a new car instead of giving it to famine relief. (Indeed, the alternative does not occur to them.) This way of looking at the matter cannot be justified. When we buy new clothes not to keep ourselves warm but to look "well-dressed" we are not providing for any important need. We would not be sacrificing anything significant if we were to continue to wear our old clothes, and give the money to famine relief. By doing so, we would be preventing another person from starving. It follows from what I have said earlier that we ought to give money away, rather than spend it on clothes which we do not need to keep us warm. To do so is not charitable, or generous. Nor is it the kind of act which philosophers and theologians have called "supererogatory"—an act which it would be good to do, but not wrong not to do. On the contrary, we ought to give the money away, and it is wrong not to do so.

I am not maintaining that there are no acts which are charitable, or that there are no acts which it would be good to do but not wrong not to do. It may be possible to redraw the distinction between duty and charity in some other place. All I am arguing here is that the present way of drawing the distinction, which makes it an act of charity for a man living at the level of affluence which most people in the "developed nations" enjoy to give money to save someone else from starvation, cannot be supported. It is beyond the scope of my argument to consider whether the distinction should be redrawn or abolished altogether. There would be many other possible ways of drawing the distinction—for instance, one might decide that it is good to make other people as happy as possible, but not wrong not to do so.

Despite the limited nature of the revision in our moral conceptual scheme which I am proposing, the revision would, given the extent of both affluence and famine in the world today, have radical implications. These implications may lead to further objections, distinct from those I have already considered. I shall discuss two of these.

One objection to the position I have taken might be simply that it is too drastic a revision of our moral scheme. People do not ordinarily judge in the way I have suggested they should. Most people reserve their moral condemnation for those who violate some moral norm, such as the norm against taking another person's property. They do not condemn those who indulge in luxury instead of giving to famine relief. But given that I did not set out to present a morally neutral description of the way people make moral judgments, the way people do in fact judge has nothing to do with the validity of my conclusion. My conclusion follows from the principle which I advanced earlier, and unless that principle is rejected, or the arguments shown to be unsound, I think the conclusion must stand, however strange it appears.

It might, nevertheless, be interesting to consider why our society, and most other societies, do judge differently from the way I have suggested they should. In a well-known article, J. O. Urmson suggests that the imperatives of duty, which tell us what we must do, as distinct from what it would be good to do but not wrong not to do, function so as to prohibit behavior that is intolerable if men are to live together in society.[3] This may explain the origin and continued existence of the present division between acts of duty and acts of charity. Moral attitudes are shaped by the needs of society, and no doubt society needs people who will observe the rules that make social existence tolerable. From the point of view of a particular

---

[3]J. O. Urmson, "Saints and Heroes," in *Essays in Moral Philosophy,* ed. Abraham I. Melden (Seattle: University of Washington Press, 1958), p. 214. For a related but significantly different view see also Henry Sidgwick, *The Methods of Ethics,* 7th edn. (London: Dover Press, 1907), pp. 220–21, 492–93.

society, it is essential to prevent violations of norms against killing, stealing, and so on. It is quite inessential, however, to help people outside one's own society.

If this is an explanation of our common distinction between duty and supererogation, however, it is not a justification of it. The moral point of view requires us to look beyond the interests of our own society. Previously, as I have already mentioned, this may hardly have been feasible, but it is quite feasible now. From the moral point of view, the prevention of the starvation of millions of people outside our society must be considered at least as pressing as the upholding of property norms within our society.

It has been argued by some writers, among them Sidgwick and Urmson, that we need to have a basic moral code which is not too far beyond the capacities of the ordinary man, for otherwise there will be a general breakdown of compliance with the moral code. Crudely stated, this argument suggests that if we tell people that they ought to refrain from murder and give everything they do not really need to famine relief, they will do neither, whereas if we tell them that they ought to refrain from murder and that it is good to give to famine relief but not wrong not to do so, they will at least refrain from murder. The issue here is: Where should we draw the line between conduct that is required and conduct that is good although not required, so as to get the best possible result? This would seem to be an empirical question, although a very difficult one. One objection to the Sidgwick-Urmson line of argument is that it takes insufficient account of the effect that moral standards can have on the decisions we make. Given a society in which a wealthy man who gives 5 percent of his income to famine relief is regarded as most generous, it is not surprising that a proposal that we all ought to give away half our incomes will be thought to be absurdly unrealistic. In a society which held that no man should have more than enough while others have less than they need, such a proposal might seem narrow-minded. What it is possible for a man to do and what he is likely to do are both, I think, very greatly influenced by what people around him are doing and expecting him to do. In any case, the possibility that by spreading the idea that we ought to be doing very much more than we are to relieve famine we shall bring about a general breakdown of moral behavior seems remote. If the stakes are an end to widespread starvation, it is worth the risk. Finally, it should be emphasized that these considerations are relevant only to the issue of what we should require from others, and not to what we ourselves ought to do.

The second objection to my attack on the present distinction between duty and charity is one which has from time to time been made against utilitarianism. It follows from some forms of utilitarian theory that we all ought, morally, to be working full time to increase the balance of happiness over misery. The position I have taken here would not lead to this conclusion in all circumstances, for if there were no bad occurrences that we could prevent without sacrificing something of comparable moral importance, my argument would have no application. Given the present conditions in many parts of the world, however, it does follow from my argument that we ought, morally, to be working full time to relieve great suffering of the sort that occurs as a result of famine or other disasters. Of course, mitigating circumstances can be adduced—for instance, that if we wear ourselves out through overwork, we shall be less effective than we would otherwise have been. Nevertheless, when all considerations of this sort have been taken into account, the conclusion remains: we ought to be preventing as much suffering as we can without sacrificing something else of comparable moral importance. This conclusion is one which we may be reluctant to face. I cannot see, though, why it should be regarded as a criticism of the position for which I have argued, rather than a criticism of our ordinary standards of behavior. Since most people are self-interested to some degree, very few of us are likely to do everything that we ought to do. It would, however, hardly be honest to take this as evidence that it is not the case that we ought to do it.

It may still be thought that my conclusions are so wildly out of line with what everyone else thinks and has always thought that there must be something wrong with the argument somewhere. In order to show that my conclusions, while certainly contrary to contemporary Western moral standards, would not have seemed so extraordinary at other times and in other places, I would like to quote a passage from a writer not normally thought of as a way-out radical, Thomas Aquinas.

> Now, according to the natural order instituted by divine providence, material goods are provided for the satisfaction of human needs. Therefore the division and appropriation of property, which proceeds from human law, must not hinder the satisfaction of man's necessity from such goods. Equally, whatever a man has in superabundance is owed, of natural right, to the poor for their sustenance. So Ambrosius says, and it is also to be found in the *Decretum Gratiani*: "The bread which you withhold belongs to the hungry; the clothing you shut away, to the naked; and the money you bury in the earth is the redemption and freedom of the penniless."[4]

I now want to consider a number of points, more practical than philosophical, which are relevant to the application of the moral conclusion we have reached. These points challenge not the idea that we ought to be doing all we can to prevent starvation, but the idea that giving away a great deal of money is the best means to this end.

[4]*Summa Theologica*, II-II, Question 66, Article 7, in *Aquinas, Selected Political Writings*, ed. A. P. d'Entreves, trans. J. G. Dawson (Oxford: Basil Blackwell, 1948), p. 171.

It is sometimes said that overseas aid should be a government responsibility, and that therefore one ought not to give to privately run charities. Giving privately, it is said, allows the government and the noncontributing members of society to escape their responsibilities.

This argument seems to assume that the more people there are who give to privately organized famine relief funds, the less likely it is that the government will take over full responsibility for such aid. This assumption is unsupported, and does not strike me as at all plausible. The opposite view—that if no one gives voluntarily, a government will assume that its citizens are uninterested in famine relief and would not wish to be forced into giving aid—seems more plausible. In any case, unless there were a definite probability that by refusing to give one would be helping to bring about massive government assistance, people who do refuse to make voluntary contributions are refusing to prevent a certain amount of suffering without being able to point to any tangible beneficial consequence of their refusal. So the onus of showing how their refusal will bring about government action is on those who refuse to give.

I do not, of course, want to dispute the contention that governments of affluent nations should be giving many times the amount of genuine, no-strings-attached aid that they are giving now. I agree, too, that giving privately is not enough, and that we ought to be campaigning actively for entirely new standards for both public and private contributions to famine relief. Indeed, I would sympathize with someone who thought that campaigning was more important than giving oneself, although I doubt whether preaching what one does not practice would be very effective. Unfortunately, for many people the idea that "it's the government's responsibility" is a reason for not giving which does not appear to entail any political action either.

Another, more serious reason for not giving to famine relief funds is that until there is effective population control, relieving famine merely postpones starvation. If we save the Bengal refugees now, others, perhaps the children of these refugees, will face starvation in a few years' time. In support of this, one may cite the now well-known facts about the population explosion and the relatively limited scope for expanded production.

This point, like the previous one, is an argument against relieving suffering that is happening now, because of a belief about what might happen in the future; it is unlike the previous point in that very good evidence can be adduced in support of this belief about the future. I will not go into the evidence here. I accept that the earth cannot support indefinitely a population rising at the present rate. This certainly poses a problem for anyone who thinks it important to prevent famine. Again, however, one could accept the argument without drawing the conclusion that it absolves one from any obligation to do anything to prevent famine. The conclusion that should be drawn is that the best means of preventing famine, in the long run, is population control. It would then follow from the position reached earlier that one ought to be doing all one can to promote population control (unless one held that all forms of population control were wrong in themselves, or would have significantly bad consequences). Since there are organizations working specifically for population control, one would then support them rather than more orthodox methods of preventing famine.

A third point raised by the conclusion reached earlier relates to the question of just how much we all ought to be giving away. One possibility, which has already been mentioned, is that we ought to give until we reach the level of marginal utility—that is, the level at which, by giving more, I would cause as much suffering to myself or my dependents as I would relieve by my gift. This would mean, of course, that one would reduce oneself to very near the material circumstances of a Bengali refugee. It will be recalled that earlier I put forward both a strong and a moderate version of the principle of preventing bad occurrences. The strong version, which required us to prevent bad things from happening unless in doing so we would be sacrificing something of comparable moral significance, does seem to require reducing ourselves to the level of marginal utility. I should also say that the strong version seems to me to be the correct one. I proposed the more moderate version—that we should prevent bad occurrences unless, to do so, we had to sacrifice something morally significant —only in order to show that even on this surely undeniable principle a great change in our way of life is required. On the more moderate principle, it may not follow that we ought to reduce ourselves to the level of marginal utility, for one might hold that to reduce oneself and one's family to this level is to cause something significantly bad to happen. Whether this is so I shall not discuss, since, as I have said, I can see no good reason for holding the moderate version of the principle rather than the strong version. Even if we accepted the principle only in its moderate form, however, it should be clear that we would have to give away enough to ensure that the consumer society, dependent as it is on people spending on trivia rather than giving to famine relief, would slow down and perhaps disappear entirely. There are several reasons why this would be desirable in itself. The value and necessity of economic growth are now being questioned not only by conservationists, but by economists as well.[5] There is no doubt, too, that the consumer society has had a distorting effect on the goals and purposes of its members. Yet looking at the matter purely from the point of view of overseas aid, there must be a limit to the extent to which we should deliberately slow down our economy; for it might be the case that if we gave away, say, 40 percent of our Gross National Product, we would

[5]See, for instance, John Kenneth Galbraith, *The New Industrial State* (Boston: Houghton Mifflin, 1967); and E. J. Mishan, *The Costs of Economic Growth* (New York: Praeger, 1967).

slow down the economy so much that in absolute terms we would be giving less than if we gave 25 percent of the much larger GNP that we would have if we limited our contribution to this smaller percentage.

I mention this only as an indication of the sort of factor that one would have to take into account in working out an ideal. Since Western societies generally consider one percent of the GNP an acceptable level for overseas aid, the matter is entirely academic. Nor does it affect the question of how much an individual should give in a society in which very few are giving substantial amounts.

It is sometimes said, though less often now than it used to be, that philosophers have no special role to play in public affairs, since most public issues depend primarily on an assessment of facts. On questions of fact, it is said, philosophers as such have no special expertise, and so it has been possible to engage in philosophy without committing oneself to any position on major public issues. No doubt there are some issues of social policy and foreign policy about which it can truly be said that a really expert assessment of the facts is required before taking sides or acting, but the issue of famine is surely not one of these. The facts about the existence of suffering are beyond dispute. Nor, I think, is it disputed that we can do something about it, either through orthodox methods of famine relief or through population control or both. This is therefore an issue on which philosophers are competent to take a position. The issue is one which faces everyone who has more money than he needs to support himself and his dependents, or who is in a position to take some sort of political action. These categories must include practically every teacher and student of philosophy in the universities of the Western world. If philosophy is to deal with matters that are relevant to both teachers and students, this is an issue that philosophers should discuss.

Discussion, though, is not enough. What is the point of relating philosophy to public (and personal) affairs if we do not take our conclusions seriously? In this instance, taking our conclusion seriously means acting upon it. The philosopher will not find it any easier than anyone else to alter his attitudes and way of life to the extent that, if I am right, is involved in doing everything that we ought to be doing. At the very least, though, one can make a start. The philosopher who does so will have to sacrifice some of the benefits of the consumer society, but he can find compensation in the satisfaction of a way of life in which theory and practice, if not yet in harmony, are at least coming together.

POSTSCRIPT

The crisis in Bangladesh that spurred me to write the above article is now of historical interest only, but the world food crisis is, if anything, still more serious. The huge grain reserves that were then held by the United States have vanished. Increased oil prices have made both fertilizer and energy more expensive in developing countries, and have made it difficult for them to produce more food. At the same time, their population has continued to grow. Fortunately, as I write now, there is no major famine anywhere in the world; but poor people are still starving in several countries, and malnutrition remains very widespread. The need for assistance is, therefore, just as great as when I first wrote, and we can be sure that without it there will, again, be major famines.

The contrast between poverty and affluence that I wrote about is also as great as it was then. True, the affluent nations have experienced a recession, and are perhaps not as prosperous as they were in 1971. But the poorer nations have suffered as least as much from the recession, in reduced government aid (because if governments decide to reduce expenditure, they regard foreign aid as one of the expendable items, ahead of, for instance, defense or public construction projects) and in increased prices for goods and materials they need to buy. In any case, compared to the difference between the affluent nations and the poor nations, the whole recession was trifling; the poorest in the affluent nations remained incomparably better off than the poorest in the poor nations.

So the case for aid, on both a personal and a governmental level, remains as great now as it was in 1971, and I would not wish to change the basic argument that I put forward then.

There are, however, some matters of emphasis that I might put differently if I were to rewrite the article, and the most important of these concerns the population problem. I still think that, as I wrote then, the view that famine relief merely postpones starvation unless something is done to check population growth is not an argument against aid, it is only an argument against the *type* of aid that should be given. Those who hold this view have the same obligation to give to prevent starvation as those who do not; the difference is that they regard assisting population control schemes as a more effective way of preventing starvation in the long run. I would now, however, have given greater space to the discussion of the population problem; for I now think that there is a serious case for saying that if a country refuses to take any steps to slow the rate of its population growth, we should not give it aid. This is, of course, a very drastic step to take, and the choice it represents is a horrible choice to have to make; but if, after a dispassionate analysis of all the available information, we come to the conclusion that without population control we will not, in the long run, be able to prevent famine or other catastrophes, then it may be more humane in the long run to aid those countries that are prepared to take strong measures to reduce population growth, and to use our aid policy as a means of pressuring other countries to take similar steps.

It may be objected that such a policy involves an attempt to coerce a sovereign nation. But since we are not under an obligation to give aid unless that aid is likely to be effective in reducing starvation or malnutrition, we are not under an obligation to give aid to countries that make no effort to reduce a rate of population growth that will lead to catastrophe. Since we do not force any nation to accept our aid, simply making it clear that we will not give aid where it is not going to be effective cannot properly be regarded as a form of coercion.

I should also make it clear that the kind of aid that will slow population growth is not just assistance with the setting up of facilities for dispensing contraceptives and performing sterilizations. It is also necessary to create the conditions under which people do not wish to have so many children. This will involve, among other things, providing greater economic security for people, particularly in their old age, so that they do not need the security of a large family to provide for them. Thus, the requirements of aid designed to reduce population growth and aid designed to eliminate starvation are by no means separate; they overlap, and the latter will often be a means to the former. The obligation of the affluent is, I believe, to do both. Fortunately, there are now so many people in the foreign aid field, including those in the private agencies, who are aware of this.

One other matter that I should now put forward slightly differently is that my argument does, of course, apply to assistance with development, particularly agricultural development, as well as to direct famine relief. Indeed, I think the former is usually the better long-term investment. Although this was my view when I wrote the article, the fact that I started from a famine situation, where the need was for immediate food, has led some readers to suppose that the argument is only about giving food and not about other types of aid. This is quite mistaken, and my view is that the aid should be of whatever type is most effective.

On a more philosophical level, there has been some discussion of the original article which has been helpful in clarifying the issues and pointing to the areas in which more work on the argument is needed. In particular, as John Arthur has shown in "Rights and the Duty to Bring Aid" (included in this volume), something more needs to be said about the notion of 'moral significance'. The problem is that to give an account of this notion involves nothing less than a full-fledged ethical theory; and while I am myself inclined toward a utilitarian view, it was my aim in writing "Famine, Affluence, and Morality" to produce an argument which would appeal not only to utilitarians, but also to anyone who accepted the initial premises of the argument, which seemed to me likely to have a very wide acceptance. So I tried to get around the need to produce a complete ethical theory by allowing my readers to fill in their own version—within limits —of what is morally significant, and then see what the moral consequences are. This tactic works reasonably well with those who are prepared to agree that such matters as being fashionably dressed are not really of moral significance; but Arthur is right to say that people could take the opposite view without being obviously irrational. Hence, I do not accept Arthur's claim that the weak principle implies little or no duty of benevolence, for it will imply a significant duty of benevolence for those who admit, as I think most nonphilosophers and even off-guard philosophers will admit, that they spend considerable sums on items that by their own standards are of no moral significance. But I do agree that the weak principle is nonetheless too weak, because it makes it too easy for the duty of benevolence to be avoided.

On the other hand, I think the strong principle will stand, whether the notion of moral significance is developed along utilitarian lines, or once again left to the individual reader's own sincere judgment. In either case, I would argue against Arthur's view that we are morally entitled to give greater weight to our own interests and purposes simply because they are our own. This view seems to me contrary to the idea, now widely shared by moral philosophers, that some element of impartiality or universalizability is inherent in the very notion of a moral judgment. (For a discussion of the different formulations of this idea, and an indication of the extent to which they are in agreement, see R.M. Hare, "Rules of War and Moral Reasoning," *Philosophy and Public Affairs* I, no. 2 [1972].) Granted, in normal circumstances, it may be better for everyone if we recognize that each of us will be primarily responsible for running our own lives and only secondarily responsible for others. This, however, is not a moral ultimate, but a secondary principle that derives from consideration of how a society may best order its affairs, given the limits of altruism in human beings. Such secondary principles are, I think, swept aside by the extreme evil of people starving to death.

JOHN ARTHUR

Arthur argues that utilitarian theories like Singer's fail to give enough weight to the rights of the affluent. He proposes an alternative, a duty of benevolence, which sometimes obligates the affluent not to exercise their right to consume.

1. Is Arthur's contention that Singer fails to account for individuals' rights correct? How important are these rights?

2. Do persons have a special moral relationship to their own goals or projects? Why?

3. For Arthur, positive rights arise only contractually. Contrast this with Aiken's "right to be saved from starvation."

4. Can starving people justifiably expect or demand benevolence?

John Arthur is Assistant Professor of Philosophy at the University of Tennessee at Nashville, where he specializes in ethics and political philosophy.

Rights and the Duty to Bring Aid

I

There is no doubt that the large and growing incidence of world hunger constitutes a major problem, both moral and practical, for the fortunate few who have surpluses of cheap food. Our habits regarding meat consumption exemplify the magnitude of the moral issue. Americans now consume about two and one-half times the meat they did in 1950 (currently about 125 lbs. per capita per year). Yet, meat is extremely inefficient as a source of food. Only a small portion of the total calories consumed

This article has not been previously published.

by the animal remains to be eaten in the meat. As much as 95 per cent of the food is lost by feeding and eating cattle rather than producing the grain for direct human consumption. Thus, the same amount of food consumed by Americans largely indirectly in meat form could feed one and a half billion persons on a (relatively meatless) Chinese diet. Much, if not all, of the world's food crisis could be resolved if Americans were simply to change their eating habits by moving toward direct consumption of grain and at the same time providing the surpluses for the hungry. Given this, plus the serious moral problems associated with animal suffering,[1] the overall case for vegetarianism seems strong.

I want to discuss here only one of these two related problems, the obligations of the affluent few to starving people. I begin by considering a recent article on the subject by Peter Singer, entitled "Famine, Affluence, and Morality" (reprinted in this volume).[2] I argue that Singer fails to establish the claim that such an obligation exists. This is the case for both the strong and weak interpretations of his view. I then go on to show that the role of rights needs to be given greater weight than utilitarian theories like Singer's allow. The rights of both the affluent and the starving are shown to be morally significant but not in themselves decisive, since obligations of benevolence can and often do override rights of others (e.g., property rights). Finally, I argue that under specific conditions the affluent are obligated not to exercise their rights to consume at the expense of others' lives.

II

Singer's argument is in two stages. First, he argues that two general moral principles are and ought to be accepted. Then he claims that the principles imply an obligation to eliminate starvation. The first principle is simply that "suffering and death from lack of food, shelter and medical care are bad."[3] This principle seems obviously true and I will have little to say about it. Some may be inclined to think that the existence of an evil in itself places an obligation on others, but that is, of course, the problem which Singer addresses. I take it that he is not begging the question in this obvious way and will argue from the existence of evil to the obligation of others to eliminate it. But how, exactly, does he establish the connection? It is the second principle which he thinks shows that connection.

The necessary link is provided by either of two versions of this principle.

[1]Peter Singer, *Animal Liberation* (New York: New York Review of Books/Random House, 1975).

[2]Peter Singer, "Famine, Affluence, and Morality," *Philosophy and Public Affairs,* I, no. 3 (Spring 1972).

[3]Ibid., p. 24 (in this volume).

The first (strong) formulation which Singer offers of the second principle is as follows:

> if it is in our power to prevent something bad from happening, without thereby sacrificing anything of comparable moral importance, we ought, morally, to do it.[4]

The weaker principle simply substitutes for "comparable moral importance" the phrase "any moral significance." He goes on to develop these notions, saying that:

> By 'without sacrificing anything of comparable moral importance' I mean without causing anything else comparably bad to happen, or doing something that is wrong in itself, or failing to promote some moral good, comparable in significance to the bad thing we can prevent.[5]

These remarks can be interpreted for the weaker principle by simply eliminating "comparable" in the statement.

One question is, of course, whether either of these two principles ought to be accepted. There are two ways in which this could be established. First, they could be shown, by philosophical argument, to follow from reasonably well established premises or from a general theory. Second, they might be justified because they are principles which underlie particular moral judgments the truth of which is accepted. Singer doesn't do either of these explicitly, although he seems to have the second in mind. He first speaks of what he takes to be the "uncontroversial appearance" of the principles. He then applies the principles to a similar case in which a drowning child requires help. Singer argues, in essence, that since the drowning is bad and it can be avoided without sacrificing something of moral significance, it is obligatory that the child be saved. He claims further that both the strong and weak versions are sufficient to establish the duty. Dirtying one's clothes, for example, is not of "moral significance" and so does not justify failure to act. The last part of his paper is devoted to the claim that the analogy between the case of the child and starving people is apt in that geographical distance and others' willingness to act are not acceptable excuses for inaction.

III

My concern here is not with these latter issues. Rather, I want to focus on the two versions of the second principle, discussing each in terms of (1)

[4] Ibid.

[5] Ibid. I assume 'importance' and 'significance' are synonymous.

whether it is plausible, and (2) if true, whether it establishes the duty to provide aid. I will deal with the weak version first, arguing that it fails at step (2) in the argument.

This version reads, "if it is in our power to prevent something bad from happening without thereby sacrificing *anything* morally significant we ought morally to do it." Singer later claims that:

> Even if we accept the principle in its moderate form, however, it should be clear that we would have to give away enough to ensure that the consumer society, dependent as it is on people spending on trivia rather than giving to famine relief, would slow down and perhaps disappear entirely.[6]

The crucial idea of "morally significant" is left largely unanalyzed. Two examples are given: dirtying one's clothes and being "well dressed." Both are taken to be morally *in*significant.

It could perhaps be argued against Singer that these things *are* morally significant. Both, for example, would be cases of decreasing aesthetic value, and if you think aesthetic values are intrinsic you might well dispute the claim that being "well dressed" is without moral significance. There is, however, a more serious objection to be raised. To see this, we need to distinguish between the possible value of the *fact* of being "well dressed" and the value of the *enjoyment* some persons receive and create by being "well dressed" (and, of course, the unhappiness avoided by being "badly dressed").

That such enjoyment and unhappiness are of some moral significance can be seen by the following case. Suppose it were possible that, by simply singing a chorus of "Dixie" you could eliminate all the unhappiness and embarrassment that some people experience at being badly dressed. Surely, doing that would be an act of moral significance. It would be good for you to do so, perhaps even wrong not to. Similarly, throwing mud on people's clothes, though not a great wrong, is surely not "without *any* moral significance."

It seems then, that the weak principle (while perhaps true) does not generally establish a duty to provide aid to starving people. Whether it does in specific instances depends on the nature of the cost to the person providing the aid. If *either* the loss to the giver is in itself valuable or the loss results in increased unhappiness or decreased happiness to someone, then the principle does not require that the burden be accepted.

(It is interesting to ask just how much giving *would* be required by this principle. If we can assume that givers would benefit in some minimal way by giving —and that they are reasonable— then perhaps the best answer

[6]Ibid., p. 32 (in this volume).

is that the level of giving required is the level that is actually given. Otherwise, why would people *not* give more if there is no value to them in things they choose to keep?)

In addition to the moral significance of the costs that I just described, there is a further problem which will become particularly significant in considering the strong principle. For many people it is part of their moral sense that they and others have a special relationship to their own goals or projects. That is, in making one's choices a person may properly weigh the outcome that one desires more heavily than the goals that others may have. Often this is expressed as a right or entitlement.[7] Thus, for example, if P acquires some good (x) in a just social arrangement without violating others' rights, then P has a special title to x that P is entitled to weigh against the desires of others. P need not, in determining whether he ought to give x to another, overlook the fact that x is his; he acquired it fairly, and so has special say in what happens to it. If this is correct, it is a fact of some moral significance and thus would also block the inference from the weak principle to the obligation to give what one has to others. I will pursue this line of argument in the following section while considering the strong version of the principle.

IV

Many people, especially those inclined toward utilitarianism, would probably accept the preceding, believing that it is the stronger of the two principles that should be used. "After all," they might argue, "the real issue is the great *disparity* between the amount of good which could be produced by resources of the rich if applied to problems of starvation as against the small amount of good produced by the resources if spent on second cars and houses, fancy clothes etc." I will assume that the facts are just as the claim suggests. That is, I will assume that it can *not* be plausibly argued that there are, for example, artistic or cultural values which (1) would be lost by such redistribution of wealth and (2) are equal in value to the starvation which would be eliminated. Thus, if the strong principle is true, then it (unlike the weak version) would require radical changes in our common understanding of the duties of the wealthy to starving people.

But is it true, as Singer suggests, that "if it is in our power to prevent something bad from happening without thereby sacrificing something of comparable moral significance we ought morally to do it?" Here the problem with the meaning of "moral significance" is even more acute than in the weak version. All that was required for the weak principle was that we

---

[7]In a recent book (*Anarchy, State, and Utopia,* New York: Basic Books, 1974), Robert Nozick argues that such rights are extensive against state authority.

be able to distinguish courses of action that have moral significance from those that do not. Here, however, the moral significance of alternative acts must be both *recognized* and *weighed*. And how is this to be done, according to Singer? Unfortunately, he provides little help here, though this is crucial in evaluating his argument.

I will discuss one obvious interpretation of "comparable moral significance," argue it is inadequate, and then suggest what I take to be some of the factors an adequate theory would consider.

Assuming that giving aid is not "bad in itself," the only other facts which Singer sees as morally significant in evaluating obligations are the good or bad consequences of actions. Singer's strong version obviously resembles the act utilitarian principle. With respect to starvation, this interpretation is open to the objection raised at the end of part III above, since it takes no account of a variety of important factors, such as the apparent right to give added weight to one's own choices and interests, and to ownership. I now wish to look at this claim in more detail.

Consider the following examples of moral problems which I take to be fairly common. One obvious means by which you could aid others is with your body. Many of your extra organs (eye, kidney) could be given to another with the result that there is more good than if you kept both. You wouldn't see as well or live as long, perhaps, but that is not of comparable significance to the benefit others would receive. Yet, surely the fact that it is your eye and you need it is not insignificant. Perhaps there could be cases where one is obligated to sacrifice one's health or sight, but what seems clear is that this is not true in every case where (slightly) more good would come of your doing so. Second, suppose a woman has a choice between remaining with her husband or leaving. As best she can determine, the morally relevant factors do not indicate which she should do (the consequences of each seem about equally good and there is no question of broken promises, deception, or whatever). But, suppose in addition to these facts, it is the case that by remaining with her husband the woman will be unable to pursue important aspects of the plan of life she has set for herself. Perhaps by remaining she will be forced to sacrifice a career which she wishes to pursue. If the *only* facts that are of moral significance are the consequences of her choice, then she ought, presumably, to flip a coin (assuming there is some feature of her staying that is of equal importance to the unhappiness at the loss of the career *she* will experience). Surely, though, the fact that some goals are ones *she* chooses for herself (assuming she doesn't violate the others' rights) is of significance. It is, after all, *her* life and *her* future and she is entitled to treat it that way. In neither of these cases is the person required to accept as equal to his or her own goals and well-being the welfare of even his or her family, much less the whole world. The fact that others may benefit even slightly more from their pursuing another course is not in itself sufficient to show they ought to act other than they choose. Servility, though perhaps not a vice, is certainly not an obligation that all must fulfill.[8]

The above goes part way, I think, in explaining the importance we place on allowing people maximal latitude in pursuing their goals. Rights or entitlements to things that are our own reflect important facts about people. Each of us has only one life and it is uniquely valuable to each of us. Your choices do not constitute my life, nor do mine yours. The purely utilitarian interpretation of "moral significance" provides for assigning no special weight to the goals and interests of individuals in making their choices. It provides no basis for saying that though there may be greater total good done by one course, still a person could be entitled for some reason to pursue another.

It seems, then, that determining whether giving aid to starving persons would be sacrificing something of comparable moral significance demands weighing the fact that the persons are entitled to give special weight to their own interests where their future or (fairly acquired) property is at issue. Exactly *how much* weight may be given is a question that I will consider shortly. The point here is that the question of the extent of the obligation to eliminate starvation has not been answered. My argument was that however "moral significance" is best understood, it is far too simple to suggest that *only* the total good produced is relevant. If providing quality education for one's children is a goal, then (assuming the resources were acquired fairly) the fact that it is a goal *itself* provides additional weight against other ways the resources might be used, including the one that maximizes the total good. Further, if the resources to be used for the purpose are legitimately owned, then that too is something that the parent is entitled to consider.

Returning to the case of the drowning child, the same point may be made. Suppose it is an important part of a person's way of life that he not interfere. Perhaps the passer-by believes God's will is being manifested in this particular incident and strongly values noninterference with God's working out of His plan. Surely, this is especially relevant to the question of whether the person is obligated to intervene, even when the greatest good would be promoted by intervention. When saying that a person is obligated to act in some way, the significance *to the person* of the act must not only be considered along with all the other features of the act, but is also of special moral significance in determining that person's duty. More, however, needs to be said here.

Suppose, for instance, that the case were like this: A passer-by sees a child drowning but fails to help, not for the sake of another important goal but rather out of lack of interest. Such situations are not at all uncommon,

[8]For an argument that servility is wrong, see Thomas Hill, "Servility and Self-Respect," *The Monist,* VII, no. 4 (January 1973).

as when people fail to report violent crimes they observe in progress. I assume that anyone who fails to act in such circumstances is acting wrongly. As with the case of the utilitarian principle discussed earlier, the drowning child also represents a limiting case. In the former, *no* significance is assigned to the woman's choice by virtue of its being *hers.* Here, however, the interests of *others* are not weighed. An acceptable principle of benevolence would fall between the two limiting cases. The relative moral significance of alternative acts could then be determined by applying the principle, distinguishing acts which are obligatory from charitable ones.

In summary, I have argued that neither the strong nor the weak principle advanced by Singer provides an adequate solution to the issue of affluence and hunger. The essential problem is with his notion of "moral significance." I argued that the weak principle fails to show any obligations, given the normal conception of factors which possess such significance. I then argued that the strong principle (which is close to act utilitarianism) is mistaken. The basic objection to this principle is that it fails to take account of certain aspects of the situation which must be considered in any adequate formulation of the principle.

V

As I suggested earlier, a fully adequate formulation of the principle of benevolence depends on a general theory of right. Such a theory would not only include a principle of benevolence but also give account of the whole range of rights and duties and a means to weigh conflicting claims. In this section, I discuss some of the various problems associated with benevolence, obligation, and rights. In the final section, I offer what I believe to be an adequate principle of benevolence.

One view, which has been criticized recently by Judith Thomson,[9] suggests that whenever there is a duty or obligation there must be a corresponding right. I presume we want to say that in some cases (e.g., the drowning child) there is an obligation to benevolence, but does this also mean that the child has a *right* to be aided? Perhaps there is only a semantic point here regarding "right," but perhaps also there is a deeper disagreement.

I suggest that, whether we call it a "right" or not, there are important differences between obligations based on benevolence and other obligations. Two differences are significant. First, the person who has the obligation to save the drowning child did not *do anything* that created the

[9]Judith Jarvis Thomson, "The Right to Privacy," *Philosophy and Public Affairs,* IV, no. 4 (Summer 1975).

situation. But, compare this case with a similar one of a lifeguard who fails to save someone. Here there is a clear sense in which the drowning victim may claim a right to have another do his utmost to save him. An agreement was reached whereby the lifeguard *accepted* the responsibility for the victim's welfare. The guard, in a sense, took on the goals of the swimmers as his own. To fail to aid is a special sort of injustice that the passer-by does not do. It seems clearly appropriate to speak of the lifeguard's failure to act as a case of a right being violated.

A second important point regarding the drowning child example and rights is that the passer-by is not *taking positive steps* in reference to the child. This can be contrasted with an action that might be taken to drown a child who would not otherwise die. Here, again, it is appropriate to describe this act as a violation of a right (to life). Other violations of rights also seem to require that one act, not merely fail to take action—for example, property rights (theft) and privacy rights (listening without leave). The drowning child and starvation cases are wrong not because of acts but the failure to act.

Thus, there are important differences between duties of benevolence and others where a right is obviously at issue. Cases of failing to aid are not (unlike right violations) either instances of positive actions that are taken or ones in which the rich or the passer-by has taken responsibility by a previous act. It does not follow from this, however, that strong obligations are not present to save other persons. Obviously, one ought to aid a drowning child (at least) in cases where there is no serious risk or cost to the passer-by. This is true even though there is no obvious right that the child has to be aided.

Furthermore, if saving a drowning child requires using someone's boat without their permission (a violation of property right), then it still ought to be done. Duties to bring aid can override duties not to violate rights. The best thing to say here is that, depending on the circumstances, duties to aid and not to violate rights can each outweigh the other. Where actions involve both violation of rights and failing to meet duties to aid (the lifeguard's failing to save), the obligation is stronger than either would be by itself. Describing the situation in this way implies that although there is a sense in which the boat owner, the affluent spender, and the passer-by have a right to fail to act, still they are obligated not to exercise that right because there is a stronger duty to give aid.

Some may be inclined to say, against this, that in fact the passer-by does not have such a right not to help. But this claim is ambiguous. If what is meant is that they ought to help, then I agree. There is, however, still a point in saying owners of food have the right to use the food as they see fit. It serves to emphasize that there is a moral difference between these cases and ones where the object of need is *not* legitimately owned by anyone (as, for example, if it's not another's boat but a log that the drowning child needs). To say that the property right is *lost* where the principle of benevolence overrides is to hide this difference, though it is morally significant.

Other people might be inclined to say about these situations that the point of saying someone has a right to their food, time, boat or whatever is that others ought not to intervene to force them to bring aid. A person defending this view might accept my claim that in fact the person ought to help. It might then be argued that because they are not violating a right of another (to be saved) and they have a (property) right to the good, others can't, through state authority, force them to bring aid.

This claim obviously raises a variety of questions in legal and political philosophy, and is outside the scope of the present paper. My position does not preclude good samaritan laws, nor are they implied. This is a further question which requires further argument. That one has a moral right to x, but is obligated for other reasons not to exercise the right, leaves open the issue of whether others either can or should make that person fulfill the obligation.

If what I have said is correct, two general points should be made about starvation. First, even though it may be that the affluent have a right to use resources to pursue their own goals, and not provide aid, they may also be strongly obligated not to exercise the right. This is because, in the circumstances, the duty to benevolence is overriding. The existence and extent of such an obligation can be determined only by discovering the relative weight of these conflicting principles. In the final section, I consider how this should be done.

Second, even if it is also true that the passer-by and the affluent do not violate a right of another in failing to help, it may still be the case that they strongly ought not do so. Of course, their behavior could also be even worse than it is (by drowning the child or sending poisoned food to the hungry and thus violating their rights). All that shows, however, is that the failure to help is not the *most* morally objectionable course that can be imagined in the circumstances. This point hardly constitutes justification for failing to act.

VI

I argued earlier that neither Singer's weak principle nor the utilitarian one is what we are after. The former would imply (wrongly) little or no duty of benevolence, and the latter does not take seriously enough the rights and interests of the affluent. What is needed is a principle which we may use to determine the circumstances in which the needs of others create a duty to bring aid which is more stringent than the rights of the affluent to pursue their own interests and use their property as they desire.

The following principle, while similar to the utilitarian one, seems to be most adequate: "If it is in our power to prevent death of an innocent without sacrificing anything of *substantial* significance then we ought morally to do it." The problem, of course, is to determine exactly what is meant by "substantial significance." I assume there are no duties present that arise out of others' rights, as, for example, those of one's children to be provided for. Considerations of that sort would lead beyond the present paper. My concern here is limited to instances in which there is a question of bringing aid (where no obvious right to the aid is present) or using resources for other (preferred) ends.

There are two questions which are important in deciding whether what is being given up by the affluent is of substantial significance. First, we might specify *objectively* the needs which people have, and grant that the duty to bring aid is not present unless these needs have already been met. Included among the needs which are of substantial significance would be those things without which a person cannot continue to function physically—for example, food, clothing, health care, housing, and sufficient training to provide these for oneself.

It also, however, seems reasonable that certain psychological facts ought to be weighed before a person is obligated to help others meet their needs. For example, if you cannot have an even modestly happy life without some further good, then surely that, too, is something to which you are entitled. This suggests a second, *subjective* standard that should also be employed to determine whether something is of no substantial significance and so ought not be consumed at the expense of others' basic needs. The best way to put this, I believe, is to say that "if the lack of x would not affect the long-term happiness of a person, then x is of no substantial significance." By "long-term happiness" I mean to include anything which, if not acquired, will result in unhappiness over an extended period of one's life, not just something the lack of which is a source of momentary loss but soon forgotten. Thus, in a normal case, dirtying one's clothes to save a drowning child is of no substantial significance and so the duty of benevolence is overriding. If, however, selling some possession for famine relief would mean the person's life *really is* (for a long period) less happy, then the possessions are of substantial significance and so the person is not wrong in exercising the right of ownership instead of providing aid. If the possessions had been sold, it would have been an act of charity, not fulfillment of a duty. The same analysis can be provided for other choices we make —for example, how our time is spent and whether to donate organs. If doing so would result in your not seeing well and this would make your life less happy over time, then you are not obligated to do so.

If what I have said is correct, then duties of benevolence increase as one's dependence on possessions for living a happy life decreases. If a person's long-term happiness does not depend on (second?) cars and fancy clothes, then that person ought not to purchase those goods at the expense of others' basic needs being unfulfilled. Thus, depending on the psychological nature of persons, their duties of benevolence will vary.

The question of the actual effect of not buying a new car, house, clothes, or whatever on one's long-term happiness is of course a difficult one. My own feeling is that if the principle were to be applied honestly, those of us who are relatively affluent would discover that a substantial part of the resources and time we expend should be used to bring aid. The extent of the obligation must, finally, be determined by asking whether the lack of some good *really would* result in a need not being met or in a less happy life for its owner, and that is a question between each of us and our conscience.

In summary, I have argued that Singer's utilitarian principle is inadequate to establish the claim that acts to eliminate starvation are obligatory, but that such an obligation still exists. The rights of both the affluent and the hungry are considered, and a principle is defended which clarifies the circumstances in which it is a duty and not merely charitable to provide aid to others whose basic needs are not being met.

JAN NARVESON

Narveson considers two popular and plausible moral responses to world hunger—the Conservative and Liberal responses. He argues, from two different moral perspectives, that the Liberal response is more reasonable and so there is a moral duty to alleviate hunger.

1. Notice his discussion of the foundation of ethical principles and his critique of the abuse of "self evident" arguments.

2. How are claims about human nature related to moral rules?

3. How does his criterion of "reasonable morality" relate to Watson's claim that morality may be irrational?

4. Legal coercion, he says, may be used to enforce morality. Should moral action to alleviate world hunger be enforced by law?

Jan Narveson, Professor of Philosophy at the University of Waterloo, is the author of Morality and Utility *as well as various articles on ethics and political philosophy.*

Morality and Starvation

People need to eat, and some are starving. Others have more than they need, even more than they could possibly eat; and they could grow still more, if so inclined. Are those with more-than-enough morally obligated to assist those with less-than-enough? That is the main question I wish to discuss here.

It is important to distinguish this question from others which lie to varying degrees beyond the province of this treatment. For example, there

This article has not been previously published.

are such issues as whether it is in the interest of one party to feed another, especially when the interests in question are national interests, the parties in question politically organized states. There is the question of whether it is possible, practically speaking, to do anything about the problem, and if so, then which are the best things to do. And there is the important issue of whether many or perhaps all forms of aid might not be self-defeating in the long run. Obviously, these are all questions which might have to be faced in one circumstance or another. Perhaps if State A feeds starving State B, then B will be able to provide A with benefits which A could not otherwise enjoy. Or perhaps if A feeds B, then some time later B will make war on A; or B will impose its political system on an unwilling A, ungratefully enough; or perhaps if the B's all starve, then the A's will be able to acquire some dandy vacation spots on the now-vacant B-premises. Again, having decided that it ought to help out the B's, A might find that it is not all that easy to help. The B's government might be corruptly diverting all the supplies to its own avaricious officials, or for political reasons of its own refusing to admit that there is a problem and not allowing food into the troubled areas. (I am told it is useless to send food to Bangladesh, and that the Romanian government confiscates and sells for its own profit CARE packages intended for starving flood victims. Examples multiply before one's troubled eyes.) And if successful, the effect of one's aid program might be to enable the B's to reproduce uninhibitedly, leaving the next A generation with a problem unmanageably greater than that presently faced and hopefully solved by the current A's. All of these problems may arise, and one or several be crucial to a nation contemplating the unfortunate condition of people in another. (Some may arise for a nation contemplating the unfortunate condition of some of its own citizens.) But how much difference they make, indeed whether they make any difference at all, will depend on one's answer to the question I am concerned to discuss. If one judges that there is no obligation at all, then one will decide what to do purely on the basis of national interest. If we conclude that there is a very stringent obligation to feed the less fortunate, then most or even all considerations of self-interest may be brushed aside—even the self-defeating character of one's efforts might be ignored on some views of the matter. So the moral question seems to be the fundamental one, the one on which a decision must be made whatever else there might be to consider. And if either nations or individuals show no sign of having even considered the question we are to consider here, then for reasons which will be brought out later in this essay we will be justified in attributing to them the moral outlook which seems most appropriate to their actual behavior. In that sense, the moral question is the one which, once any of us thinks of it, becomes inescapable for all.

Some people will find it absolutely obvious, self-evident, that we have the obligation to provide the essentials of life to those unable to do so themselves if we are able to do so. But others find it far from self-evident. They may even find the contrary position self-evident. On the face of it, there is disagreement. It could be only on the face of it, for we might find that when all the facts are in, the apparent disagreement has disappeared. For example, one person might believe we have this obligation, but that it would be canceled or counteracted by the fact that one's efforts were self-defeating or that the objects of one's aid then rose up against their benefactors. And another person who claimed that we don't have this obligation might believe that the reason we don't have it is that efforts at charity are always, human nature being what it is, self-defeating and that people are inevitably ungrateful. This second person might agree that if people could be relied upon simply to enjoy the benefit without thereupon creating a further avalanche of problems for the benefactors, then we would have this obligation. Once the evidently factual issue of whether the people to be aided are or are not likely to do those things is sorted out —which may be very difficult, of course—then it would turn out that these two people agreed, so far as the basic moral issue is concerned. However, while apparent disagreement may not be real, we certainly can't assume this. Indeed, insofar as experience can inform us about such things, I think it likely that there is real disagreement, and not merely disagreement about secondary issues. That is to say, even where all else is equal and known to be so, I suspect we will still find people who do not agree on our basic question. What are we to say to them? (If you are on one side of this issue, what would you say to someone who was on the other side?)

It is, as I have implied, not uncommon for people to find one view or another on these issues "self-evident." But when there is disagreement among those who have considered the issue, the claim that one side is self-evident tends at least to be unhelpful, and probably irritating. If a proposition is self-evident, after all, then one would think that it ought to be seen to be so by any reasonable being who troubles to acquaint himself with its meaning. So if Pro tells Con that Con's position is "self-evidently" false, then Pro is in effect telling Con that Con is either being unreasonable or doesn't know what he's talking about. Either of which may be true, of course; but it is not reasonable, let alone good manners, to assume either or both of these things, especially in the case of someone with whom one has been discussing the question in an apparently intelligible way.

We need not reject the possibility that some position or other is, after all is said and done, self-evident. Even so, the doing and saying of what needs to be "said and done" may be a great deal. If something self-evident lies at the bottom of this matter, then, it is reasonable to suppose that it must be rather far down, and thus that a good deal of overlay needs removing before we are in a position to see what it is. And if nothing, even at bottom, strikes us as self-evident, we may not reach agreement; but perhaps we can reach appreciation of the alternative positions.

There is a considerable spectrum of possible views about the question of feeding the starving. At one end, it conceivably could be held that we not only have no duty to feed those who cannot feed themselves, but that we have a positive duty not to do so. At the other, there would be the view that we not only have a duty to feed those who cannot feed themselves, but that in fact this duty precedes our duty or even our right to feed ourselves and our immediate loved ones. Both positions, I imagine, will strike most people as amazing, on the face of it—which does not, of course, prove that they are wrong, but does invite reflection on the cause of the amazement. Light will be shed both on that and on the main question by considering two positions which will not only strike nearly everyone as far less extreme, but which will probably strike many people, in each case, as the truth, even the obvious truth, on the matter. These are as follows; and since we will be concerned with them at some length, I will supply labels for them, viz., 'Conservative' and 'Liberal' respectively.

> 'Conservative': We do not have any duty to feed those less fortunate than ourselves, though doing so is perfectly permissible and perhaps even admirable.

> 'Liberal': We do have a duty to feed those unable to feed themselves, but not at the expense of severely constricting ourselves or those close to us, or those to whom we have various specific and special obligations.

There is a point in the middle at which the difference between these positions becomes purely semantic. Conservative can go so far as to allow that if feeding the hungry would cost us really nothing at all, not inconvenience us in the slightest, then we really ought to do it even though it still isn't strictly a "duty": it's just that it would be a pretty poor show, morally, if under those circumstances we didn't. And Liberal can allow that, really, all sorts of other things take precedence over the duty to feed the starving: for instance, giving one's spouse some sheer luxury as an anniversary present, or indulging in a $50 gourmet dinner on the ground that one owed it to oneself as an educational experience. The difference between thinking that an act which costs essentially nothing is a duty and thinking that, while not a duty, it is still something one should be ashamed of oneself for not doing, seems either infinitesimal or nonexistent. This illustrates the flexibility of moral expressions, and should caution us against too quickly assuming that apparently disagreeing views really do differ. But there are various ways in which we can pry these two positions apart and keep them there. First, we can insist that the person who claims it is his duty to do something must agree that it is something which you must do even if you don't want to or don't feel like it, and in possible cases that it ought to be done at nonnegligible cost to oneself. And second, there is the important question whether it would be morally proper for governments to support the effort, using money derived from taxation (for example). What these have in common is that a certain amount of coercion, even if mild, is envisaged as being acceptable as a way of getting the job done. Conservative, on the other hand, maintains that the use of coercion of any kind is not acceptable as a way of getting the well-fed to help feed the needy. (But just where one draws the line between coercion and, say, persuasion or inducement is not easy to say, a point to which we will revert below.)

Now the question arises, on what might our two stated positions be founded? But by 'founded' here we mean two different things, both relevant in this essay. First, a moral principle is sometimes (usually) "founded on" another, more general one, and in this sense our job is to see what the most basic principle underlying the stated one might be. And second, a principle may be founded upon a general outlook and on some facts, conjectures, or facets of the human situation—some theory of human nature, for example, and some theory of what morality and moral concepts amount to or are all about. Getting into the latter gets us into various deep (or at least muddy) waters, of course; but getting into them is the point of moral philosophy, so we can hardly shun it here.

Starting with 'foundations' in the first sense, let us look at our two views in turn. What underlies the Conservative position? There need not be a unique answer to this, of course, for a great number of distinguishable basic principles could imply the Conservative position. However, the one which seems to me much the most challenging and attractive is what has come to be called the "libertarian" position. According to it, each person has the right to do whatever he pleases, provided only that he refrain from harming or forcibly restricting the liberty of others. Thus, the reason why we have no duty to feed the starving is that we do not, in failing to feed them, harm them: we simply fail to help them, which is a different matter entirely. Morality, on this conception, is entirely "negative": it requires you not to do certain things, but it doesn't require you to *do* anything at all, except things which you have deliberately undertaken to do, e.g., by making a promise. And the starving in distant places have not been put into that situation by us. (Sometimes, of course, they have—as when we defoliate their landscape. But we are addressing ourselves to the more usual cases in which it is not owing to our actions that they are in bad shape.) As they have not been put there by us, we have no duty to repair their situation. Only by acts of our own do we acquire positive duties; otherwise, we have only the negative duty to keep off the persons and property of others. Feeding the starving is a nice thing to do, it may be granted; but it is not a duty. Or—what comes to the same thing—the starving do not, as such, have a right to our aid.

This explanation of the Conservative position also explains why the extreme position first mentioned will not do. For in denying not only that we have the duty to help others, but even that we have the right to do so, it contradicts the libertarian postulates. Some of us may wish to help the starving, and so long as the starving don't mind being helped, to deny us even the right to do so is to deny us some liberty which we can enjoy without harming anyone, namely the liberty to help others if we are so inclined. Of course, proponents of the extreme position would usually hold it on the ground that helping others only makes things worse in some way, or eventually violates someone else's rights. But special circumstances would have to hold to validate that justification. In many cases, presumably, it simply would not be true that helping A implies harming some B. (A more interesting defense of the extreme thesis would take the line, say, that helping others is simply wrong because it violates an ideal of self-sufficiency. I will advert to that idea briefly later on.)

On the libertarian view, the very notion of possessing something is such that if I legitimately possess x, then nobody may take x from me without my voluntary consent. I may give it to anyone I please, or exchange it with someone for an agreed return (e.g., in money), or I may let it lie rusting in the back yard. (There is disagreement about whether I may burn it or bury it or rip it up. But I do not see how a restriction along that line can easily be defended on strict libertarian lines, and will assume that the right to dispose of my property as I please extends to a right to destroy it, so long as I don't thereby harm others—e.g., by getting smoke in their noses.) How do I legitimately acquire property? One way, of course, is to have others give it to me, either as a gift or in exchange for something which I've agreed to give in return. In addition, I can make it, provided that the materials from which I make it are mine or have been legitimately borrowed. Finally, I can simply find it, it not being previously owned by anyone else. These ways exhaust the list of legitimate acquisition methods. Beyond them, there is theft: taking it from someone who has no duty to part with it. In particular, the libertarian view implies no right to equal distribution, or even to an equal chance to acquire: transferences of property are legitimate if and only if all parties to the transfer agree to it, no matter what the structural pattern of holdings which may result from the transfer. In particular, therefore, no State has any business taxing people for purposes of property redistribution, social welfare maintenance, or any other ends except that of providing for security of person and property. Needless to say, it may not do so simply in order to relieve the starvation of miscellaneous strangers.[1]

[1]My sketch of the "libertarian" position is inspired by Robert Nozick's extremely interesting book, *Anarchy, State, and Utopia* (New York: Basic Books, 1974). Those unsympathetic to this sort of position should read this book and not trust my account—Nozick is far better able to speak for himself than I for him. For some questions, see also my critical notice in *Dialogue,* XV (1976).

My "Liberal" position is not so easy to generalize. Most people who accept my "Conservative" position on feeding the hungry would also, I think, accept the basic picture of its moral outlook given above, but among those who accept the "Liberal" view there is wide divergence. And this divergence comes in at the level of the most basic principles. Still, there are a number of general principles—what we might call the "middle principles" of liberalism—on which there is very wide if not universal agreement, at least with respect to the broad outlines if not in detail. First, it is agreed that there are a number of civil liberties to which everyone has the right and which it is therefore the duty of governments to secure and respect. (With much of this the libertarian would also agree, of course.) But second, and equally important (in some circumstances more important, in others, less), it is the duty of Society to secure to each individual, so far as possible: (a) equality of opportunity at the highest feasible level, and (b) at least a minimal level of welfare, depending on the wealth of the society. What this minimal level is, of course, is hard to say, and could reasonably vary with a number of factors, especially that of the society's general level of wealth. In all advanced industrial societies, this would include reasonable medical care, a good enough supply of food to enable the individual not only to stay alive but also to function with reasonable physical efficiency, minimal shelter and clothing, and in general, enough of the essentials of life to enable him to get on and to take at least some advantage of the opportunities the society otherwise provides for economic and cultural advancement. The basic point is that the society's government has not only the right but the duty to provide these things, and since it must do so through taxation, has the right to tax people in order to do it. And there is the question whether it extends beyond that society's borders, which will be discussed below.

As I say, just what the fundamental principle is which implies these things is a matter of considerable disagreement. I want to mention two theories on the matter, one of which is currently the subject of a great deal of discussion and admiration, the other of which goes back at least a century and a half and has had varying popularity; it is currently rather unpopular—though I believe that, in fact, the two may well be equivalent! The first theory is stated in terms of rights and says that there are two basic principles: (1) that everyone has the right to maximum equal civil liberty, religious, political, and intellectual, and (2) that with regard to the division of economic goods, equality is to be regarded as the point of departure or norm, and departures from it are justified only if (a) the favored offices or positions are open to everyone on a basis of fair equal opportunity and competition, and (b) they work out to the benefit of the least favored—indeed, to their maximum benefit. Thus, the poorest members of the society are to be made as well off as possible—attempting to make them still better off, if the point of maximum justice has been reached, would in fact make them worse off, e.g., by depressing the level of capital investment to the point where their income basis would deteriorate.[2] The second theory is not stated in terms of rights, though it can easily enough be reformulated in those terms. It is the theory of classical Utilitarianism and it simply says that individual acts and social institutions are to be rated by their contribution to the general happiness, where the latter is to be understood as the sum of the happinesses of each person. In other words, a "unit" of happiness for any person is equal to a "unit" of happiness for any other person, and the idea is to maximize the net sum or balance of positive units.

On the two-principles theory, we ought to help the starving if we can because they have a *right* to be as well off as they can be made without making others worse off than they. On the utilitarian theory, we ought to help the starving if we can because (and if) the amount which the starving gain by being enabled to continue living is more than the rest of us (collectively) lose by giving them some of our produce. Both theories, note, allow that in some conceivable circumstances it would be permissible not to help starving people. But these would have to be extreme circumstances; in fact, they would be effectively limited to circumstances in which transferring food to the starving would cause others to be at least as badly off as the starving persons.

I have remarked that I think that the two theories are really equivalent. This is an overstatement, actually. What I mean, more accurately, is that utilitarianism plus certain assumptions would imply the first theory, and that those assumptions are fairly plausible, up to a point, and are appealed to by defenders of the first theory. It would be a lengthy matter, and out of place, to try to prove this here, but very briefly the "certain assumptions" in question are these: Suppose that the utility associated with a unit increase in food, clothing, and other economic goods decreases as the amount already possessed by the person being considered increases—what is called the "declining marginal utility" of wealth. And suppose also that beyond a certain point of advancement in economic goods, the ability to engage in activities protected by the civil rights becomes a greater source of utility than any economic activity. Given these two assumptions, we will have the result that in any moderately advanced societies, the protection of civil liberties at a high equal level is of first priority, and the maximization of the economic welfare of the worst off will be second, as the two-principles theory says. And these are, in fact, the very assump-

---

[2]The "two principles" view is, of course, that of John Rawls as developed in his now celebrated book, *A Theory of Justice* (Cambridge, Mass.: Harvard University Press, 1971). My claims about the utilitarianism of his theory are developed in a paper, "Rawls and Utilitarianism," presented at the Canadian Philosophical Association meetings in Toronto, June 1974, and elsewhere, but currently unpublished.

tions appealed to. So it seems likely that there is a good deal of agreement between the utilitarian and the two-principles adherent, even at a very fundamental level.

As to rights, the utilitarian can say two things. First, he can say that, if you like, there is one absolute natural right possessed by everyone, and that is the right to have one's utility counted equally with others. Second, as to more specific rights, he can define a right as follows: 'A has a right to x' means 'other people should be compelled, if necessary, to provide x to A.' There are two kinds of rights which it is important to distinguish: "liberty" rights, or rights to *do,* in which what the rightholder has a right to is freedom to perform certain actions if he wishes and if he can—and on the other hand, "claim" rights, which are rights to *have* certain things and to be given them if one doesn't already have them. My definition covers both types. Where x is 'the liberty to perform action y if A wishes,' the meaning of the claim that this is a right is that others must provide A with that liberty if he doesn't already have it, i.e., others must avoid interfering with A's doing y if A tries to do it. Where x is a good—e.g., food or property or a service—then the definition says that others should be compelled, if necessary, to give A that good or do him that service. Now, under what circumstances, for any given x, will it be the case that a given A does have the right to x? From the utilitarian's point of view, this will be so whenever the social cost of compelling people (if necessary) to provide A with x is exceeded by the benefit to A of so compelling them. And to apply this to our present question, it will be the case that the starving have a right to be given food over others if those others are sufficiently well supplied so that making them part with enough food to enable the starving to live diminishes their well-being less than it improves that of the starving.[3] It seems plausible to suppose that this condition is fulfilled whenever the well-supplied are, for instance, getting so fat that they must frequently resort to dieting, or must burn or bury or store large amounts of food in order to keep prices up for farmers, and so on.

It will be noted that I have indiscriminately applied the two-principles theory, as well as the utilitarian theory, to the case of feeding the starving even when those who are starving are in a different country and hence not under the same government as those who are potential suppliers of food to them. This is intentional. It is obvious, of course, on the utilitarian theory that it makes no fundamental difference whatever whether A and B are under the same government or not when the question is whether B should feed A if he can. (It makes, as I have pointed out before, a whole lot of difference to the question of whether B *can* feed A, of course; but

---

[3]My account of utilitarianism on this matter, including approximately the proposed definition of rights, is more fully developed in Chapter 7 of my *Morality and Utility* (Baltimore: Johns Hopkins Press, 1967). But see also my article mentioned in note 7 below.

that is just an influencing fact, not a factor with basic moral significance.) But the two-principles theory tends to be stated as the fundamental charter for governing "a Society," and it is natural to interpret this as meaning that it applies only to the borders of a given political locale or country. However, I shall assume here, again without attempting to defend it at length, that this is not so, and that for purposes of moral theory, we may consider the entirety of mankind, insofar as all humans are capable of communicating and having other relations with each other, to be one "Society." It will, of course, usually be practically impossible for a particular country to take measures to maximize the welfare of the worst-off class of another country, and since it is impossible, the government of the country in question has a perfectly good excuse for not doing so, in most cases. But it sometimes is politically and otherwise possible for one country to feed the starving of another, and when that is so, I believe that the two-principles theory should be read so as to imply that it has a duty in justice to attempt to do so. (The reason for so reading it will come out below.)

Here, then, we have a rather breathlessly brief review of two major political/moral views. They differ substantially on our central question. How is one to choose between them? Or is it even possible to make a rational choice? Clearly, it will again be impossible to do justice to either of them in the small space available here. But we must, clearly, try to say at least a little about the foundations, in the second sense of 'foundations' distinguished above, of the respective views. However inadequately, then, I turn now to this project, in hopes that a few salient pointers can be uncovered and in expectation of not finally settling the issue.

Defenders of the libertarian theory, with its Conservative implication for our question, tend to appeal to natural rights as the basis of their view. But appeals of that kind are notoriously obscure. Sometimes they seem simply to be appeals to self-evidence of the kind objected to at the outset. As noted there, the trouble is that people seem to disagree about the matter. Some find it obvious, self-evident, that they have a moral duty to help people who are starving; others find the very reverse self-evident. If we have nothing better than self-evidence to appeal to at this point, we are unlikely to reach agreement.

There is also a subtler maneuver on the part of natural-rights advocates which we must watch out for here. It might be said that those who are starving owing to no fault of their own do *not* have the natural right to our aid, and this might seem persuasive. Now, denials of rights play a very important role in moral arguments. If I can establish that you have no right to my doing so-and-so, then I have also undercut the main (according to many theorists, the only) basis for saying that I have the duty to you to do so-and-so. The trick is that the premise of this argument is a denial of *natural* rights. But if we think there are no such things as "natural" rights, that rights simply are not "natural," whatever that may mean, then the argument will not prove what it sets out to; for what we would need to be shown is that the starving person has no right at all to our aid.

We must also consider the idea that natural rights, or whatever, are founded on certain aspects of "human nature." For example, it may be said that all humans are by nature free beings, who make their own decisions, have their own values, and guide their own actions, and therefore that to force them to do what they don't want to do is a violation of their nature. Certainly, there is something attractive about this sort of argument; and surely, we may feel, there must be some foundation in human nature for fundamental moral principles. True, perhaps: but the question is, how does it work? If we look at the argument just stated, for instance, there seem to be two major defects in it. In the first place, the premise simply isn't true, or at least not obviously so. People do not always make their own decisions, they do not always act according to their own decisions or values, and they do not, as we are constantly being reminded, always even *have* "their own values." So what does it mean to say that they do all these things 'by nature'? That they have the capacity to do so? Perhaps. But they also have the capacity to be slaves, sycophants, and zombies, so that seems to get us nowhere. It leads, in fact, to the other defect, which is that the premise doesn't seem to imply its conclusion. The conclusion, after all, says that it is wrong to keep people from doing as they want to, whereas the premise says only that they do, or at least have the capacity to do, what they want to do. In *this* argument, at least, there seems to be the notorious "is-ought" gap which ethical theorists have been so concerned about for the past century or two.[4]

What we need, evidently, is a conception of morality, a view of what it is all about. A very big order indeed, it may be said. And truly; but not so big that we can do nothing but gape in awe at its enormity. At least part of the answer may perhaps be fairly readily forthcoming. Indeed, there is fairly wide agreement on some parts of the answer. And it may be that those parts are enough.

In the first place, a morality will be expressible as a set of rules or directives: 'When in circumstances C, do such-and-such', or '. . . the thing to do is so-and-so'. It may also, or even alternatively, be expressed as a set of ideals of character. But even so, these ideals must have implications for

---

[4]Readers unacquainted with the literature on these matters would do well to delve into any good anthology of recent ethical writings, such as Kenneth Pahel and Marvin Schiller, eds., *Readings in Contemporary Ethical Theory* (Englewood Cliffs, N.J.: Prentice-Hall, Inc., 1970).

action: 'be this sort of person' must imply 'do the sort of things this sort of person would do, or the sort of things that will make you that sort of person'.

In the second place, the rules of a morality are not solely for the direction of one's own behavior. They will express what one would direct others to do as well. Indeed, in the end, they are the rules or principles by reference to which one will criticize or appraise the behavior of anybody, not just oneself. In this sense, they are rules for groups, and ultimately for the "group" which includes *everybody,* or at least everybody who is capable of understanding and communicating about rule-governed action. (Note that they are not necessarily the rules "of" the group: others may or may not accept the rules you think are the right ones to govern everyone's behavior.)

Are there any other important conditions to impose here? At this point, there is enormous controversy among moral philosophers.[5] However, for present purposes, we do not need to add more conditions. Instead, we simply turn to the question of finding a *reasonable* morality. It might be asked whether morality must be reasonable, or whether it even should be. The answer to the first question is that the moralities of various persons and groups are often very unreasonable indeed, so in that sense morality does not have to be reasonable; and the answer to the second question, which you may regard as rather high-handed if you wish, is that it's hard to see what it would mean to say that morality *should* be *un*reasonable. The point of thinking about things is to find reasons for them, and the point of thinking about moralities is to find reasons for them. If one doesn't want to be reasonable about such things, then presumably one won't waste one's time reading philosophical articles about them.

Well, what would make a morality "reasonable"? Confining the question to one's own point of view for the moment, the answer would seem to be that it is reasonable insofar as its adoption would promote a good life for oneself, preferably the best life possible. Much could be and has been said about that aim, but we can't and won't dwell on it here. Instead, we now need to remember that a morality is proposed as a set of rules to govern *every*one's behavior. This brings up the difficulty that other people, being different, may not have the same views about the good life, and so

[5]Among the main figures in this controversy are, on the one hand, R. M. Hare, *Freedom and Reason* (Oxford: Clarendon Press, 1963), and on the other hand, G. J. Warnock, *The Object of Morality* (London: Methuen and Co., Ltd., 1971). But see also the interesting article by Peter Singer, "The Triviality of the Debate Over 'Is-Ought' and the Definition of 'Moral,' " *American Philosophical Quarterly,* 10 (1973) 351–56. The version I have used is somewhat more like Hare's but also borrows some interesting ideas from David Gauthier. See the latter's "Rational Co-operation," *Nous,* 8 (1974), 53–65. But I take my argument to be virtually an interpretation of Kant's fourth example of the Categorical Imperative in *Foundations of the Metaphysics of Morals,* second edition.

may be inclined toward different rules. If the rules one proposes are unreasonable from other people's points of view, then it is unreasonable to expect them to accept such rules. But if they are not accepted by others, then one's adoption of them will be to that extent unworkable; particularly so since these are informal rules or principles, not rules which are enforced by some authority. It seems, then, that a rational or reasonable morality will be one which it is reasonable for you to adopt, given that it is reasonable for everyone else to adopt as well: in short, one which it is reasonable for everyone, collectively, to adopt.

It is perhaps from such a starting point that we begin to see the point of such ideas as fairness and such equality as is called for by morality. If we are trying to generate a reasonable code of conduct, then we shall have to look at it from the point of view of each affected party, and not only from our own. We shall have to ask questions of the form, 'If I were he, then what would it be reasonable for me to accept?' And since the results of such reflection are going to influence one's own eventual choice of principles, we may say that going at it this way generates a sympathetic attitude, if one didn't have it in the first place.

Even though this skeletal sketch is quite incomplete, let us see whether it does not already give us some insight into the problem at hand. When we have the conception that morality is a set of principles which everyone is to find acceptable and which governs everyone's actions, including one's own, with no candidates left out of the field for consideration, then it becomes clear that we will always, in the case of each possibility, be making a trade-off between certain advantages and disadvantages. To illustrate, consider the system of pure egoism, where each person may do whatever he likes and no conduct can be criticized. This has the signal attraction of unlimited freedom for oneself—and how could that fail to be attractive? If the good life is the one in which all of our wants are satisfied, how can it not be a good thing to be able to do whatever one wants? But then, it has the outstanding demerit of being exposed to the depredations of others: since they can do whatever they want, they can do whatever they want (and can) to you. Whatever attractions freedom may have had, this disadvantage must surely outweigh it.

Now let us consider the "libertarian" system underlying our 'Conservative' view. This system, we noted, incorporates the minimal constraint that one is to inflict no harm on others; helping others is entirely voluntary and never an obligation, unless there has been an explicit previous arrangement requiring it. Here again, we have a system which carries with it a huge "plus" on the score of liberty—unsurprisingly, since that is the whole idea of it. Furthermore, it does not have the disadvantage of pure egoism, since others are restricted from harming you and interfering with your legitimate actions. You may sleep securely on your property, if you are well-to-do, and the rabble without will simply have to stay there.—Yes, but what if you are one of the rabble? Things will then look rather different. It's all very well to reflect that if you had a lot of property, then it would be safe. But what if, owing to extreme misfortune in one's choice of parents, or weather, you don't have any property or lose what you do have? Of course, you will be free to go and work for somebody who does have some, thus exchanging your labor for the necessities of life. But (1) you are thus in a pretty poor bargaining position, often, and may well find yourself working eighteen hours per day for crumbs, the alternative being starvation; and (2) it may be that you are in an enormous area where there simply isn't enough for many people, and nothing you can do will get you what you need. Not to mention (3) that you may lack the skills, education, etc., which would make your labor salable. Now, libertarianism offers very cold comfort to you in such circumstances. It says that you can do two things: (1) beg, or (2) starve. You may not, for instance, insist, nor may you steal or fight. Acceptance of such a morality by people in such circumstances, one must surely conclude, would not be reasonable. If we really are free to accept any morality, subject only to the conditions set out above, then why accept this one?

Now some people, of stoical natures, will at this point say that one should accept this option despite its discomforts because of a moral ideal of self-sufficiency. No person of dignity will resort to coercion simply to keep body and soul together: we are better off, our souls are in better condition, if we accept whatever is ours, and if it is not enough, then die in silence like a man. The trouble is, to invoke this "ideal" at this point is either question-begging or irrelevant. It is question-begging if it is invoked as if it were an outcome of the process we are now going through, for the question is where we do come out with whatever we had before we went into it. No "peeking" to the back of the book is possible, and this because the book is *not written* yet. From our austere point of view, there are *no* self-evident, "natural" rights. And on the other hand, if the "ideal" is invoked as a personal ideal, then it is irrelevant. We are not asking whether people who happen to have an ideal of self-sufficiency and will therefore not ask for help, and will refuse any help if offered, ought nevertheless to have the food shoved down their throats. What we are asking is only whether any reasonable person, whatever his ideals, could accept a universal morality which would not allow people who, through no fault of their own, are starving to death and who would gladly accept help if offered, to do so even though others could readily aid them. And *this* is what, I am arguing, it would not be reasonable for all to accept. For there is a better one, a better deal. The better morality says that our freedom to acquire more property than our neighbor will still be protected, but subject to a constraint. The constraint is that one must be willing to contribute a certain amount of one's wealth to those in undeserved misfortune, once one gets beyond a certain minimal amount—a fraction which perhaps increases as one gets more and more. Under this system, you get most of the advantage of the libertarian system, but you also get the protection implicit in knowing that so long as there is enough for everybody, you will get at least enough to keep you going. (Or at least, you will get a chance to acquire it by work of a type which you are able to do, and then if you can't work, you will be outrightly given some.) A morality incorporating this sort of provision has a far better chance of universal acceptance than the other one.

The foregoing arguments are bound to be misleading. All of us, after all, have been brought up with, or may have become converted to (with or without argument) some or other morality; our very thought and habits are permeated with acquired and impressed moral ideas, explicitly known or only subconsciously accepted. When we talk of considering the advantages and disadvantages of various "packages" of moral principles, then, it will be exceedingly difficult to distinguish this activity from that of considering, for instance, the advantages and disadvantages of various brands of new car. But in considering the new car, we properly include moral considerations of many kinds: for instance, that if the car is lethal to many others, then that is a demerit. In choosing moral packages, on the other hand, we presume no antecedent, "natural" morality, but only that we are shopping around for a reasonable set of principles by which to govern our interactions with other reasonable beings.[6] Perhaps the project of doing this in a really thoroughgoing way is unachievable. Even if it is, however, it may be that approximations to it can be made which, for many purposes, are good enough. And I contend that the present one, for the purpose of assessing our obligations to relieve starvation, is enough. I address myself, after all, to the food-rich people of northern North America. In Canada, we can grow twenty times what we need, if we like; even in the populous United States, probably at least three or four times. And we know what things are like in India, in the sub-Sahara, and in Bangladesh. (Those who don't know can readily enough find out if they wish; and if they don't wish, then they aren't eligible for the present consideration, owing to ignorance of relevant facts.) There is not much difficulty in coming to realize that, in similar circumstances, we would find a morality of 'nobody needs to help anybody' an unreasonable one. And this is all that I am trying to do.

My conclusion is very thin, and there are many complex issues which remain, many of which will be reasonably thought by many people to be the only really important ones. But that is because those people are already

---

[6]This characterization leaves animals out of the picture, perhaps arbitrarily. How far is unclear: are some animals rational? Arguably. See, for comparison, Tom Reagan, "The Moral Basis of Vegetarianism," *Canadian Journal of Philosophy* (Autumn 1975).

persuaded of at least as much, and probably far more, than I have been trying to establish. One of these further points is too important to ignore, however. This is the reasonability of attaching conditions to foreign aid intended for humanitarian purposes. There are two different types of such conditions to consider. One is the sort of condition that says, "We'll feed you, but only if you join our party (make our enemies your enemies, etc.)." I don't have space to discuss this point at which no such conditions are reasonable: for it will deny the very sort of freedom which we ourselves rightly insist upon, thus giving life to others but only of a degraded form. The other sort of condition says, "We'll give you food, but on condition that you restrict your population growth to the point where the problem will eventually disappear instead of mushrooming to proportions which nobody can handle." This type of condition, where it is relevant, seems to me reasonable. It is not reasonable to have a morality which makes it a duty to do self-defeating acts. And if your feeding me now means that in twenty years there will be five more in the same circumstances, then your aid *has* been self-defeating. (The political objections which have been made against insistence on reasonable programs of birth control impress me, thus far, as despicable hypocrisy.)

Nor have I considered the question of degrees and limits, though it is related to the question about population control. I have not, for instance, considered utilitarianism, as described above, in detail. There are strong arguments why a system for evaluating principles of the type I have described would not lead to the choice of utilitarianism; discussing these at this point is far beyond the province of this paper. But supposing that all those arguments were ultimately rebutted and utilitarianism did remain as the best candidate, what would it imply? Would it, for instance, imply that we should, as Christ said, "sell all that we have and give it to the poor"? No, since we should then become poor ourselves and those we gave it to would have the same problem about us as we started out having with them. Would we take all that everyone has and divide it equally? No, I think, for many reasons, the main one of which is that the relation between one's happiness, one's possessions, and the activities by means of which one acquires those possessions, is too intimate and complex to allow detaching the possessions as completely separate things, available for redistribution without any untoward side effects. No, because one can be happy though relatively poor. No, because you can't make people not care about the things they have. And so on. But this does not tell us *how* great the disparity in wealth must be between A and B before A has the duty to keep B going when B can't do so himself.[7] The only thing I would say about

    [7]For some rather heretical further speculations on these matters, see Jan Narveson, "Aesthetics, Charity, Utility, and Distributive Justice," *Monist,* 56 (1972), 527–51.

this question right now is: whatever that line of disparity is, we are above it in relation to the Sahel, to Bangladesh, and the other known regions of starvation in the world.

WILLIAM K. FRANKENA

Frankena begins by locating the world hunger issue in the conceptual framework of moral philosophy. He then argues that the Principle of Beneficence and the Principle of Justice (or something like them), which tell us that we ought to try to alleviate starvation, should be adopted as rules of our positive social morality.

> *1.   Pay particular attention to his analysis of prudent action and to his distinction between 'duty' and 'obligation'.*

> *2.   He distinguishes between aretaic and deontic morality. How would an aretaic morality address this issue? Would it be preferable?*

> *3.   Recipients of food aid, he claims, should not be coerced into limiting procreation. Most other essayists seem to disagree. Is such coercion acceptable?*

> *4.   It is implied that a world state may be necessary to solve the world hunger problem. What do you think? Would Watson agree? Would Hardin agree?*

William K. Frankena, Roy Wood Sellars Professor of Philosophy at the University of Michigan, is the author of Ethics *and* Three Historical Philosophies of Education. *He also delivered the Carus Lectures to the American Philosophical Association in 1974.*

This article has not been previously published.

Moral Philosophy and World Hunger

Should a nation or society as fortunate as ours, or individuals and groups belonging to such a fortunate country, whether their fortune is of their own making or not, act to prevent or alleviate hunger in countries that are much less fortunate—where, say, large numbers of people are dying or suffering greatly for lack of food or in peril of doing so—whether their misfortune is of their own making, of our making, or neither? Is it in any way right, obligatory, "oughty," or even good, for us to act or be disposed to act across countries or nations in such a way as to reduce or eliminate hunger, disease, suffering, or death? This, or something like it, is our question. Our purpose, as I understand it, is not so much to answer it with a definite yes or no, qualified or unqualified, or to tell Americans just what they should do, but rather to discuss certain questions of a general philosophical and somewhat theoretical nature relating to this problem. At least, this is all I shall try to do. I shall not deal with all of the questions raised by the editors, and I shall take them up in my own way, referring to them as EQ1, EQ2, etc.*

In a little book called *Ethics* I discuss ethical egoism, the divine command theory, various deontological views, utilitarianism, and the ethics of love, concluding that we should recognize two basic principles of morality: the Principle of Beneficence, which tells us not to bring about evil or harm and to promote good, and the Principle of Justice, which tells us to treat people equally. I suggest, among other things, that we should treat people equally (wherever they live) "except when unequal treatment can be justified by considerations of beneficence (including utility) or on the ground that it will promote greater equality in the long run." Then I say:

> It is in the light of the preceding discussion . . . that we must try to solve such social problems as education, economic opportunity, racial integration, and aid to underdeveloped countries, remembering always that the principle of beneficence requires us to respect the liberty of others. Our discussion provides only the most general guidelines for solving such problems, of course, but most of what is needed in addition is good will, clarity of thought, and knowledge of the relevant facts.[1]

I also say that the ideal state of affairs is one in which everyone in the world has the best life he or she is capable of. Now, having reflected further on our present topic and other similar matters, I believe that things are not quite so simple as this passage implies, even if we stick to providing general

---

*In our original invitation to contributors, we suggested several questions for consideration. Mr. Frankena specifically labels them EQ1, EQ2, etc.

[1]W. K. Frankena, *Ethics,* 2nd ed. (Englewood Cliffs, N.J.: Prentice-Hall, Inc., 1973), p. 52. I should also have referred to Chapter 5.

guidelines. I recognized this a bit later in talking about the application of my two principles, but only briefly.[2] I am glad, therefore, to have this occasion to review some of the problems involved in dealing with topics of the kinds referred to, starting more or less from scratch.[3] In a way, my main point will be that more is needed than some basic principles, the will to act on them, clear thinking, and relevant factual knowledge. It should be emphasized, however, that very often our trouble in solving problems like those in question here is simply that we are not sure of our basic principles, lack the will to live by them, fail to think carefully, or do not have or even seek the necessary factual information. Action can turn awry or lose its name for any of these reasons and often does. I only hope that what follows will not just sickly o'er with the pale cast of thought whatever native hue of resolution we may have, but will show instead that moral philosophy can and should illuminate even enterprises of great pitch and moment.

I

"Is action to alleviate world hunger a prudential issue (justified solely on grounds of political expediency) and not a moral issue at all?" This question (EQ1) implies that not all issues about what we should do are moral ones. They may be legal, prudential, religious, aesthetic, etiquettical, baseballish, and so on. Now, it is hardly plausible to think that our issue here is simply one of aesthetics, of etiquette, or the rules of some club or game. It might, however, be thought of as a question of international law, in which case it could be settled by an inquiry into the law of nations to see if it includes a rule enjoining other nations to feed, if necessary, the people of a starving one. In this connection it is interesting to observe that the UN Declaration of Human Rights of 1948 ascribes to everyone "the right to a standard of living adequate for the health and well-being of himself and of his family, including food. . . ."[4] Certainly many people think of our issue as a prudential one, arguing that we should feed other countries if and only if it is to our own enlightened self-interest and does not entail too big a sacrifice on our part. There *is* such a prudential question

---

[2]Ibid., pp. 46–47, 53–54.

[3]For other discussions of my two principles, see Frankena, "The Concept of Social Justice," in R. B. Brandt, ed., *Social Justice* (Englewood Cliffs, N.J.: Prentice-Hall, Inc., 1962), pp. 1–29; "Some Beliefs About Justice," a Lindley Lecture (University of Kansas, 1966); "The Principles and Categories of Morality," in J. E. Smith, ed., *Contemporary Philosophy, Second Series* (New York: Humanities Press, 1970), pp. 93–106.

[4]*Human Rights,* a UNESCO symposium (New York: Columbia University Press, 1949), Article 25, p. 278.

and the answer may well be yes, at least sometimes; whether it is yes or no depends on the facts in the case. Those who hold that our issue is wholly prudential may do so on either of two grounds. They may subscribe to ethical egoism in general, and then their position stands or falls with that of the ethical egoist, which we cannot debate here.[5] Or they may contend that, while we should act on nonegoistic principles in our relations to fellow citizens, such principles are not binding across national boundaries and we may and should be egoists in dealing with peoples in other countries. Such a combination of altruism and egoism strikes me as simply incredible; it implies, among other things, that while it is morally wrong for me to cause a fellow American to starve, even if doing so is to my interest, it is not morally wrong for me or for the United States to cause Africans or Britons to starve, even if we are not at war with them, if it is in our interest to do so. Even if we have no moral obligation to alleviate starvation elsewhere, it seems clear to me that it is morally wrong for us to bring it about knowingly. As for the view that our issue is a religious one—theologians do often think of it as a question of divine law, and hence as a kind of legal question, but this does not prevent its being also a moral issue, as I shall argue it is (and as most theologians would agree).

There is still another nonmoral way of viewing our issue. This is to claim that statements like "We should do something about world hunger (WH)" are just hypothetical imperatives in Kant's sense, saying only that we should do so if or because doing so is necessary to achieve some end we have. Such a view need not be egoistic; it might hold that one should act to alleviate WH because it is necessary to prevent the unhappiness of others. Then it assumes that we want to prevent the unhappiness of others in a nonegoistic way. But it still insists that we ought to act to feed hungry peoples if and only if *we want* to promote their happiness, not because it is morally right or good to do so. And then the answer to our opening question is simply, "Yes, but only if it is necessary to achieve some purpose we have," and we have only to look to see whether this is so or not. If it is not, then it is not true that we ought to alleviate WH. This view also can take two forms. One is to contend that all Oughts and Shoulds are merely hypothetical in this sense or should be so understood.[6] In this form, the view is tantamount to a rejection of morality as this has usually been conceived, and so raises issues we cannot go into now.[7] In any case, it is

---

[5]See Frankena, *Ethics,* pp. 17–22.

[6]Cf., e.g., Phillipa Foot, "Morality as a System of Hypothetical Imperatives," *Philosophical Review,* LXXXI (1972), 305–316.

[7]I do go into them in *Three Questions About Morality,* to be published by the Open Court Press.

not obvious that the Oughts or Shoulds of law, art, etiquette, and religion are or should all be understood as hypothetical or self-referential in the sense proposed. The other form of the view is to maintain that, even though this is not so in the case of action within a country, in the case of action across national boundaries there is no Ought or Should unless such action is needed or helpful in our achieving our ends, altruistic or selfish, charitable or prudential. I see no good reason for adopting this view; if there are nonhypothetical Oughts or Shoulds about how we should treat each other, why can there not be nonhypothetical ones about how we should treat people in other countries? At any rate, it is hard to see how *moral* Oughts can apply only to our relations to other Americans; as Kant, Warnock, and many others have held, it seems to be characteristic of moral Oughts that they apply to our relations to all rational beings, if they apply at all.[8] It is true, of course, that I have duties to members of my family or nation that I do not have to those of other families or nations, but my basic moral duties must be duties I have toward all persons as persons.

The title of an article on our topic reads "What Happened to 'America the Beneficent'?"[9] Now, suppose that we really were a benevolent and humanitarian people, not in the sense of having a strong sense of duty to help other peoples who are in trouble, but in the sense of simply wanting to do so even at the cost of a considerable sacrifice on our part. Then it would not be necessary to raise any moral issue here; having such a strong desire for the welfare of others, we could ask simply what we must do to bring it about—what we can do and how to do it. We might ask what we should do, but the answer must be a mere hypothetical imperative like "You should send a million bushels of wheat to Bangladesh (if or since you want to help the people there)." Then hypothetical imperatives would suffice to tell us what to do, if supplemented by factual knowledge about the means of accomplishing our ends. Like the title referred to, however, our present inquiry presupposes precisely that we are not sufficiently benevolent in this sentimental (or, as Kant called it, "pathological") way, and this is why we must raise the issue of morality. For morality is *necessary* just when our nonmoral motivations are inadequate. Its principles, whether these are conceived of as aretaic or as deontic, are essentially such as to apply to us even when what they enjoin or recommend is not what we want to do and is not a means to what we want.

[8]Cf., e.g., G. J. Warnock, *The Object of Morality* (London: Methuen and Co. Ltd, 1971), pp. 143–52.

[9]S. Rosenfeld, *Sat. Rev. World*, I.D. 18, 1973. I do not here mean to imply that D. Riesman is mistaken when he says, "The ordinary American is characteristically generous," *Time*, June 2, 1975, p. 4.

II

Before we proceed to EQ2, we must say something about two other questions. First, when is an issue a moral one? We must have some answer to this question if we are to answer EQ1. It is, however, a very complex question that has been much discussed in recent moral philosophy, and cannot be adequately dealt with here.[10] I shall say only that, as I understand the nature of morality, a moral question or judgment is at least *relevant* whenever the conduct or life of a person or rational being, insofar as it is voluntary, impinges, or may impinge directly or indirectly, on the feelings, beliefs, happiness, well-being, etc., of other persons or rational beings. This is true, it seems to me, independently of the existence of any divine command, social contract, positive social code, or personal aim or commitment. If this is so without any important qualification, then it obviously follows, in answer to EQ1, that the existence of WH does raise a moral issue. Moral judgments are at least relevant to what we do or do not do about it, e.g., if we voluntarily help to bring it about.

At this point, however, we must ask our second question: What reasons are there for denying that moral judgments can be applied to actions and dispositions that have effects across national boundaries? Four lines of thought strike me as needing attention. One is to argue that Ought implies Can—that there is nothing morally right or wrong about our not doing what we cannot do—and that there simply is not anything we can do about the lives of people in other countries. But, even if we agree that Ought always implies Can, at least in morality (which may be disputed), it is surely clear that we can do something, as individuals or groups or as a nation, about WH, if we are willing to sacrifice a bit. It may be true that we cannot do much to alleviate it without great cost or sacrifice, but that is another question. At most, if this is true, it can serve to excuse us from doing what we should; it does not show that it is not true that we should do it. In any case, it is true that we can do something, for we can at least act so as to make matters worse for other countries.

The second line of thought is more complicated. This is to argue that morality follows the flag in the sense of applying only between people whose flag it is, except perhaps when they are traveling or working in other countries in a private capacity. Briefly, the idea here would be that the very institution of the sovereign nation-state is calculated to remove the welfare of the people of each such nation-state from the area of the moral concern of the peoples of the others; that, when a people like the Bangladesh accept

[10]For discussion by myself and others, see G. Wallace and A. D. M. Walker, eds., *The Definition of Morality* (London: Methuen and Co. Ltd., 1970).

or proclaim their independence as a nation, they are in effect saying that they and they alone are morally (as well as legally) responsible for what happens to them; and that, when a people thus attain sovereign statehood, other peoples are absolved from any responsibility they may have had toward the one in question. Such, it might be claimed, is the nature of that Leviathan, the national state. Much could be said about this view of our matter. Even if one accepts the implied notion of a plurality of sovereign nation-states, one can doubt that any existing state is absolutely autonomous even legally, if one believes that there is such a thing as international law.[11] In any case, however, I see no reason for accepting this theory unless legal autonomy entails moral nonresponsibility. But it seems clear that it does not; within a given state, for example, two individuals may be legally independent of each other without its following that moral judgments do not apply to what they do to one another.

A third theory would maintain that morality depends entirely on the existence of an actual social contract, i.e., that A and B cannot have moral duties or rights with respect to each other, or stand in moral relations of any kind, if they have not made a contract with each other, at least implicitly. Hobbes talks in this way some of the time. However, even if law does presuppose the existence of an actual contract in this way—and this may be questioned—it does not follow that morality does; in fact, it is not clear that morality presupposes even a hypothetical contract.[12] At any rate, it is hard to see how the view that morality involves an actual compact of some kind can find a place for our belief that moral judgments apply to what we do to animals, infants, fetuses, assailants, enemies, etc. This is one reason why I answered the previous question as I did.

Similarly, one might contend that the making of moral judgments presupposes the existence of a positive social morality of rules enforced by social sanctions of praise and blame, that such positive moralities exist only within national boundaries, and that, therefore, moral judgments cannot be made about relations with foreign countries and their peoples.[13] In reply, it may be pointed out that, even if the existence of international law can be denied, it can hardly be denied that there is, or at least may be, a positive international morality, a kind of bar of world moral opinion that cannot always be lightly flaunted.[14] Later I shall contend that we ought to have such a positive international morality and that it should include a clause about WH. In any case, it is not true that the making of moral

---

[11]For an interesting view here, see H. Fain, "The Idea of the State," *Nous,* VI (1972), 15–26.

[12]See, however, J. Rawls, *A Theory of Justice* (Cambridge, Mass.: Harvard University Press, 1971).

[13]The nature of a positive social morality will be explained later.

[14]See the UN Declaration quoted earlier.

judgments requires the prior existence of a positive code of rules; if it did, we would not be able to judge the code itself on moral grounds, as reformers and new generations are constantly doing.

As far as I can see, therefore, we may stick to our claim that the existence of WH does raise a moral issue. Of course, even if one admits this, one can still ask, "Why should we do the moral thing about WH?" But this *is* a different question, and, while the answer is not easy, it is part of the more general problem of why we should be moral about anything, which also cannot be dealt with here.[15]

III

Suppose we agree, then, that WH raises a moral issue, not just a prudential or emotional one, and also that some favorable moral judgment is applicable if we seek to prevent or alleviate it, and some unfavorable one if we do not. It certainly does not seem at all plausible to say that helping to do something positive about it is morally bad, wrong, or even indifferent, though, of course, there may be bad or wrong ways of going about it, as well as unwise or inefficient ones. Even then, some rather different approaches are possible. The editors' second question focuses on this diversity: "If the issue is indeed a moral one, is the action properly seen as a moral duty, or merely an act of charity?" For acting to lessen WH may be seen as a moral duty or it may be seen merely as an act of charity; as C. I. Lewis might have put it, it can be regarded as a "requirement of the moral" or it can be regarded as a "gift."[16] Others might prefer to say that it is good but not obligatory.[17] Actually, however, there are several alternatives here, not just two, even if we do not count the approaches covered in Sections I and II. A number of philosophers, for example, have distinguished between duties in the strict sense, obligations proper, and what we (merely) ought to do.[18] The first, they contend, presupposes roles and rules defining those roles; thus, a father has certain duties (and rights) because of the rules of the institution of the family defining his role. The second presupposes a promise or agreement of some sort; one has an obligation proper if and only if one has made at least a tacit agreement to do some-

---

[15]See Frankena, *Ethics*, pp. 114–16.

[16]C. I. Lewis, *The Ground and Nature of the Right* (New York: Columbia University Press, 1955), p. 84.

[17]See, e.g., A. Bain, *The Emotions and the Will*, 3rd ed. (New York: D. Appleton and Co., 1875), p. 292; M. G. Singer, *Generalization in Ethics* (New York: Alfred A. Knopf, 1961), p. 186.

[18]Cf., e.g., E. J. Lemmon, "Moral Dilemmas," *Philosophical Review*, LXXI (1962), 139–43; R. B. Brandt, "The Concepts of Obligation and Duty," *Mind*, LXXIII (1964), 374–93; Frankena, *Ethics*, p. 47.

thing.[19] If we have a duty or obligation, these writers say, then we ought, other things being equal, to do the thing in question, but there are things we ought to do that are not duties or obligations proper. When one has a duty or obligation to someone else—and there always is such a someone else *to* whom one has a duty or obligation proper[20]—then that someone else has a *right* to the thing involved; but, where one simply ought to do something, this is not so. When one simply ought to do something, what is presupposed is not any agreement or any social rule sanctioned by praise and blame, but only some "principle," like those of beneficence or equal treatment, which may but need not be a part of our positive social morality at all. On this view, an action is right to do if it is not wrong, and it can be wrong in any of three ways: by violating a duty, an obligation, or an Ought.

Now, I think we can, and to some extent do, recognize this threefold distinction in the context of our problem, though it must be admitted that both philosophers and ordinary people often use "duty," "obligation," "ought," and "right" as if they were synonymous—and "good," "ethical," "moral," etc., as well. Then we may ask whether we have an *obligation* proper to feed the hungry peoples of other countries, and the answer must be: not unless we have made some kind of agreement to do so, which may be, but in general is not, the case. Again, we may ask whether we have a *duty* to feed them, and then the reply will be that we have a strict duty if and only if we occupy some socially defined role that requires us to feed them in something like the way that being a father requires one to feed one's children. Most of us do not occupy any such role, however, though such a role may, of course, be assigned to someone, as in the case of Joseph in the *Bible,* or of Herbert Hoover in our own history. It cannot be maintained, then, in any blanket fashion, that fortunate people or nations have either a duty or an obligation in these strict senses to feed unfortunate ones.

We must, however, amend the tripartite account we are using in one important way. Many societies have what is called a "positive social morality" in the sense of having a code of moral rules that are acknowledged, taught, and enforced by sanctions of praise, blame, punishment, ostracism, etc.[21] In fact, morality has generally presented itself in this form in modern western culture, and the so-called new moralities of today usually call for the abolition of such social codes in favor of more personal ideals or "value-systems." An example of what I mean is provided by Harry Truman's description of the society in which he grew up:

[19]Or, perhaps, if one has accepted a benefaction.

[20]Unless one can have a duty or obligation to oneself.

[21]See H. L. A. Hart, *Law, Liberty, and Morality* (London: Oxford University Press, 1963), pp. 20, 22.

> [My mother] was always a woman who did the right thing, and she taught us . . . that, too. We were taught that punishment always followed transgression, and where she was concerned, it always did. . . . In those days . . . people thought more of an honest man than any one thing, and, if a man wasn't honest, he wouldn't stay long in the neighborhood. They would run him out.[22]

Now, it seems clear that in such a society we would say (or would have said) that a person had a duty or obligation to be honest, not just that he ought to be, even when no agreement or special social role was involved. In such a society certain kinds of conduct are publicly demanded of or extracted from a person, though not necessarily by the use of legal sanctions; moral rules are different from legal rules (though the two often overlap) but, as J. O. Urmson remarks, they are more like public laws than like private ideals.[23] In fact, Locke called them a kind of law: "the law of opinion and reputation."[24] They are within "the call of duty" in this sense, not "beyond" it.

If this is so, then, if either in our own code or in an international one we acknowledge, teach, and sanction a rule requiring us to do something about WH, we can still say that we have a duty or obligation to do so. The next question is whether we do have, teach, and sanction any such rule. The answer I believe is not clear; in some ways it seems we do and in some not. Perhaps some of us do, some do not, and others are uncertain. Indeed, it is probably just because the answer is unclear that we are discussing our topic; we seem to be trying to make up our minds whether we should or should not acknowledge, teach, and sanction such a rule, i.e., whether we should make (or keep) it as a part of our positive morality. Let us therefore go on with our review of alternative approaches.

The next alternative is to regard feeding the hungry in other countries as being something we *ought* to do if we can, though not as a strict duty or obligation. Then it is still something it is morally wrong not to do when we can, *ceteris paribus*. Should we accept some "principle" to this effect or some more basic principle that has such a consequence? Here we must first say a word about situational ethics. One kind of "situation ethics" involves accepting some general principle like "Love!" or "Promote the general welfare," as, for example, Joseph Fletcher's does. It could say yes to our question. A really extreme situationalist, however, would disown appealing to any general rule, principle, or "value" whatever, and would say no to our question. On such a view one simply looks at the situation (or

[22]Merle Miller, *Plain Speaking: an Oral Biography of Harry S. Truman* (New York: G. P. Putnam's Sons, 1973), pp. 46–48.

[23]J. O. Urmson, "Saints and Heroes," in A. I. Melden, ed., *Essays in Moral Philosophy* (Seattle: University of Washington Press, 1958), p. 213.

[24]*Essay Concerning Human Understanding*, Book II, ch. xxviii.

Situation) in all its aspects and then "sees" or "decides," depending on whether one is an intuitionist (what Sidgwick called a "perceptual intuitionist") or an existentialist, what one should do. It seems to me, however, that, unless one is taking the moral point of view in this process, one cannot make a moral judgment; one's conclusion or decision will simply be a function of one's desires and one's beliefs about the facts in the case. And, while the moral point of view is not exactly a principle like "Love is a virtue" or "We ought to treat people equally," it is something general, the same for all situations, so that the thing to do is not dictated merely by the particular situation being faced.

The situationalist may be right in thinking that moral situations usually involve conflicting considerations pointing to different moral conclusions about what actually to do, and that, when this is so, the solution must consist in an appeal to "perception" or in a decision, not in a deduction from a principle or rule. But this need not always be the case, and even when it is, it must still be some kind of Gen[25] that tells us that a certain consideration is a reason for thinking one should or should not act in a certain way. Gens may give us the pros and cons even when they do not give us the definitive answer. Thus the fact that people are starving may be a consideration in favor of feeding them in every situation of which it is a part—it cannot be such a consideration in one situation and not in another, though it may sometimes be outweighed by other considerations. But to acknowledge this is to acknowledge a principle of the kind in question.

At any rate, unless we are willing to espouse an extreme situation ethics, it seems plausible that we should accept some principle telling us, directly or by implication, that we ought to try to alleviate starvation if we can. As has been intimated, such a principle will not necessarily imply that we are actually doing wrong if we do not so act whenever someone is starving, for it may sometimes be overruled by some other principle with which it conflicts—or by some duty or obligation. In other words, it need not be absolute; it may, in W. D. Ross's sense, be a *prima facie* principle, requiring us always to act in a certain way in a situation of a certain sort when we can and when it is not outweighed by some other Gen.[26] Even if one accepts such a principle, however, there are at least three different alternatives one may take, depending on what one thinks about making the principle a part of our positive social or international morality in the way

[25]I use the word "Gen" to cover any kind of rule, principle, standard, norm, "value," or whatever, that may apply or be relevant to more than one action, situation, person, etc., e.g., "Stealing is wrong," "Sincerity is a virtue," and "The fact that doing A harms someone counts as a reason for regarding A as wrong."

[26]W. D. Ross, *The Right and the Good* (Oxford at the Clarendon Press, 1930), pp. 17–34.

described earlier: (a) One may hold that it should be made a rule of our positive morality in this way, and that, when it is not overruled by a conflicting rule, we should sanction it with praise for actions conforming to it and blame for actions contrary to it. (b) One may hold that, while we should make it such a rule and praise actions conforming to it, we should not blame contrary actions—that is, that we should praise people when they feed the hungry but not blame them when they do not (even though they are doing wrong if they do not do so when they are able to and the principle is not overruled by some other Gen). Or (c) one may maintain —some new moralists certainly would—that although we indeed ought to help feed the hungry of the world, there should be no publicly sanctioned moral rule to this effect, national, subnational, or international; the whole matter should be regarded as an affair of private conscience or individual ideal, whether we agree about it or not. If one takes position (a), one will claim we have a duty or obligation to relieve WH, but if one takes (b) or (c), one will deny this—and will be taking the alternative in question.

I myself believe that we cannot do without some kind of positive moral- ity that operates both within and across national boundaries and that it should include something, perhaps a clause or a corollary, about helping to deal with WH, and sanction this with blame for not helping as well as praise for helping. Human nature being what it is, people need some kind of policing by others that does not take the form of civil law and is not supported—or is supported only in part—by legal sanctions and the arms of the law. I doubt, therefore, that we can be satisfied with the alternative being considered if we mean to be realistic about what we are like, at least as long as circumstances like the present energy and food situations remain such as to tempt us not to act as we should. Now, however, we must recognize yet another alternative. Let us call concepts like duty, obligation, oughtness, rightness, wrongness, and having a right, and the judgments in which they appear, *deontic* ones, and concepts like moral goodness and badness, virtue and vice, and the judgments in which they appear, *aretaic.* Then one might go so far as to contend—any ethics of virtue and some new moralities would—that aretaic terms and judgments are or should be basic in morality, not deontic ones. Without going that far, one might argue that morality has or should have two parts, a deontic and an aretaic part, and that the business of helping with WH belongs or should belong to the aretaic part. Either way, one would hold that it is not a duty or obligation, or even something we ought to do, but only that it is morally good, and possibly even supererogatory, saintly, or heroic. One might then still re- gard it as wrong to help cause other peoples to starve, but one would claim that it is not wrong in any sense to refrain from doing something more positive. That, one would leave to the good Samaritan. One would probably not even allow that it is morally *bad* to refrain from doing something positive; one certainly would insist that starving peoples have no right to our assistance.

This aretaic view of our subject could take at least two forms. At any rate, though this is not usually recognized, the positive morality of a society might be aretaic rather than deontic; it is sometimes thought that this was true of the social morality of the Greeks. That is, it might consist, not of publicly sanctioned rules, but of publicly inculcated virtues or ideals of virtue or goodness. If so, then one might hold that the aretaic principle of helping starving people should be part of such a publicly promoted ethics of virtue, being sanctioned at least by the use of praise and maybe by the use of dispraise (and "faint praise") if not of blame. On the other hand, one might deny that any principle or clause about helping starving peoples should be thus publicly supported; while agreeing that it is morally good or virtuous to help them, one would then insist that helping them is or should be left to individual ideals and not made a matter of social morality in any way.

As I said, I believe that we must have some kind of positive social morality, national and/or international, bearing on the question of dealing with WH. But since we cannot here debate the merits of deontic versus aretaic views of the matter, I shall not discuss them further, though I am still inclined to favor the former.[27] I doubt that a purely aretaic positive morality carries enough "clout" to be realistically regarded as sufficient. In any case, it seems that the actions it would urge on all of us as distinct from those it would ask only from some of us, would very largely coincide with those a deontic public morality would demand of us.

IV

The view I have been favoring is that we should recognize one or more basic moral principles, aretaic or deontic, which would constitute our primary morality (PM), and in some way, erect at least a minimal positive social morality (PSM) upon them, possibly by incorporating some of our basic principles of their corollaries into a public code of rules or tables of virtues and vices, possibly in some indirect way such as is taken by rule-utilitarians,[28] including in this public code something about WH or at least about aid to needy or suffering countries. One may then ask which principles we should take as our PM. As indicated earlier, I argued elsewhere for

[27]For something on this issue, see Frankena, *Ethics,* pp. 62–67. In any case, I do have doubts about taking a purely aretaic line on the subject of WH.

[28]On rule-utilitarianism, see *Ethics,* pp. 39–41.

taking as basic two coordinate principles: the Principle of Beneficence (PB), which, other things being equal, requires passing unfavorable moral judgments on acts or dispositions of inflicting evil or harm and favorable ones on acts or dispositions or preventing or removing it or of doing good; and the Principle of Justice (PJ), which, other things being equal, requires passing favorable moral judgments on acts or dispositions of treating people equally and unfavorable judgments on opposite ones. Here I leave open the question whether such judgments should be basically aretaic or deontic, i.e., whether the principles should take the form "We ought (or have a duty or obligation) to act beneficently and to treat people equally," or the form "Benevolence and justice are moral virtues (or morally good)."[29] Either way, I think, they—certainly the PB and perhaps the PJ too, though I am less sure of this—imply that WH should not be a matter of moral indifference to us, either as individuals or as a nation. This I shall not argue for. However, I suggested at the outset that, for dealing with problems like WH, more is needed than just some basic principles, a will to act on them, logical thinking, and factual knowledge, and I now want finally to explore this subject, which is partly brought up by EQ3 ("Who is obligated to act —a nation or individuals only?"). I shall talk mainly in the deontic terms I am accustomed to, but what I shall say can readily be transposed into an aretaic key.

To whom do moral principles apply, whom are they supposed to guide? Moral agents, of course, and first of all, individual human beings like us. But organized groups, including states or organized nations, are also moral agents in a sense, since, although they are not themselves persons, they are composed of persons and can act only through the actions of persons. All such agents should be guided by moral principles, if not directly or proximately, then at least indirectly or ultimately. This does not yet give us the answer to EQ3, however, for it may still be that only individuals or only nations should try to do something about WH, or only voluntary associations of individuals or nations. For a more complete answer we must see what basic principles of morality are to be understood as telling us. Just what is their role, the role of PM?

The most natural way to interpret a moral principle is to construe it as an act-principle, as I did in the passage quoted in my introduction, i.e., to read it as a Gen to which an agent is to appeal directly in each situation on which it bears, simply by looking at the facts and asking what the principle, in the light of the facts, calls for. This is the procedure of the act-utilitarian, of course, but it is also followed by most deontologists.

---

[29]One might hold that we *ought* to be just and nonmaleficent, but that being positively beneficent is (only) good or virtuous.

However, it raises problems. The difficulties of act-utilitarianism are well known, having been pointed out both by deontologists and by rule-utilitarians.[30] But there are difficulties in my modified deontological view also, if my principles are interpreted simply as act-principles, as I in effect recognize a page or two after the passage referred to; and these are not entirely avoided by adopting a larger number of more specific principles like those of W. D. Ross. About the PB for example, M. G. Singer writes:

> One major objection to this principle is that if consistently adhered to, it would lead to moral fanaticism, to the idea that . . . every occasion is momentous. . . . Now this . . . is . . . absurd. . . . One . . . would die from moral perplexity.

He also objects that, according to that principle, if I had but one ticket to a concert and knew that Q would appreciate the concert more than I, then I ought to give Q my ticket.[31] As for my PJ, it would seem to say that, if I feed my children, I ought likewise to feed children everywhere, since I am to treat everyone equally. I would either have to sell all that I have and give it to all children equally or stop feeding mine. The latter alternative reminds me of what one of his players said about Vince Lombardi's being democratic: "Oh, sure! He treats us all equally—like dogs."

One might reply, as an ethics of virtue would, that the basic principles of morality are not act-principles anyway but disposition-principles; they tell agents not to do certain sorts of acts but to cultivate and manifest certain dispositions or traits of character. As Leslie Stephen put it, "The moral law . . . has to be expressed in the form, 'be this,' not in the form, 'do this.' "[32] It is not clear, however, that this move helps us to deal with the sorts of difficulties just indicated, since character-traits must be manifested in action, and dispositions like benevolence and justice will express themselves in much the same acts as will the corresponding act-principles. At any rate, there is an alternative way of taking basic principles, as the rule-utilitarians have seen. This is to take them as principles for the designing, assessment, and modification of social institutions, practices, roles, and rules, not as principles for determining directly what to do.[33] The idea here would be that society, national and/or international, should have or set up a system of institutions, legal, social, economic, which is such that, if

[30]E.g., by W. D. Ross, *The Right and the Good*, pp. 34–39; R. B. Brandt, *Ethical Theory* (Englewood Cliffs, N.J.: Prentice-Hall, Inc., 1959), pp. 380–91.

[31]M. G. Singer, *Generalization in Ethics*, pp. 184–86.

[32]Leslie Stephen, *The Science of Ethics* (New York: G. P. Putnam's Sons, 1882), p. 155.

[33]I.e., as "critical morality" in Hart's sense, or as "principles for institutions" in Rawls's sense. See Hart, *Law, Liberty, and Morality*; Rawls, *A Theory of Justice*.

individuals, groups, and nations act according to the rules of that system, then the requirements of beneficence and justice will be met insofar as this is feasible.[34] Given such a system, individuals and other moral agents could and should determine what to do, not by themselves appealing directly to basic moral principles, but by looking to the rules of the system. Their actions would be judged only by the rules and the rules would be judged only by the principles, much as the Lowells speak only to the Cabots and the Cabots speak only to God.

It is certainly possible to conceive of a society in which the institutions would be of this sort, and there would be no call for any agent to apply basic principles directly to his, her, or its actions. In such a society, the difficulties described above would not arise, even if the PB and the PJ were the principles of its PM. For example, given the necessary natural resources, an adequate economic system, and the institution of the family, then, if I feed my children, Jones his, Smith hers, etc., all of our children will come out fed, and, ideally at least, no one need worry about other people's offspring.[35] In a way, the institution of the family is calculated, among other things, to help us to apply, or rather to obviate the necessity of applying, the PJ directly. In a somewhat similar way, but on a larger scale, it might be that the institution of national states is calculated, when functioning ideally, to solve or to obviate problems about beneficence and justice across boundaries. At any rate, one may suppose that there is some possible system of institutions that would do so, one which would then also dispose of the problem of WH, at least if natural resources permitted.

Even if we assume that natural resources suffice for feeding everyone, present or future (though perhaps only if some sort of population control is practiced), it is obvious that our international society does not have such a failsafe system of institutions. In fact, our problem arises just because this is not the case: the question is precisely what we should do in the absence of such a system. But now we see that there are at least two alternatives, depending on how we take our basic principles. One is that every agent is to do whatever he, she, or it can, consistently with other moral requirements, to see that people everywhere are adequately or at least minimally well fed, applying the basic principles of morality directly. The other is that every agent (individual, group, or nation) is to act according to the rules of the system or systems there are and, especially and urgently, to do what he, she, or it can do to bring into existence a system that will get everyone fed, hopefully at not too great a cost in terms of other goods. Which of these two moral policies should we adopt in dealing with such

[34]Here I am thinking, as is usual, that institutions and roles are constituted or defined by sets of rules.

[35]Cf. Frankena, *Ethics,* p. 54.

problems as WH, etc.? A plausible case can be made for choosing the second. As Narveson says:

> It may be allowed ... that in this day and age especially, isolated acts of charity on an individual basis, or even extensive and moderately popular solicitations such as those made by the International Red Cross ... must be rather ineffective by comparison with the potential of government action, and that therefore we would perhaps do better to engage in and support political activity towards the end of getting humanitarian programs of famine relief, medical aid, social and economic aid to underdeveloped countries adopted as basic and serious public policy than to send in a cheque now and again to our favorite charitable organization.[36]

Here I should want to add that we ought to engage in and support international as well as national activity toward getting such programs into effect. Indeed, it does seem to me that what is most imperative is for all of us to do what we can to bring into existence a national and international set of institutions such that, if all agents act on its rules (or fulfill their respective roles), then everyone's basic needs will be supplied insofar as nature permits. There is at least this much truth in the second line of thought discussed in Section II.

Even though he says what he does in the passage quoted, Narveson himself ends by saying that we seem ultimately to have but two alternatives:

> Either we literally do everything we can: which, in the case of many of us, would mean not ten dollars or two or three per cent of our incomes, but probably sixty or seventy per cent. Or we make a judgment that the importance of the kind of life we have set out to live is greater than the amount of suffering preventable by depriving ourselves of the means to live it.[37]

And, while he seems to think we should also follow the first course of reaching for our wallets, he argues that the second is more defensible than moralists have thought. I do not deny that there is some truth in this contention, as many of us certainly assume in practice, but it seems to me that there is a third alternative, namely, the one I sketched with the help of my first quotation from him, and that it is the one to emphasize.

It seems to me, however, that as long as things are as they are, we cannot take principles like the PB and the PJ simply as institution-or-rule-principles but must treat them also as act-principles to be applied by us directly. Whatever the problems it involves, some direct action on our parts is called

[36]Jan Narveson, "Aesthetics, Charity, Utility, and Distributive Justice," *Monist,* 56 (1972), 530.

[37]Ibid., p. 551.

for in addition to doing what we can to improve the institutions of the world. It is, moreover, not only necessary under the circumstances; we are in some sense morally better persons if we act directly than if we act only following the requirements of institutions within which we live, however beneficent and just these may be. But I have no formula for determining just how much of what kind of direct action is called for, or for determining how we should divide our efforts between direct action and the improvement of social institutions. I do believe, as I suggested earlier, that direct action, even across national boundaries, should be made part of our "law of opinion and reputation" in some way and not left wholly to private conscience, though some room—as much as possible—should be provided for moral autonomy too, since the ideal moral agent is an autonomous one. But if what I have been saying more recently is anywhere near the mark, the main body of our PSM should consist of institutions whose rules may not even be corollaries of the principles of beneficence and equality, but whose operations are nevertheless beneficent and just, e.g., perhaps the family and, in some improved form, the nation-state.

V

What precedes is all I have done by way of an answer to EQ3 and I have space for only a word or two about EQ4, 5, and 6. EQ4 asks: "Are affluent nations and societies only obligated to help when it requires no significant national or personal sacrifice?" I would argue that morality may require sacrifices, and even if there is something to Narveson's contention, we should sometimes help people in other countries even if it involves giving something up, whether we do it by direct action or by indirect means. And in reply to EQ5 ("Should such action be carried out with political interests and considerations in mind?"), we should not help only those who are our allies, for to do so is to let prudence override morality. However, if we must choose between helping an ally and helping a neutral, there is no reason in principle why we may not prefer the ally, especially if aid is part of the agreement we made with her. EQ6 is more difficult: "Should such action be made contingent upon the successful implementation of a plan by the receiving nation to curtail its population growth?" It seems other nations do have some kind of responsibility to feed themselves and not to be a burden on us; this is one of the obligations of political independence. Moreover, if our aiding them entails serious sacrifice on our part, we have some kind of right to ask them to do what they can to lighten our load.[38] I have also hinted that a policy of population control may be needed as a part of the system of institutions we should seek to make operative in the

---

[38]Cf. Bain, *The Emotions and the Will*, pp. 298–99.

world. Still, finally, the quality of morality is not strained; perhaps it need not come down like a cloudburst, but it should sometimes drop as the gentle rain from heaven. Besides, we must respect the beliefs and the liberty of others, even—and maybe especially—when we are feeding them. We dare not take advantage of their hunger to compel them to do what they do not yet believe to be right.

There is another question that might be raised: whether we can do what should be done without creating a world state. I have tried to assume that we can, but nothing I have said is incompatible with the view that we cannot.

WILLIAM AIKEN

Aiken maintains that persons have a moral right to be saved from starvation, which is derived from the general right—the right to be saved from preventable death due to deprivation. Recognition of this right, he claims, would substantially alter the moral debate on world hunger.

1. He suggests that the normative mode of reference to rights is more fundamental than the descriptive mode. Is this true?

2. How strong is this right? Does it ever override other moral or legal rights?

3. What changes in our normal beliefs would recognition of such a right entail?

4. Should we recognize this right in a world already overcrowded?

William Aiken teaches philosophy at Chatham College. He recently completed his doctoral dissertation, "Starvation, Morality, and the Right to Be Saved."

The Right to Be Saved from Starvation

I

Human beings who have the same needs, fears, pains, and wants as you and I are starving to death. The advocates of triage, the Neo-Malthusians, and the lifeboat "ethicists" seem to forget this obvious fact. Those "hopeless masses" of the Hungry World are just individual persons who are hungry, sick, and dying. They need help. Through no fault of their own they cannot get enough to eat. They can do nothing but ask for help from

This article has not been previously published.

persons of the Affluent World. And if they do ask for help, are they merely begging for charity? Are they merely pleading for us to be benevolent? Are they merely crying out for some merciful supererogatory crumbs from our overabundant tables?

The belief that a person in dire need has no stronger claim against those who can help him or her than a plea for benevolence (which is no real claim at all) is unacceptable. Dire need creates obligations and rights. Starving persons have a moral right against those who are in a position to help them. Their suffering is not simply a harmful by-product of a morally permissible omission on the part of others. It is a *wrong* committed against them. It is a violation of their moral right. It is a reprehensible neglect of moral duty.

The right to be saved from starvation is derived from the more general moral right, the right to be saved from preventable death due to deprivation. This general right is based on human need. A person involuntarily undergoing extreme deprivation which would lead to his or her death has a moral right to the goods and services required to prevent that death. The sufferer has this right against any and all who are in a position to provide the necessary goods and services, since the sufferer's need puts them under an obligation to prevent his death.

II

No doubt many readers will find the above assertions controversial. It will be argued that moral rights result from promises or from special roles and relationships—not from human need alone. In fact, some will argue that a 'need right' is either a misuse of the term 'right' or, if not a misuse, then a frustratingly vague use which can only muddy the waters of good clear analysis. In section III, I will show that a need right as a moral right is not problematic. I will show this by making it clear exactly what is and what is not being said when a need right is claimed as a moral right.

Other critics of need rights will argue that any formulation of a proposed need right is doomed to failure because of inherent vagueness; that careful specification of conditions of ascription and the determination of stringency are impossible. However, basing a moral right on the criterion of need does not necessarily condemn us to wishy-washy generalizations which are impractical, inflexible, and inapplicable. The problem which has arisen with the lack of specificity is not due to the nature of need rights, but to the lack of careful analysis of this type of right by moral philosophers. In section IV, I will discuss the relevant considerations involved in specifying one type of need right, the right to be saved from preventable death due to deprivation.

Finally, some critics may object that the ascription of the right to be saved[1] to dying persons will not benefit them. It would be maintained by these critics that even if we ascribe such a right, we still would not know what to do about deprivation situations like world hunger. Why, they would ask, confound the moral issue with talk of nonenforced "moral" rights—why not simply concentrate on what we ought to do? In section V, I will address this criticism and argue that talk of rights is significant for moral deliberation (and ultimately personal action) on deprivation situations.

III

According to some critics, to say there is a right to be saved from preventable death due to deprivation is to misunderstand the meaning of the term 'right.' A right, it would be maintained, involves public rules, prescriptive institutions, and enforcement procedures with specified sanctions. The paradigm use of the term 'right' is in the expression 'legal right' in which a power, immunity, liberty, or privilege is specified under a valid legal rule and enforced by legal sanctions. This paradigmatic use of rights talk functions solely from within the descriptive mode; it speaks of those rights which *are* ascribed by rules. Any moral rights there might be must conform to this paradigm; that is, A has a right to x only if public rules ascribe x to A and enforce A's right to x. For example, the right a child has to loving support from his parents is a right generally acknowledged by popular moral rules and enforced by public opinion. Since the right to be saved is not ascribed and protected by law or popular moral rules, then it would not be a right at all.

Often claims of right are made which are not rights actually ascribed or protected by public rules. For example, the right to have an abortion was claimed before this right was recognized by either popular moral rules or legal rules. Currently, the right to privacy, the right to adequate health care, and the right to death with dignity are all being claimed independently of the actual public rules. There are four ways to account for this apparent nondescriptive mode of reference to rights.

The first way is just to say that this is a misuse of the term 'right.' A second way is to label claimed rights mere 'claims of right' which are *not* rights until so designated by public rules. They are possible candidates for rights but they are not rights; for example, the right to privacy is really only a possible candidate for the right to privacy. If a law is passed which ascribes and protects a candidate for right, then it will become a legal right.

---

[1]The elliptical expression, 'the right to be saved', will be used interchangeably with the expression, 'the right to be saved from preventable death due to deprivation'.

It may also become a moral right (in the sense of being ascribed and protected by a popular moral rule), but this process is more complicated. It is mysterious how mores, morals, and popular moral opinions which ascribe some claims as moral rights (but exclude many others) become accepted as moral rules in the first place; but it is even more mysterious (even baffling) to try to explain how newly proposed candidates for rights would become ascribed and protected by these popular rules. Does it just happen? Is an expensive advertising campaign the most effective way to transform a candidate for a right into a right? But how they become ascribed is not important to this account. All that matters is that claims of moral right are not rights until they are ascribed and protected by public rules.

A third way to account for the apparent nondescriptive modes of referring to rights is to argue that the appearance is often illusory. Some claims of right (though not all) which are not ascribed by human rules (legal or moral) are ascribed by Natural or Divine Law. These rights, Natural Rights, are enforced by Nature, Providence, or eschatological rewards and punishments. So at least some of the claims of right which appear not to be ascribed and protected by rules are, in fact, ascribed and protected by some 'higher law.'

There is a fourth way to account for these claims of right and that is to say that they are *not* rights in the descriptive mode of reference, but they *are*, nonetheless, rights in another mode—the normative mode. The normative mode refers to rights which ought to be protected by public rules, conditions permitting. The human rights listed in the United Nations Declaration of Rights are rights in this normative sense.[2] Rights which are ascribed by public rules may or may not be rights in the normative sense. The right of a slave owner to dispose of his 'human property' at will is not, in my opinion, a right which ought to be protected by public rules; rights like the right to adequate health care are. This fourth way to account for these references to rights does not, like the other three, relegate all legitimate talk of rights to the descriptive mode. The right to be saved from preventable death due to deprivation (like the right to death with dignity) is a moral right in this normative sense and not in the popular morality sense.

In an important way the normative mode of reference to rights is more fundamental than the descriptive mode. Founding Fathers, reformers, judges, and even legislators (to some extent) must consider which claims of right *ought* to be protected by public rules and which rights presently protected by rules *ought not* to be so protected (e.g., should the right to own handguns or the right to unlimited procreation be removed from the list

[2]UNESCO, *Human Rights* (Westport, Conn.: Greenwood Press, 1973) pp. 273–80.

of rule-protected legal rights?). Positive law and popular moral rules need not be interpreted anew, criticized, or changed. But when they are and when the interpreter, criticizer, or changer appeals to what ought to be the case regarding rights—then the normative mode is being used to make judgments about rights in the descriptive mode. The normative mode must be used to determine which rights we should protect by rules.

Determining which claims of right ought (morally) to be protected by rules is difficult. Not every claim of right is a claim that can be morally justified (e.g., I have a right to rule the world). To determine if a claim is a justified one we must appeal to moral principles. If a binding moral principle justifies my claim to x, then I have a moral right to x (in the normative sense) which ought to be protected by rules. Once this right is protected by rules, I have a right to x in the descriptive sense. Naturally, persons differ as to which moral principles are binding: are Liberty principles, Equality principles, Benevolent principles? Thus, they will differ as to which claims are morally justified and so which moral rights persons have.

In the normative mode all claims of right (both those presently protected by public rules and those not protected) are on an equal footing. All claims of right are justified by appeal to moral principles. The claim of right is only as strong as its justifying principle. Many of our legal and popular moral rights are based on the negative *in rem* right (a general right of noninterference) to liberty which is justified by appeal to a moral principle that promotes maximal individual liberty for all. The right to be saved (which is not presently protected by rules) is a positive *in rem* right (a general right of entitlement *to* certain goods) which is justified by appeal to a moral principle that promotes maximal individual welfare for all. Since life (which the right to be saved is designed to preserve) is required for the exercise of the right to liberty, I would place priority upon the welfare principle over the liberty principle, making it, in many cases, the binding principle when the resultant rights come into conflict. But this need not be maintained in order to argue that some welfare rights ought to be protected. As long as both principles are understood to be good ones, then rights based on liberty (like the right to privacy) and rights based on welfare (like the right to adequate health care) ought to be enforced by public rules (either popular moral or, in some cases, even legal rules).

I have shown that the right to be saved from preventable death due to deprivation (a need right) is a moral right—albeit, in the normative, not descriptive, mode of reference. Speaking of rights in the normative mode does not result in a misuse of the term 'right,' nor does it result in a misunderstanding of the concept of right. It is different from the paradigmatic use (in the descriptive mode) but it is, nonetheless, a proper one. In fact, it appears to be more fundamental.

IV

It is not uncommon for persons who assert that there are human rights which are based on need alone to avoid specificity or careful discussion of these rights. It is as if they would have us just "look at that mother's face" or just "listen to that child's cry" and we would know (intuit? grasp? infer? feel?) that needy persons do have a right to our assistance. Critics are correct to level the charge of vagueness at these assertions. They would ask a list of questions: How are needs distinguished from wants and wishes? How needy does one have to be in order to have such a right? Who, if anyone, is this right correctly claimed against? Why should your need obligate me—I didn't put you in that condition? How is this right balanced against other rights—like my right to control my property?

Even to maintain that the right to be saved from preventable death due to deprivation is a plausible candidate for a moral right which ought to be protected by rules, the typical vagueness surrounding rights based on need must be avoided. In this section, I will demonstrate the manner in which such a right can be specified. I do not intend for this to be a complete specification, but at least it should show that vagueness is not inherent in claims of right based on need.[3]

The right to be saved from preventable death due to deprivation can be justifiably claimed by or on behalf of any individual in a condition of extreme deprivation such that without assistance from others that individual will die as a result of the deprivation.[4] Pure cases of death due to deprivation are rare because in typical cases, like starvation, the sufferer is gradually weakened by the deprivation and eventually dies from a deprivation-related disease (pneumonia, dysentery, etc.). However, if the deprivation is the *dominant factor* leading to the sufferer's death, then the sufferer may claim relief from this deprivation as a moral right.

The right to be saved from preventable death due to deprivation differs from other rights based on need (e.g., the right to adequate housing, the right to employment, etc.) in that identifying it does not require distinguishing needs from wants and wishes. This need right is clearly grounded upon a need—the need for the goods or services *necessary* to stay alive.

However, the sufferer cannot justifiably claim this right if he has voluntarily placed himself in a condition of deprivation by knowingly refusing to prevent foreseeable and preventable consequences of his actions. Thus if he *could*, but willingly does *not*, obtain the goods required to maintain

[3]See William H. Aiken, Jr., "Starvation, Morality, and The Right To Be Saved" (Ph.D. diss., Vanderbilt University, 1977).

[4]I will not consider here the problems involved with fetuses' rights. Individuals, as identified in this essay, are *born* persons.

himself (by work, for example) then he has voluntarily placed himself in the condition of deprivation and thus cannot justifiably claim the right to be saved from preventable death due to deprivation (though he may ask for charity). This allows for suicide by deprivation (e.g., a hunger strike or a refusal of medical treatment) as well as prevents abuse of the claim of a right to be saved. It is important to realize that the *sufferer* must have voluntarily placed himself in the condition of deprivation. If another person places the sufferer in that position, then failure to save the sufferer is a violation of his right to be saved. This is an important distinction for it rebuts the common argument that we have no duty to save starving children if their parents knowingly overprocreate with the foreseeable consequence that at least some of their children will die of starvation. If parents knowingly place their child in a condition of dire need (by having an excess of children), we nonetheless have a duty to that child to save him from starvation.

The right to be saved from preventable death due to deprivation is a right against others. It is a general positive right and so is claimable against all persons who satisfy three minimal conditions: an epistemological condition, an 'ought implies can' condition, and an 'equivalent need' condition. If *no one* satisfies these conditions, then the claim of right cannot justifiably be made.

In order to be obligated to provide the goods and services to the sufferer one must be aware of the sufferer's condition of extreme need. A person starving to death on a desert island whose plight is unknown to the rest of the world cannot claim the moral right to be saved from starvation. The right to be saved and the obligation to save are, like other rights and obligations, concepts dependent in meaning upon there being a social context (of at least a minimal form). There must be knowledge of a person's need before one can be obligated to help that person. However, we have at least some moral responsibility to become aware of the needs of others. The intentional cultivation of ignorance of the needs of others for the purpose of avoiding the obligation to save them is as reprehensible as the cultivated ignorance of an investor who buys into a loan shark operation and then says, "I don't want to know how you get it—as long as my profits are high, I'm happy."

The second minimal condition is the 'ought implies can' condition. In order to be obligated to save the sufferer one must have the means to remedy his condition, that is, have the goods or the capability to render the services required to alleviate the condition of the sufferer. I can only be obligated to save you if I *can* save you. Thus, if you are dying for need of a blood transfusion of a very rare type of blood and I am available for a transfusion, but my blood type is incompatible with your blood type and thus of no use to you, then no matter how severe your need is, I have no duty to save you because I cannot provide you with the goods you need. However, any person of the right blood type who knows of your condition and who is available to provide a transfusion has a moral duty to save you.

"Having" goods normally means "possessing" goods—or at least, having legal access to those goods. Thus, if I do not have legal access to the goods required to save you, I cannot save you. However, since the 'ought implies can' condition is a logical one, and since I *could* steal to acquire the necessary goods, then theft is not *formally* excluded. "Robin Hoodism" is sometimes morally justified, especially when those who possess and own the goods have, like the Sheriff of Nottingham, acquired them unjustly. I may also be justified in taking others' goods if those who have the goods are exceptionally neglectful of their moral duties to save others. For instance, suppose a natural disaster destroys a village, leaving only one large house; the owner refuses shelter for the seriously injured on the grounds that it is, after all, *his* house. In this instance, the townspeople may, with moral justification, take over the house. However, the normal association of 'have' with 'possess' or 'have legal access to,' should be maintained in most cases.

The 'ought implies can' condition is often used to defend inaction in the world hunger situation since, it is claimed, we simply cannot feed everyone. If it becomes true that persons cannot be saved from starvation (that is, if the world population outruns the *world's* food-producing capacity), then there can be no moral right to be saved from starvation. Naturally, this level of "impossibility" involves several complicated issues, for example, the distribution of food, the strength of property rights over moral rights, the unequal quality of diet among peoples of different regions of the world, the amount of food inefficiently utilized on meat production, etc. The point of "impossibility" may be rapidly approaching if the present increase in birth rate in the famine-stricken areas of the world continues and if the affluent nations continue to improve their diets by increasing the consumption of inefficiently produced animal products. But the point of impossibility is far off if an equitable means of production and redistribution is effected.

This 'ought implies can' qualification is included as a formal condition. However, it should be noted that it does not mean 'ought if convenient' or 'ought if I feel charitable.' It means 'ought if at all possible.'

The third condition is the equivalent need condition. It states that a person is not obligated to save another if he cannot render the service or supply the goods without involving himself in a position of equivalent or more extreme need than that of the sufferer for whom the services and goods are granted. This is called the 'equivalent need' condition. If the only way to save you of dying of dehydration is to give you my canteen of water and thus bring about my own death by dehydration, then obviously I have no duty to save you. Similarly, if to save you from feeezing to death I must give you my only coat and thus freeze to death myself, then I have no moral duty to save you. This condition prevents the appeal to lifeboat situations of *extreme* scarcity from serving as counterexamples to the right to be saved from death due to deprivation. The ethics of extreme scarcity is perhaps different from the ethics of moderate scarcity or moderate abundance. Be that as it may, there are *very* few situations in which the scarcity is so extreme as to warrant appeal to "lifeboat ethics" (which is, in my opinion, the same as prudent self-interest). One situation of such scarcity might be the case of the clotting factor for hemophiliacs. Another might be the use of a dialysis machine for those with kidney failure. But very few cases demonstrate this extreme scarcity. The world hunger situation is not yet—*pace* the opinion of many—a lifeboat situation. It is more of a problem of distribution, use, and waste of food than it is of scarcity of food.

Until it is true that I cannot help another without putting myself in an equivalent position of need (that is, dying of deprivation), I have a *prima facie* obligation to honor others' right to be saved from preventable death due to deprivation.

Some have maintained that there is a fourth minimal condition which a potential helper of a person in need must satisfy in order to be obligated to act—the condition of being the 'last resort'. Richard Brandt suggests such a condition in his book, *Ethical Theory*.[5] He specifies that it is only in cases where "we are the only one in a position to help" that we have a moral obligation to assist a person in dire need and that the person in need has a right to our assistance.

There is a danger in adopting this 'last resort' condition since it poses an additional epistemological difficulty, that is, the determination of whether or not I am the last resort. Beyond this, it is an undesirable condition because it will justify inaction where more than one person *could* act but where no one *is* acting. In most emergency situations there is more than one potential assistor. For instance, five persons may simultaneously come across a drowning child. Each would be obligated to act if he were the last resort, but since no single one *is* the last resort, then all five may refuse to act, claiming that it is not their duty to act any more than it is the duty of the other four and so each one would be justified in not acting. If this condition is placed on the right to be saved, the child could drown and none of the five spectators could be held morally accountable. But surely the presence of another person at an accident site does not automatically relieve me of a moral duty to assist the victim in need, any more than

[5] R. B. Brandt, *Ethical Theory* (Englewood Cliffs, N.J.: Prentice-Hall, 1959), p. 439.

the presence of one police officer called to the scene of a bank robbery relieves other officers in the area from attempting to apprehend the suspects. The condition of last resort is too strong; it is not a minimal condition for obligation.

The moral right to be saved from preventable death due to deprivation is not an absolute right. Rights which are not absolute are sometimes called '*prima facie* rights' or 'rights *prima facie*.' I will call them '*prima facie* rights,' meaning only that such rights are not absolute. This right to be saved is a claim which, other things being equal, and provided that there is no conflict of it with another right or obligation, is one that we ought to act in accordance with or honor. Of course, the difficult cases are those in which there is a conflict of rights or obligations; for instance, when your right to be saved from preventable death due to deprivation comes into conflict with my right to control my goods in the way I desire. There are two ways to describe rights in conflictual situations.

One way is to make all *prima facie* rights "maybe rights." When one "maybe right" is judged to override another, then it becomes a right. In effect, this approach says that two conflicting *prima facie* rights at first glance both look like rights—but later we see that one really is a right and the other is not. The overridden "maybe right" ceases to have any claim upon us. So if my "maybe right" to control my goods overrides your "maybe right" to my assistance, then I have a right and you no longer have anything—you cease to have a legitimate claim against me.[6] Rights are, in effect, determined by right actions.

The second way to approach the conflict of *prima facie* rights is to see *prima facie* rights as legitimate moral claims. When these claims come into conflict and we must choose to act on one, the other (overridden) one remains a legitimate claim even though it would be wrong, in this circumstance, to act on it. Although it is a legitimate moral claim, it is not a justified moral claim in this circumstance. Thus *prima facie* rights are not "maybe rights"; and even though they are rights that are defeasible, when they are defeated, they remain legitimate claims. Honoring one *prima facie* right may excuse us from honoring other conflicting ones. But though we are excused, the conflicting claims remain legitimate claims.[7] For instance, if I am forced to hit and kill you with my car in order to avoid hitting a dozen children, then your *prima facie* right not to be killed remains a legitimate claim upon me—only in this instance, I am excused from honoring it. The former position would result in your "maybe right" not to be killed disappearing altogether.

[6]This, or something like it, is suggested by W. D. Ross in *The Right and the Good* (Oxford at the Clarendon Press, 1930), Chapter II.

[7]I derive this position from A. I. Melden's views in "The Play of Rights," *Monist,* 56 (1972), 479–502.

The right to be saved from preventable death due to deprivation is a *prima facie* right in the second sense, and so I can be excused from acting on a sufferer's legitimate claim to assistance. There are excusing conditions to my obligation. If we lived in a world where our obligations did not conflict with other obligations and rights, then there would be no excuse for failing to save others in need. But we do not live in that type of moral world. Obligations conflict. Some obligations are less stringent than others; some are overridden and some are defeated. The obligation to save others from death due to deprivation also comes into conflict with other obligations. Sometimes it is overridden and we are excused from acting on it. There are, it seems, at least two conditions which can excuse us from providing others with the goods and services required by them to be saved from preventable death due to deprivation—although both of these conditions are difficult to describe precisely.

The first excusing condition is this: if rendering the goods and services required to save another from death involves an *unreasonable* amount of cost to the giver, then the giver is excused from aiding the sufferer. By cost I do not mean only expense, but also effort, risk, and sacrifice. The obvious difficulty with this condition is the unfixed nature of the 'unreasonable' criterion. What is an unreasonable amount of cost? Surely if I am not a good swimmer, then risking my life in the pounding surf to save you from drowning would be an unreasonable risk. So too, if by helping you I place myself in a similar, but not quite equivalent, position of deprivation, then this too would be an unreasonable amount of cost. But at what point, precisely, does a cost become unreasonable and thus provide me with an excusing condition to fail to act on your claim against me? Some would suggest that the cut-off point is the point of marginal utility. Others would suggest that it is not until the point of complete egalitarian distribution. Others would suggest the point is the level of slight inconvenience. This cut-off point may not be determinable outside of the context of an actual situation. But some suggestions can be made.

The stringency of the obligation to save others, and thus the strength of the right to be saved, should be seen as standing in inverse proportion to the cost of the goods or services to the actor. Thus, if all that I need do to save you from drowning is to reach out my hand, then my duty to save you is more stringent and your claim of right stronger than if I must swim to reach you. The greater the cost to the actor, the less stringent the duty. Once the actor reaches a state of equivalent need, the obligation has ceased altogether.

As the claim against me decreases in strength according to the cost of the action to me, the duty to honor that claim (by acting upon it) becomes more easily overridden by my other moral duties. For instance, my duty to provide for my family would override my duty to save your starving family if by saving your family I seriously endanger my family's health. The greater the cost to me, the more easily my duty is overridden by my other moral duties.

Perhaps the determination of the degree of cost to me which is an unreasonable amount of cost could be made by finding that point in a particular situation where any other conflicting moral duty I have overrides the duty to save the person in need. At this point of cost I would be excused from the obligation because any conflicting duty would override it. It would still be debatable as to whether or not this point of cost is above or below the point of marginal utility; but at least this criterion allows for flexibility. Flexibility in this matter is desirable because different persons have different moral duties, some of which do and some of which do not conflict with the duty to save persons in dire need. For those persons with few conflicting moral duties, the point where the cost becomes unreasonable (and thus the point where one is excused from performing the saving act) will be higher than for those who have many conflicting moral duties. A greater amount of effort, risk, sacrifice, and expense will be required of that person with fewer conflicting moral duties because there will be less to justify his being excused from acting.

This flexible criterion of unreasonable cost accounts for the general impression that persons who have much in the way of goods but little in the way of moral responsibilities ought to give more to assist persons in need. It also allows for the performance of acts beyond the call of duty (that is, supererogatory acts), for if a person takes an unreasonable risk or sacrifices an unreasonable amount, then he is truly acting nobly or even saintly. It is important to allow for the distinction between obligations and acts of supererogation since without it all persons would be required, by duty, to be moral saints. This would make morality unattainable by the majority of humans—and perhaps even irrelevant to human action.

There is another excusing condition to the obligation to save persons from preventable death due to deprivation. If one has no access to an effective method of making the goods and services available to the sufferer, then one is excused from the obligation to save the sufferer. For example, if a government intentionally prevents the delivery of food relief to starving persons within that nation, then one possible method of delivering the food would be to destroy that government by declaring war on it. Another would be to smuggle the food in with the knowledge that most of it would be confiscated. Another would be to drop packages from high flying aircraft with the hope that at least some of them reached the ground undamaged and were then received by those who need them. Each of these methods is a *possible* means of delivering the food but none of them is particularly *effective*. In this case, where no effective means of distributing the food is available, we would be excused from the obligation to save the starving persons in that nation. Of course, it might be that we have other moral responsibilities to find or to establish an effective method. We might even be required to coerce that government into permitting us to distribute the food necessary for the lives of persons within that nation; but this would be another type of moral responsibility, and justification of it would require a separate argument.

The term 'effective' is an evaluating notion and as such it creates in this excusing condition, as in the previous one, a flexible criterion. The stringency of the obligation to save persons in dire need is proportional to the effectiveness of the available method of providing the goods and services required by the persons in need. But this flexibility is not necessarily undesirable. For instance, there is a general opinion among moral philosophers that distance provides a relevant moral consideration; that is, if a person is starving on your doorstep he has a stronger claim to assistance from you than does someone who is living on the other side of the world. Although the claim that distance alone makes a difference is popular, it is difficult to justify other than by appeal to moral intuitions. But with the effectiveness of the method of distribution playing a role in determining the strength of the duty to save persons in dire need, it is easily seen that the duty to the man on your doorstep is stronger than the duty to the person across the world. All that is required of you to deliver the necessary food to the man on your doorstep is to walk to the kitchen and bring back some food from the refrigerator. But to deliver the food to the person in India, for example, you must depend upon a complex network of international relief; however, since there are effective relief organizations (CARE, Ox-Fam, etc.), we are not *entirely* excused from our obligation. There are other elements, in addition to distance, involved in determining effectiveness (e.g., political sovereignty); but it certainly is one element. Although voluntary organizations like CARE are effective methods, they are not very effective. Much more effective methods of food distribution are needed if all those dying of hunger are going to be saved. As suggested before, we may have some responsibility to see to it that obstacles impairing the effective commission of our obligations are removed—be they obstacles presented by our own or another government's action.

The flexibility of the effectiveness condition also accounts for the insight expressed in the proposed 'last resort' condition for obligation mentioned above. If I *am* the last resort, for instance, if I am the only person near enough to a pond to save a drowning child, then I have a more effective method of acting (owing to my physical proximity) than do others. So I cannot be excused from acting. If there are others with more effective methods, I may be excused. But if there are other persons with *equally* effective methods of providing goods or services, then none of us is excused from his or her obligation to act (by the effectiveness condition). Not being the last resort does not necessarily excuse me from by obligation, but it may.

In this lengthy section, I have tried to show that moral rights based on need are not necessarily doomed to failure because of vagueness—that at least one such right is specifiable, the right to be saved from preventable death due to deprivation.

V

Recognition of the right to be saved from preventable death due to deprivation would clarify many traditional problem cases for moral philosophers. In addition to the 'drowning child' case and the 'accident victim' case, it would also be useful in deciding on cases of euthanasia like the Karen Quinlan case, where the issue seems not to be whether the right violated by unplugging a respirator is the right to life (that is, the right not to be killed unjustly), but is rather the right to be saved from preventable death due to deprivation. As the instruments for keeping people (both terminal patients and newborns) alive improve in technological capability, the deliberations of ethicists will increasingly be confused without the recognition of this moral right.

But the one area where recognition of this moral right will have the most impact on moral deliberation is the world hunger issue. Since starving to death is a form of death due to deprivation, and since death due to this cause is preventable (at least at present), then persons who are starving to death have a *prima facie* moral right to be saved. There *is* a moral right to be saved from starvation.

But has any benefit been gained by admitting that there is such a moral right? Does the recognition of this right tell us what we *ought* to do about the problem of world hunger and the massive death toll that famine is reaping in the sub-Sahara and in India? Certainly, the recognition of this right by itself will not solve the difficult problem of making moral choices. But it does, I believe, substantially change the moral arena in which such decisions must be discussed. In order for us to know that we *ought* to provide someone with the goods and/or services he needs to stay alive, we must know that his *prima facie* moral right overrrides all other rights in this circumstance and that we are not excused from honoring his right. Unfortunately, we have no automatic procedure to discover what we ought to do when there is a conflict of *prima facie* rights. But even though recognition of this right to be saved will not tell us, *a priori*, what we ought to do in every circumstance, it does have several important implications for the world hunger situation.

Giving aid to persons who are in need is not always merely an act of charity to which the recipient should respond with gratitude. That people are starving is not merely a signal to exercise our duties of benevolence and thereby become better persons (that is, persons with better moral characters). Those starving people have a claim of right against us. As the situation is seen today by affluent nations like the United States, giving aid to starving peoples is a matter of charity. And so, when Third World Nations demand assistance from us in the world food conferences, we scream with indignation about the ungrateful beggars. After all, one cannot demand charity. All one can do is plead for it. Recognition that there is a moral right to be saved from starvation would at least rid us of any illusions about our "good deeds."

With recognition of the moral right to be saved from starvation, it will be seen that the world hunger problem cannot be solved simply by appeal to prudential considerations. For instance, it is in the grain-producing nations' best economic interest to control carefully the amount of grain that is sold on the world market in order to insure that the prices remain high. Since the demand for food is rapidly becoming as high as the demand for petroleum products, the grain-producing nations have an exceptionally valuable resource with which to balance trade deficits, to utilize as a political tool to insure friendly governments, and with which to gain power over potentially threatening nations. It is definitely not in their prudential interest simply to give food away or to sell it at less than competitive prices, for this would be to waste a valuable commodity from which great profits could be made. This dual use of the food weapon as an economic and political tool becomes questionable if persons have a moral right to be saved from starvation. If failing to assist starving persons is a neglect of a moral obligation, then we cannot, without proper justification of our omission, avoid being morally reprehensible for following prudential guidelines.

Recognition of this right to be saved from starvation would transform the debate about aiding hungry people from one of charity-in-abundance to one of conflicting *prima facie* moral rights. The arena for moral decision would become the adjudication of conflicting claims. This shift of arena alone would substantially affect the world hunger issue. For example, the popular 'population explosion' argument, which does not see the issue as a conflict of rights, would be seen to be inadequate. This argument runs something like this: if you feed x number of starving persons now they will, in some period of time, procreate at such a rate that the population will be doubled and so too will the total amount of human misery due to starvation. So failure to feed people now will diminish the total amount of human suffering.

Besides the difficulties involved in predicting a continued geometrical increase in population according to present trends, this approach is misguided. It addresses the problem as one would the rat population in a city slum: if we kill x number of rats now we can avoid having to kill 2x number next year. Except for appeal to the omission–commission distinction and the supposed crucial moral distinction between the two, the case of people in the first argument is the same as the case of rats in the second. Since it is immoral to simply exterminate several million starving people (it violates their right not to be killed unjustly), it is best to "let nature take its course"—that is, it is right to let these people die even though we could prevent their deaths. By ignoring the right to be saved from starvation and thereby avoiding the conflict of rights, the 'population argument' suggests that the intentional reliance on starvation as a means of population control is a moral alternative. But it is *not*, other things being equal, a moral alternative. It is a violation of a moral right which must be justified. The real moral difficulty that underlies the population problem is a fundamental conflict of two moral rights: the right to procreate (which is deduced from the generally recognized right to freedom) and the right to be saved from starvation. If the population exceeds the food supply, then either the right to procreate must be overridden by the right to be saved or vice versa. I would advocate mandatory birth control (say, after the birth of two children) before I would support the intentional reliance upon starvation as a means of population control. But I need not defend this position in order to make the general point that there is a conflict of rights here which must be resolved by offering good moral reasons why one right should override another.[8] If the moral arena of the world hunger debate were the arena of conflicts of rights (as it should be), the 'population explosion' argument would not be as sheltered from criticism as it presently is.

Another argument which would be eliminated by the recognition that the issue is a matter of a conflict of rights is what I shall call the 'it's mine' argument. The revival of the deification of property rights with its distinguished prophets is of no small consequence for the world hunger issue. The 'it's mine' argument simply says, "the goods in question are *mine* and I may do as I please with them without thereby incurring moral blame." This theory can only be maintained seriously if it presupposes that property rights are absolute rights. But it seems absurd (without the sophistical backing of Natural Law) to claim that any moral right is absolute. If

[8]Some leaders in famine-stricken nations may not see that the right to procreate conflicts with the right to be saved from starvation. They need to be convinced of this. However, if they persist in avoiding population control programs, I do not think that tying food relief to population control is the most moral alternative. An inducement with favorable trade agreements or developmental assistance would be better alternatives. Other goods than food should be used to bribe neglectful governments into action to curb population growth.

property rights are *not* seen as absolute rights, then there will be situations in which my *moral* claim (we are not talking about legal entitlement nor about what extent of coercion is justifiable) to goods in my possession can be overridden by others' moral claim to those goods. My property rights may come into conflict with another's need right and may be overridden by it. One could maintain that property rights always override need rights without the supposition of property rights being absolute, yet this would need a very sophisticated *moral* defense. Since there is a conflict between property rights and need rights, the standard of measurement of the strength of each right must be morally defensible. The suggested inflexible priority of property rights over need rights would require its advocates to defend it against a host of counterexamples. (For example: Does my right to possess a gold-plated toilet seat override someone else's right to a survival quantity of food? Does my right to own all the oxygen in, around, and above New York City, if I could figure out a way to capture it and bottle it, override the residents of that city's right to be saved from death due to deprivation of oxygen? Etc.)

The problems cited in the above paragraph result from considering the world hunger issue as a conflict of rights. But the 'it's mine' argument would not even require us to examine this problem. By ignoring the conflict of rights, the 'it's mine' argument supposes that the only moral issue involved is the goodness of the moral character of the person who could, if he chooses, aid the starving. The starving have absolutely no claim (moral or otherwise) to aid; refusing to give aid is morally permissible, though it is perhaps being "less than a Minimally Decent Samaritan" (as Judith Thomson would say).[9]

The final and most important aspect of recognizing the moral right to be saved from starvation and of seeing the world hunger issue in terms of a conflict of moral rights, is that the burden of proof has been shifted from those in need of food to those who could give food. The needy no longer must supply reasons why they should be helped (e.g., by promising favorable trade, by making compromising political concessions). Rather, those who can assist the hungry must explain why they are *not* acting. It would no longer be morally acceptable merely to let people die and then claim moral innocence. Not honoring the right to be saved from starvation by giving the required goods and services would require giving excusing reasons and offering moral justifications for inaction. This would involve weighing moral duties and balancing claims. No longer would it be taken for granted that as long as you do not harm someone directly, you are morally blameless. This applies to the drowning child case, the accident

---

[9]Judith Thomson, "A Defense of Abortion," in J. Feinberg, ed., *The Problem of Abortion* (Belmont, Calif.: Wadsworth Publishing Co., Inc., 1973), pp. 121–39.

victim case, and especially to the world hunger issue. Inaction, the omission to act, must be justified when the need of another is extreme (to the point of death). The question is not "Why should I send money to save starving people?" but rather "If I am not sending money, why am I not?" I must offer reasons. I must show that there are excusing conditions which apply. I must justify my inaction.

JOSEPH FLETCHER

Fletcher argues that food assistance must not be given indiscriminately. For those countries which have exceeded their carrying capacity, assistance is, in the long run, harmful. Even though we could, we ought not to assist them.

1. *Notice that Fletcher does not exclude giving food to all underdeveloped nations, but only to those which have exceeded their carrying capacity. How can one determine precisely that point at which the carrying capacity is exceeded?*

2. *His argument is a utilitarian one. But he comes up with a different prescription than either Narveson or Singer, who also rely on utilitarian arguments. How do we account for this difference?*

3. *His discussion is set within the practical limits of the present-day political world where there is an unequal distribution of food and raw materials. Does this make his essay more "realistic" than some of the others in this volume?*

4. *Would Fletcher's argument justify destroying surplus food rather than giving it to certain starving people?*

Joseph Fletcher is Visiting Professor of Medical Ethics at the Virginia School of Medicine. Author of the well-known Situation Ethics, *he has written numerous articles on ethical problems in biomedical fields.*

This article has not been previously published.

Give If It Helps
But Not If It Hurts

"Philosophers Are Back On The Job," said Peter Singer recently, in a magazine piece about the revival of normative ethics.[1] He meant that the apparent death of ethical–political discussion among philosophers has ended, and that "wisdom lovers" are in fact ready for enterprises somewhat more humanistic than their once-fashionable language analysis. Aristotle was right all along; politics is ethics writ large, and thus it is that the debate about helping the hungry, especially feeding them, is an excellent arena for showing what being "back on the job" amounts to.

Ethically regarded, famine relief is not a particularly complicated or knotty problem. As in everything else, any proposition about a person's or group's or country's obligation to help hungry or starving people has to satisfy three reasonable requirements: (1) that it is based on facts, data, evidence, (2) that it is logically consistent, and (3) that its foreseeable consequences are defensible. (These canons do not apply to astrology, for example, nor do they fit some kinds of "sharing" either.)

The more-or-less official foreign aid policy of the United States, as reflected in the literature and history of the U.S. Agency for International Development, stands on three legs—emergency aid, developmental assistance, and population control. This policy is, as we shall see, rationally acceptable, but acceptable only *if and when* it is qualified by an essential discrimination between needs arising from catastrophe or underdevelopment, on the one hand, as over against needs arising from high fecundity and an irrational fertility rate. In some cases, we shall argue, population control should not only be encouraged but stoutly required as a condition or precondition of help.

Just as there are three requirements for valid obligation and three legs to American foreign aid, there are also three kinds of aid. They are: (1) *developmental assistance,* helping underdeveloped countries educationally and technically to accumulate capital and raise their standard of living; (2) *emergency famine or disaster relief,* as when earthquakes, floods, typhoons, or atypical droughts occur—an instance being when a hurricane hit Honduras recently, and (3) *relief for countries suffering chronic famine* because their birth rate exceeds their actual or potential productivity. In this last case we ought not to help, it will be argued, until a workable and sincere commitment is made contractually to reduce such a country's fertility.

One religious activist, in a show of Jamesian tough-mindedness, has asked his fellow promoters of feed-the-hungry programs, "But have the tough questions been faced?"[2] He lists as tough questions to face such

[1] *The New York Times Magazine,* July 7, 1974, v. 6–7, pp. 17–20.

[2] Richard W. Gillett, "World Hunger and Future Christian Response: The Issues," *The Witness* (an Episcopal social concerns magazine), October 1975, p. 5.

things as inequitable global distributions of food, equivocal government policies, big agricultural corporations, and outrageous overconsumption (in America). However weighty, these are all socio-political factors. He asks nothing in the basic, biological order; nothing ecological. His appraisal never asks whether some countries have exceeded their carrying capacity by spawning more mouths to feed than the ecology allows.

We will contend that in at least a few cases certain countries have exceeded their biological carrying capacity, and that therefore to give them food is immoral. The writer just quoted appeals to the "right to eat," but we shall reject any notion that rights are self-validating regardless of the relativities. Our ethical "method" will be to determine right and wrong contextually or situationally, not by predetermined rules or moral imperatives; in this modality both values and judgments, along with moral claims (rights), will be treated as variable according to the shifting factors within which ethical policies and decisions are to be made. Therefore, it can be right to send food or wrong to send it, depending on the situation and the foreseeable consequences. We shall also presuppose that we ought to seek the greatest possible good for the greatest number possible.

One relief crusade is "Food For Our Neighbors," a Billy James Hargis evangelistic program which solicits money to send food indiscriminately to Bangladesh (a high-excess country) and to Mexico (a country decidedly in biological balance). They explain that they work through missionaries (which makes their ulterior motive obvious); their lack of ethical acumen is revealed in a typical appeal letter: "Pray and let your heart rule your actions. Help us save innocent children from hunger and death." It is risky to knock prayer, and we all admire plenty of heart and nobody wants children to suffer, but even if their motives were disinterested, their concern for human beings is undermined by refusing to let their brains rule.

Any suggestion that there are rational and fair conditions for generosity sets the visceral functions of many people at war with their cerebral functions. The consequence is such a high-flown but logically circular sentiment as, "We ought to feed the hungry because they are hungry." A *circulus in probando* or *petitio principii* of this kind appears in the thinking of an economist in the Food and Agricultural Organization; writing on the subject of feeding hungry peoples, he says, "It shall be done because it must be done."[3]

To ask seriously whether sharing will help or hurt shocks the superficial who have never grasped how wrong generosity can be. Such innocents are

---

[3]R. C. Tetro, quoted in T. Y. Canby, "Can the World Feed Its People?" *National Geographic*, vol. 148, no. 1 (1975), p. 31.

easily dismissed by cynics—many of the latter being admirably hard-headed but deplorably hardhearted. To be situationally realistic about generosity is not by any means to call into question the virtue of generosity, as such. And to ask, for example, what Americans ought to do for hungry Upper Voltans or Mauritanians is humane, not chauvinist. Charity begins at home, arguably, but if it stops at the water's edge, it withers into group-egoism.

If we want to ask analytic questions seriously, we should follow the advice of the mathematician Karl Jacobi; it was, "Umkehren, immer um-kehren" (invert, always invert).[4] We ought not to go on asking always, "Who would be helped by our help?" We need also to ask, "Who would be *hurt* by our help?" Relief is not always or necessarily helpful. This inversion stratagem is a very useful tool ethically. By inverting we can see that in some situations we may actually hurt people if we send them food; in some instances even nonfood assistance might at least be futile if not hurtful. In situations where reproduction has outstripped productivity, to give food would only increase the population without raising the rate of production (GNP), thus increasing the number of starving people and so producing a net loss of life and a net increase of human misery.

Sometimes we hear specious or at least secondary objections to sending food relief to famine areas—objections having to do with alleged or known misfeasance or even malfeasance in the distribution of relief, or doctrinaire and ideological protests, as in sales of grain to Russia or Poland. But these are not fundamental when compared to objections based on biological-ecological limits and imbalances.

Somebody is sure to say, as a label and perhaps as an epithet, that to reason this way is Malthusian or neo-Malthusian. The latter term fits better, if the thesis has to be christened. It has been argued by competent demographers, social biologists, climatologists, and geographers that we cannot feed everybody in the world.[5] In the analysis here, however, the thesis is that we *ought* not to feed everybody; it is therefore an ethical thesis, resting on the interface between population and the standard of living. Marx said that production and reproduction are the two basic realities of human existence; and Malthus (much earlier) saw that baby-making can nullify the supposed benefits of wealthmaking. Both, thus far, are correct.

---

[4]I am indebted to Garrett Hardin for this; from "Carrying Capacity as an Ethical Concept," in a symposium edited by George R. Lucas, Jr., "World Famine and Triage," 69 *Soundings* (Spring 1976).

[5]See such investigations as Studies of Critical Environmental Problems, *Man's Impact on the Global Environment* (Cambridge, Mass.: M.I.T. Press, 1970); Editors of the Ecologist, *Blueprint for Survival* (Boston: Houghton Mifflin Company, 1972); D. H. and D. L. Meadows, et al., *The Limits to Growth* (New York: Universe Books, 1972).

Malthus reasoned that population tends (sic) to increase faster, in a geometric ratio, than the means of production provide food. Food, he held, increases only in arithmetic ratio. And, he went on, this will result in a chronically low supply of food *except* when war, famine, and disease reduce the population *or* it is checked by "sexual restraint" (meaning late marriage and continence).[6] His "positive checks" on population (war, famine, and disease) did not include contraceptive birth control because Malthus—a "good" eighteenth-century clergyman—believed it to be immoral. (He was in much the same bind as the Pope is today, recognizing the actuality of overpopulation but forbidden by a moral rule to act rationally.)

"Neo-Malthusians" take to heart the biological tension between population and wealth, as mutually limiting factors, but they agree with William Godwin and Condorcet against Malthus that the best positive check on fertility is birth control rather than disease, war, or famine. The Reverend Mr. Malthus was an economic pessimist who believed we would *always* be impoverished by fecundity; thus the new social biology shifts away from his naturalistic pessimism to a trust in the workability of rational control. Again unlike Malthus, neo-Malthusians call for cutting down fertility, not for cutting out sex.

If a country of 25 million stomachs has exceeded its carrying capacity and fallen into chronic famine, with a vital balance of 10 births and 10 deaths annually per thousand (one million each), food would prolong the progenitors' lives and in about 20 years they would double the population. At the established balance there would then be *two* million births and deaths per year; the quantum of human suffering would have been doubled in a net loss of lives to disease and starvation. Contrary to what some relief advocates say, this neo-Malthusian analysis does not assume that such countries will never lower their birth rates; it does assume, however, that if their birth rates are not lowered to a biological balance of people and environment, they cannot escape their predicament.

In the course of this century's debate about ethics and hunger, a fairly new term has emerged, "the Fourth World." It may help this discussion along if we use "Third World" (by now a familiar label) to stand for undeveloped countries like Tanzania and underdeveloped countries like Indonesia. This grouping includes countries with national economies which have yet to achieve enough capital development and technical sophistication but nevertheless have a social-biological balance favorable to development—they have a favorable ratio between the five primary factors: population, pollution, raw materials, food supply, and industrial output. Given a socio-biological balance, development presents no great

---

[6]Thomas Robert Malthus, *An Essay on the Principles of Population as It Affects the Future of Society, with Remarks on the Speculations of Mr. Godwin, M. Condorcet, and Other Writers* (London, 1798).

obstacles. At the close of World War II, 90 percent of the world's countries were stagnant economically. Today fewer than half of them are in that class, owing mainly to developmental assistance.

The Fourth World, on the other hand, consists of about forty countries whose standard of living is at the lowest level. Among these is a small— we may be thankful—category which exceed their carrying capacity (too many people) and in consequence face chronic famine plus a paralysis of capital growth. For this bottom-of-the-barrel group we will use the name "Fifth World."

In this Fifth World group might go India, Bangladesh, Upper Volta, Senegal, Niger, and a few others. (Determining which countries are "Fifth" is a question for the requisite experts rather than for ethicists.) In any case, they are unlike the Third and Fourth World countries because they are biologically stymied, without a rationally founded hope unless they reduce their population and reconstitute their soil—the source of their food and raw materials. In that struggle the affluent (developed countries) could help the impoverished by giving assistance (growth support), but the help should not be in the form of food shipments.

"Assistance" covers "seed capital" and "pilot" equipment, which could be rented, sold, lent, or given outright, along with technical, educational, and medical training, to build their capabilities and increase the productivity of their labor. Even in cases of assistance, however, we find James W. Howe, an able spokesman for US-AID, carefully qualifying his advocacy with a statement that "assistance would be of doubtful morality (only) if it were absolutely certain that fertility could not be reduced over the decades ahead."[7] (Phrasing his statement in this way, he could in the recesses of his own mind be quite unconditional about assistance, since demographic projections cannot be "absolutely certain.")

Howe demonstrates the peculiar logic with which help-the-hungry advocates usually do their work. Having thus acknowledged that fertility is the key to successful aid, he then adds that "to assume a permanent inability to reduce births is to say there is no hope that these countries will ever escape the Malthusian dilemma." In truth, the assumption is just the opposite of what he suggests: namely, that if these countries do not escape the Malthusian dilemma by reducing their birth rates, there is no hope they can escape from a permanently hungry and starving situation.

Even if we take a global Spaceship Earth stance rather than a national-economy Lifeboat stance, we ought not to feed Fifth World peoples with

---

[7]J. W. Howe and Staff of the World Development Council, *The U. S. and World Development: Agenda for Action in 1975* (New York: Praeger Paperbacks, 1975), p. 65.

their present reproductive mores.[8] Even if we feel we ought to help Third and Fourth World countries (as I for one do), we ought not to send food to the chronic-famine countries no matter how saddened or upset we are by their plight. Undiscriminating generosity, fired by feelings of false guilt when comparing high standards of living to sub-subsistence, is appropriate only to "liberals" of the most sentimental kind. Our own wealth and ability to relieve hunger are morally irrelevant, because the consequence sometimes of feeding the starving is to make things worse in terms of human well-being. Feeding the hungry in some countries only keeps them alive longer to produce more hungry bellies and disease and death.

Calling the United States and the Soviet Union "fat cat" countries which "ought to be ashamed to be so selfish" is pure ethical rubbish, sentimental and uncritical and therefore irresponsible, if the charge is made in blanket terms without careful use of the carrying capacity criterion. Garrett Hardin's challenge, in effect, is to ask us the searching question ethically—do good intentions excuse the consequences of our actions? The Fifth World with its suffocating birth rates and depletion of its soil is deep in nihilistic immolation, and to become accessories after the fact is indefensible—if you have enough loving concern for human beings to want to minimize suffering. To minimize suffering is one important way of maximizing the good.

One school of thought about helping the world's poor offers what the unwary might take to be a way out of the neo-Malthusian dilemma. The dilemma is that famine relief helps excessive reproducers to survive and thus to increase the number of famine victims. The alleged way out of this is called "the demographic transition theory."[9] As a theory, it is both debatable and in fact much debated. Its exponents argue that with capital development and a rise of the standards of living the rate of reproduction falls. This appears to have happened as a coincidence in some times and places, but it is not uniformly the case nor causally established. The evidence supporting it is more anecdotal than scientific. In the United States, to take a rich country, its enormous technical development has been paralleled by an enormous overall population *growth.*

This theory might influence some moral judgments about offers of help to Third and possibly Fourth World countries, but if it ever applies at all to Fifth World countries it should only influence decisions to offer assistance—not food. One well-known American foundation regularly gives nearly $400,000 in grants for an irrigation project in Niger, but not one cent for food. We should be asking "invertly" what Dives' generosity does to

[8]Garrett Hardin's *Exploring New Ethics for Survival* (New York: Viking Press, 1972) set the stage for the present debate by showing us the ecological basis for "mutual coercion mutually agreed upon."

[9]A champion is Roger Revelle. See his "The Ghost at the Feast," *Science,* 186 (1974), 9.

Lazarus, not only what it does to or for Dives and his spiritual Brownie points. Even as tough-minded a person as Robert McNamara, president of the World Bank, never asks the question—perhaps because it is inexpedient to raise it, and undiplomatic.[10]

A typical instance of uncritical thinking about hunger in the world occurred at an Aspen Conference of Jews and Christians in 1974. Everybody there assumed we should aid *all* hungry people, apparently with priority going to the hungriest and most desperate—which is exactly the opposite of "triage." They made no attempt to answer the neo-Malthusian thesis, contenting themselves moralistically and piously with the saying, "As you do it unto the least of these my brethren you do it unto me."[11] On the other hand, the World Development Council (which engineered the Aspen meeting and published its proceedings) quite forthrightly confronts the neo-Malthusians by appealing to the demographic transition theory.[12]

Be it noted, however, that the World Development Council's analysts *never ask whether there are some situations in which food should not be given.* They never invert. For the most part, their promotion of the assistance principle is entirely reasonable ethically; it is "development" that concerns them chiefly—not relief. But too much of their discussion is at fault ethically because it fails to appreciate and make use of the distinctions between developmental assistance, emergency aid, and chronic famine relief. The same complaint can be lodged against Ox-FAM, a more militant organization which, like the Council, fails to make situational distinctions or allocations.[13]

The 1974 international meetings in Romania and Rome (the former on population, the latter on food) provided a striking contrast in rationality. The food conference managed to be realistic and fairly candid. The population conference in Bucharest was a shambles of both reason and honesty. It was dominated by Third and Fourth World politicians and ideologues, and their line was an undiscriminating appeal to "human rights"—an alleged right to eat and an alleged right to reproduce.

Their purple oratory appealed idealistically (philosophically speaking) to an objective moral order; they preached that we "ought" to feed the hungry just because they are hungry and regardless of the consequences.

[10]This question is the one which was not sufficiently examined in Garrett Hardin's brilliant and much-contested essays, "Lifeboat Ethics: The Case Against Helping The Poor," *Psychology Today*, 8 (1974), 38–43, (included in this volume), and "Living on a Lifeboat," *Bioscience*, 25 (1974), 561–68.

[11]Report of the Aspen Interreligious Consultation, *Global Justice and Development* (Washington, D.C.: Overseas Development Council, 1975).

[12]J. W. Howe, et al., *The U. S. and World Development*, pp. 55–71.

[13]See its lively magazine, *The New Internationalist*, edited in England by Peter Adamson.

For them ethics meant rights (claims), not responsibilities. They perpe-
trated unblushingly the most simplistic ideas about feeding and breeding.
Away from the rostrum and its microphones, comments were muttered as
asides, such as "Groceries, yes, but not without vasectomies."

Some objections to helping hungry countries fail to go as deep as the
Malthusian problem runs. Neo-Malthusians contend that when help hurts
the recipients, by increasing the number of sufferers, it is wrong to give
it. The food exists, of course. In 1970 it would have taken only 12 billion
tons of cereals to increase the caloric intake of 460 million sufferers by 250
calories each. This is about one percent of the world's consumption, less
than half of what Americans throw away, about 30 percent of what is fed
to livestock in the United States.[14] The question is not *can* we feed the
hungry of Blankland, but *should* we. It is an ethical, not a technical, question.

Giving food to the countries most destitute and bogged down in ecological suicide only deprives others that can benefit. The argument that corrupt
and elitist rulers in some lands will prevent help reaching the needy is
often true enough, on the record, but it is always a questionable assumption. Undemocratic or vicious governments sometimes strengthen their
hold by using donated food to feed the hungry, but the obverse, that *not*
feeding the starving will undermine such governments, is not too likely.
It is a mistake to suppose that the hungry and desperate will organize a
new regime; more often they fall to fighting each other. Even if a bad
government falls, there is no reason to expect its successor to be more just
or benevolent. In any case, widespread hunger is only secondarily a political issue; basically, it is a problem in social biology.

The kernel of the question appears when we face a standard appeal such
as, "look at how much of everything we have and how easily we could feed
the goat-herding people who are starving in the Sahel or sub-Saharan
Africa." (As little as 15 percent of the wheat grown in the United States
is enough to feed its population well; Kansas alone grows enough to do it.)
Ethically examined, the kernel is that whether we are rich or poor, affluent
or not, is irrelevant to the issue. It is relevant only to ask whether sharing
will help or hurt the recipients.

It is appropriate, also, to ask whether sharing will help or hurt the *donor*
as well. Assuming there is a moral gain in acts of constructive generosity,
it still remains necessary to find out at what point (1) giving "hurts" in the
sense of making a real or felt sacrifice, at what point beyond that (2)
sharing becomes dangerous to the donor, and finally at what point (3) it
would be self-destructive. In another place I have argued that we rich

---

[14]Economic Research Council, U.S. Department of Agriculture, *The World Food Situation
and Prospects to 1985* (Washington, D.C., 1974), p. 12.

Americans should individually and collectively share where it will help, at least up to the first point where we feel it, and arguably sometimes up to the second point (danger), yet not to the suicidal point.[15] But this has to do with developmental assistance to Third and Fourth World countries, whereas the present position paper deals chiefly with food relief for chronic famine in Fifth World countries.

The world as a whole is hungrier today, has far more undernourished or actually starving people in it, than probably at any time since mankind generally (not simultaneously) passed over from nomadic to agrarian societies. In a few countries which have achieved a high level of technical development in agriculture as well as in industry, people consume food to the extent of overindulgence; the average American swallows twice as much protein as the human body can use, and the steers we eat are ridiculously inefficient converters of plant to animal protein (about one pound per 21 pounds of feed).

One engaging and earnest advocate of help for the hungry, working in disregard of the distinctions being drawn here, was annoyed because John Knowles, president of the Rockefeller Foundation, had said, "Malthus has already been proved correct." She retorted, "If our agricultural resources were used rationally and distributed at all equitably, there would be enough to go around now (in the whole world)."[16] The truth is that: (1) the world's resources are not distributed equitably mainly because good soil and new materials are not distributed equitably; (2) there are no global structures politically and economically to provide a supernational distribution; (3) national sovereignty prevents a world government which might limit the consumption of rich foods and scarce energy-fuels in affluent countries; and (4) a few countries which exceed their carrying capacity are acting most irrationally and lethally by their excessive reproduction.

This is the right point at which to speak bluntly to the anti-ethics of excessive reproduction. In Bangladesh, a typically irrational country in its death-dealing fertility, seven babies are born every minute in a land with 1400 Bangladeshi per square mile. The peasant progenitors there think their children are their only security against old age, if their progeny should manage to survive. But if only two out of five survive (that is the actual situation), what they have done in every case is to doom three of their own children in order to better the parents' chances of not dying themselves. This is a ruthless numbers game, a parlay *en masse*, with human lives as chips—a gambling game of prodigal prolificity. It is almost always reinforced by religious teaching about an alleged divine approval of it. In fact, of course, they are for their own gain victimizing their own

[15]See Joseph Fletcher, "Feeding the Hungry: An Ethical Appraisal," *Soundings*, 69 (Spring 1976).

[16]Frances Lappe, "Fantasies of Famine," *Harper's Magazine*, 2:1497 (February 1975), 54.

children, as well as their countrymen collectively and whatever foreign "benefactors" might be sending them food.

Education and health care can hold down and reverse such fertility rates, as we have seen in Sri Lanka, Costa Rica, Egypt, Taiwan, and Barbados. Without eliminating the excess population, helping the Fifth World countries is inhumane and therefore immoral, a band-aid treatment to cover up the real sore. The new post-1950 China is a large-scale instance of how a high-fertility ethos centuries old can be changed. Some Quakers are now confessing that the problem is not food but fertility: "If Quaker world relief were to make a dramatic and sustained shift in such a direction, we might again provide the model for a crucial change in humanitarian efforts everywhere, and later generations might indeed 'rise up and call us blessed.' "[17]

When wondering which Fifth World countries we ought to help, it is ethically irrelevant to ask, "Do I need large portions of meat?" or "Do I need meat and bread every day?" or "How else can I get enough proteins?" Having "fasting meals" and "foodless banquets" may have some nutritional value for the overfed, but that is all. Possibly some people are brought by such sentimentalities to perceive the problem, but if they send any food for the victims of chronic famine they would be unethical.

Garrett Hardin in his *Exploring New Ethics for Survival* (already cited) embraces the act-utilitarian method of situation ethics; he expresses it in his own formulation, "The morality of an act is a function of the state of the system at the time the act is performed—this is the fundamental tenet of 'situation ethics'. "[18] He takes killing an elephant as an example; killing one this year might be moral, indeterminate two years from now, and immoral in five years. It depends on the consequences, and the consequences are shaped by the situation. To give developmental assistance or food relief, either one, without reckoning the cause or without counting the cost is irresponsible, i.e., unethical. It is simply untrue to say without reservation that "it is more blessed to give than to receive."

Therefore, it is merely sentimental to say we *can* or *could* help the starving; what counts is whether such "help" will really help. Often it will, sometimes it will not. And by the same token, to say we can or could lower the birth rate to make help effective is not good enough; we would have to say we *are* doing it, or we have done it.

Alan Berg of the World Bank has contended, "If it were not for aid there would be many more starving babies."[19] In flat contradiction we have to

[17]R. B. Crowell, "Lifeboat Ethics and the Quaker Conscience," *Friends' Journal*, 21 (May 15, 1975), 294–96.

[18]Hardin, *Exploring New Ethics for Survival*, p. 134.

[19]Quoted in Ward Greene, "Triage," *New York Times Magazine*, January 5, 1975, pp. 9ff.

say that in some countries it would be *because* of aid that there are more starving babies. Alan Gregg, a past vice-president of the Rockefeller Foundation, saw the real problem more clearly and described overpopulation as a cancer, adding that he had never heard of a cancer being cured by feeding it.[20]

[20]Alan Gregg, "A Medical Aspect of the Population Problem," *Science*, 121 (1955), 681–682.

RICHARD A. WATSON

Watson argues that in a world of scarcity the overriding moral principle of equity demands the equal sharing of food even if this leads to universal malnourishment or the termination of the species.

1. *He argues that neither the species nor future generations are the kinds of entities that can have rights, and so we should exclude them from our moral deliberations. Is he correct?*

2. *He maintains that morality may, in some cases, be irrational. Is this true? If so, then what problems does this create for moralists?*

3. *How stringent is the principle of equity? Does it override all other moral principles?*

4. *He claims that equal sharing can be accomplished only by total economic and political revolution. Is total revolution the only way to solve the world hunger problem? If so, is it justified?*

Richard A. Watson is Professor of Philosophy at Washington University, St. Louis. He is the author of The Downfall of Cartesianism *and co-author, with Patty Jo Watson, of* Man and Nature, an Anthropological Essay in Human Ecology.

This paper was written while I was a Visiting Fellow at the Center of International Studies, Princeton University. I wish to thank the Center's Director, Cyril E. Black, and Richard A. Falk for discussions and hospitality.

Reason and Morality
in a World of Limited Food

A few years ago, President Johnson said:

> There are 200 million of us and 3 billion of them and they want what we've
> got, but we're not going to give it to them.

In this essay I examine the conflict between reasonable and moral behavior in a world of limited food. It appears to be unreasonable—and conceivably immoral—to share all food equally when this would result in
everyone's being malnourished. Arguments for the morality of unequal
distribution are presented from the standpoint of the individual, the nation, and the human species. These arguments fail because, although it is
unreasonable to share limited food when sharing threatens survival, the
moral principle of equity ranks sharing above survival. I accept the principle of equity, and conclude by challenging the ideological basis that makes
sharing unreasonable.

The contrast of the moral with the reasonable depends on distinguishing
people from things. Moral considerations pertain to behavior of individuals that affects other people by acting on them directly or by acting on
things in which they have an interest. The moral context is broad, for
people have interests in almost everything, and almost any behavior may
affect someone.

If reasonable and moral behavior were coextensive, then there would be
no morality. Thus, there is no contrast at the extremes that bound the
moral milieu, reason and morality being the same at one pole, and morality
not existing at the other. These extremes meet in evolutionary naturalism:
If it is moral to treat people as animals surviving, then reason augmenting
instinct is the best criterion for behavior, and a separate discipline of
morality is extraneous. Only between the extremes can reason and morality conflict.

Between the extremes, some moralists use 'rational' to indicate conclusions that tend toward moral behavior, and 'practical' for conclusions that
excusably do not. The use of these terms often constitutes special pleading,
either to gain sympathy for a position that is not strictly reasonable but
is "rational" (because it is "right"), or that is not strictly moral but is
"practical" (because it "should" be done). These hedges hide the sharp
distinction between people and things in the context of reason and morality. The rational and the practical are obviously reasonable in a way that
they are not obviously either moral or immoral. Reasonable behavior is
either moral, immoral, or amoral. When reason and morality conflict, there
can be confusion, but no compromise.

Attacks on morality by reason disguised in practical dress are so common as to go almost without notice. The practical ousts morality as a determinant of behavior, particularly in industrialized nations. Many argue that the practical imperatives of survival preclude moral behavior even by those who want to be moral. If only it were practical to be moral, then all would gladly be so.

It is difficult to be moral in a world of limited food because the supreme moral principle is that of equity. The principle of equity is based on the belief that all human beings are moral equals with equal rights to the necessities of life. Differential treatment of human beings thus should be based only on their freely chosen actions and not on accidents of their birth and environment. Specific to this discussion, everyone has a right to an equal share of available food.

However, we find ourselves in a world about which many food and population experts assert the following:

1. One-third of the world's people (the West) consume two-thirds of the world's resources.

2. Two-thirds of the world's people (the Third World) are malnourished.

3. Equal distribution of the world's resources would result in everyone's being malnourished.

There is ample evidence that these statements are true, but for this discussion it is enough that many people in the West—particularly those who occupy positions of responsibility and power—understand and accept them.

These moral and factual beliefs drive one to this practical conclusion: Although morally we should share all food equally, and we in the West eat more than we need, equal sharing would be futile (unreasonable), for then no one would be well nourished. Thus, any food sharing is necessarily symbolic, for no practical action would alleviate the plight of the malnourished.

For example, practical action—moral as far as it goes—might be to reduce food consumption until every Westerner is just well-nourished. But if the surplus were distributed equally to the other two-thirds of the world's people, they would still be malnourished. Thus, an easy excuse for not sharing at all is that it would neither solve the nourishment problem nor change the moral situation. Two-thirds would still be malnourished, and one-third would still be consuming more than equal shares of the world's food, to which everyone has equal rights.

Another argument for unequal distribution is as follows: All people are moral equals. Because everyone has a right to be well nourished, it would be immoral to take so much food from someone who has enough as to leave him without enough. Anyone who takes the food would be acting immorally, even if the taker is starving. This argument can go two ways. One could simply say that it would be immoral to deprive oneself of what one has. But if one wanted to discredit morality itself, one could claim that morality in this instance is self-contradictory. For if I behave morally by distributing food equally, I behave immorally by depriving someone (myself) of enough food to remain well-nourished. And noticing that if all food were shared equally, everyone would be malnourished instead of just some, one might argue that it cannot be moral to deprive one person of his right to enough food so that two people have less than enough. Proper moral action must be to maintain the inequity, so at least one person can enjoy his rights.

Nevertheless, according to the highest principles of traditional Western morality, available food should be distributed equally even if everyone then will be malnourished. This is belabored by everyone who compares the earth to a lifeboat, a desert island, or a spaceship. In these situations, the strong are expected to take even a smaller share than the weak. There is no need for us to go overboard, however. We shall soon be as weak as anyone else if we just do our moral duty and distribute the food equally.

Given this, the well-nourished minority might try to buttress its position morally by attempting to solve the nourishment problem for everyone, either by producing enough food for everyone, or by humanely reducing the world's population to a size at which equal distribution of food would nourish everyone adequately. The difficulty with this is that national survival for the food-favored industrial nations requires maintenance of political and economic systems that depend on unequal distribution of limited goods.[1] In the present world context, it would be unreasonable (disastrous) for an industrialized nation to attempt to provide food for everybody. Who would pay for it? And after all, well-nourished citizens are obviously important to the survival of the nation. As for humanely reducing the world's population, there are no practical means for doing it. Thus, the practical expediencies of national survival preclude actions that might justify temporary unequal distribution with the claim that it is essential for solving the nourishment problem. Equal distribution is impossible without total (impractical) economic and political revolution.

These arguments are morally spurious. That food sufficient for well-nourished survival is the equal right of every human individual or nation is a specification of the higher principle that everyone has equal right to the necessities of life. The moral stress of the principle of equity is primar-

---

[1]See Richard Watson, "The Limits of World Order," *Alternatives: A Journal of World Policy,* I (1975), 487–513.

ily on equal sharing, and only secondarily on what is being shared. The higher moral principle is of human *equity per se*. Consequently, the moral action is to distribute all food equally, *whatever the consequences*. This is the hard line apparently drawn by such moralists as Immanuel Kant and Noam Chomsky—but then, morality is hard. The conclusion may be unreasonable (impractical and irrational in conventional terms), but it is obviously moral. Nor should anyone purport surprise; it has always been understood that the claims of morality—if taken seriously—supersede those of conflicting reason.

One may even have to sacrifice one's life or one's nation to be moral in situations where practical behavior would preserve it. For example, if a prisoner of war undergoing torture is to be a (perhaps dead) patriot even when reason tells him that collaboration will hurt no one, he remains silent. Similarly, if one is to be moral, one distributes available food in equal shares (even if everyone then dies). That an action is necessary to save one's life is no excuse for behaving unpatriotically or immorally if one wishes to be a patriot or moral. No principle of morality absolves one of behaving immorally simply to save one's life or nation. There is a strict analogy here between adhering to moral principles for the sake of being moral, and adhering to Christian principles for the sake of being Christian. The moral world contains pits and lions, but one looks always to the highest light. The ultimate test always harks to the highest principle—recant or die—and it is pathetic to profess morality if one quits when the going gets rough.

I have put aside many questions of detail—such as the mechanical problems of distributing food—because detail does not alter the stark conclusion. If every human life is equal in value, then the equal distribution of the necessities of life is an extremely high, if not the highest, moral duty. It is at least high enough to override the excuse that by doing it one would lose one's own life. But many people cannot accept the view that one must distribute equally even if the nation collapses or all people die.

If everyone dies, then there will be no realm of morality. Practically speaking, sheer survival comes first. One can adhere to the principle of equity only if one exists. So it is rational to suppose that the principle of survival is morally higher than the principle of equity. And though one might not be able to argue for unequal distribution of food to save a nation —for nations can come and go—one might well argue that unequal distribution is necessary for the survival of the human species. That is, some large group—say one-third of present world population—should be at least well-nourished for human survival.

However, from an individual standpoint, the human species—like the nation—is of no moral relevance. From a naturalistic standpoint, survival does come first; from a moralistic standpoint—as indicated above—survival may have to be sacrificed. In the milieu of morality, it is immaterial whether or not the human species survives as a result of individual moral behavior.

A possible way to resolve this conflict between reason and morality is to challenge the view that morality pertains only to the behavior of individual human beings. One way to do this is to break down the distinction between people and things. It would have to be established that such abstract things as "the people," "the nation," and "the human species" in themselves have moral status. Then they would have a right to survival just as human beings have a right to life: We should be concerned about the survival of these things not merely because human beings have an interest in them, but because it would be immoral *per se* to destroy them.

In the West, corporation law provides the theoretical basis for treating things as people.[2] Corporate entities such as the State, the Church, and trading companies have long enjoyed special status in Western society. The rights of corporate entities are precisely defined by a legal fiction, the concept of the corporate person. Christopher D. Stone says that corporate persons enjoy as many legal rights as, and sometimes more than, do individual human persons.[3] Thus, while most of us are not tempted to confuse ordinary things like stones and houses with people, almost everyone concurs with a legal system that treats corporate entities as people. The great familiarity and usefulness of this system supports the delusion that corporate entities have rights in common with, and are the moral equals of, individual human beings.

On these grounds, some argue that because of the size, importance, and power of corporate entities, institutional rights have priority over the rights of individuals. Of course, to the extent that society is defined by the economy or the State, people are dependent on and subordinate to these institutions. Practically speaking, institutional needs come first; people's needs are satisfied perhaps coextensively with, but secondarily to, satisfying institutional needs. It is argued that to put individual human needs first would be both illogical and impractical, for people and their needs are defined only in the social context. Institutions come first because they are prerequisite to the very existence of people.

A difficulty with the above argument as a support for any given institution is that it provides merely for the priority of *some* institutions over

---

[2]See Christopher D. Stone, *Should Trees Have Standing? Toward Legal Rights for Natural Objects* (Los Altos, Calif.: William Kaufmann, 1974). Stone proposes that to protect such things as national parks, we should give them legal personhood as we do corporations.

[3]Ibid., p. 47: "It is more and more the individual human being, with his consciousness, that is the legal fiction." Also: "The legal system does the best it can to maintain the illusion of the reality of the individual human being." (footnote 125) Many public figures have discovered that they have a higher legal status if they incorporate themselves than they do as individual persons.

human individuals, not, say, for the priority of the United States or the West. But it does appear to provide an argument for the priority of the human species.

Given that the human species has rights as a fictional person on the analogy of corporate rights, it would seem to be rational to place the right of survival of the species above that of individuals. Unless the species survives, no individual will survive, and thus an individual's right to life is subordinate to the species' right to survival. If species survival depends on the unequal distribution of food to maintain a healthy breeding stock, then it is morally right for some people to have plenty while others starve. Only if there is enough food to nourish everyone well does it follow that food should be shared equally.

This might be true if corporate entities actually do have moral status and moral rights. But obviously, the legal status of corporate entities as fictional persons does not make them moral equals or superiors of actual human persons. Legislators might profess astonishment that anyone would think that a corporate person is a *person* as people are, let alone a moral person. However, because the legal rights of corporate entities are based on individual rights, and because corporate entities are treated so much like persons, the transition is often made.

Few theorists today would argue that the state or the human species is a personal agent.[4] But all this means is that idealism is dead in theory. Unfortunately, its influence lives, so it is worth giving an argument to show that corporate entities are not real persons.

Corporate entities are not persons as you and I are in the explicit sense that we are self-conscious agents and they are not. Corporate entities are not *agents* at all, let alone moral agents. This is a good reason for not treating corporate entities even as fictional persons. The distinction between people and other things, to generalize, is that people are self-conscious agents, whereas things are not.

The possession of rights essentially depends on an entity's being self-conscious, i.e., on its actually being a person. If it is self-conscious, then it has a right to life. Self-consciousness is a necessary, but not sufficient, condition for an entity's being a moral equal of human beings; moral equality depends on the entity's also being a responsible moral agent as most human beings are. A moral agent must have the capacity to be responsible, i.e., the capacity to choose and to act freely with respect to consequences that the agent does or can recognize and accept as its own

[4]Stone (ibid., p. 47) does say that "institutions . . . have wills, minds, purposes, and inertias that are in very important ways their own, i.e., that can transcend and survive changes in the consciousnesses of the individual humans who supposedly comprise them, and whom they supposedly serve," but I do not think Stone actually believes that corporate entities are persons like you and me.

choice and doing. Only a being who knows himself as a person, and who can effect choices and accept consequences, is a responsible moral agent.

On these grounds, moral equality rests on the actuality of moral agency based on reciprocal rights and responsibilities. One is responsible to something only if it can be responsible in return. Thus, we have responsibilities to other people, and they have reciprocal rights. We have no responsibilities to things as such, and they have no rights. If we care for things, it is because people have interests in them, not because things in themselves impose responsibilities on us.

That is, as stated early in this essay, morality essentially has to do with relations among people, among persons. It is nonsense to talk of things that cannot be moral agents as having responsibilities; consequently, it is nonsense to talk of whatever is not actually a person as having rights. It is deceptive even to talk of legal rights of a corporate entity. Those rights (and reciprocal responsibilities) actually pertain to individual human beings who have an interest in the corporate entity. The State or the human species have no rights at all, let alone rights superior to those of individuals.

The basic reason given for preserving a nation or the human species is that otherwise the milieu of morality would not exist. This is false so far as specific nations are concerned, but it is true that the existence of individuals depends on the existence of the species. However, although moral behavior is required of each individual, no principle requires that the realm of morality itself be preserved. Thus, we are reduced to the position that people's interest in preserving the human species is based primarily on the interest of each in individual survival. Having shown above that the principle of equity is morally superior to the principle of survival, we can conclude again that food should be shared equally even if this means the extinction of the human race.

Is there no way to produce enough food to nourish everyone well? Besides cutting down to the minimum, people in the West might quit feeding such nonhuman animals as cats and dogs. However, some people (e.g., Peter Singer) argue that mere sentience—the capacity to suffer pain —means that an animal is the moral equal of human beings.[5] I argue that because nonhuman animals are not moral agents, they do not share the rights of self-conscious responsible persons. And considering the profligacy of nature, it is rational to argue that if nonhuman animals have any rights at all, they include not the right to life, but merely the right to fight for life. In fact, if people in the West did not feed grain to cattle, sheep, and hogs, a considerable amount of food would be freed for human

[5]See Peter Singer, *Animal Liberation* (New York: The New York Review of Books/Random House, 1975).

consumption. Even then, there might not be enough to nourish everyone well.

Let me remark that Stone and Singer attempt to break down the distinction between people on the one hand, and certain things (corporate entities) and nonhuman animals on the other, out of moral concern. However, there is another, profoundly antihumanitarian movement also attempting to break down the distinction. All over the world, heirs of Gobineau, Goebbels, and Hitler practice genocide and otherwise treat people as nonhuman animals and things in the name of the State. I am afraid that the consequences of treating entities such as corporations and nonhuman animals—that are not moral agents—as persons with rights will not be that we will treat national parks and chickens the way we treat people, but that we will have provided support for those who would treat people the way we now treat nonhuman animals and things.

The benefits of modern society depend in no small part on the institution of corporation law. Even if the majority of these benefits are to the good —of which I am by no means sure—the legal fiction of corporate personhood still elevates corporate needs above the needs of people. In the present context, reverence for corporate entities leads to the spurious argument that the present world imbalance of food and resources is morally justified in the name of the higher rights of sovereign nations, or even of the human species, the survival of which is said to be more important than the right of any individual to life.

This conclusion is morally absurd. This is not, however, the fault of morality. We *should* share all food equally, at least until everyone is well-nourished. Besides food, *all* the necessities of life should be shared, at least until everyone is adequately supplied with a humane minimum. The hard conclusion remains that we should share all food equally even if this means that everyone starves and the human species becomes extinct. But, of course, the human race would survive even equal sharing, for after enough people died, the remainder could be well-nourished on the food that remained. But this grisly propsect does not show that anything is wrong with the principle of equity. Instead, it shows that something is profoundly wrong with the social institutions in which sharing the necessities of life equally is "impractical" and "irrational."

In another ideological frame, moral behavior might also be practical and rational. As remarked above, equal sharing can be accomplished only through total economic and political revolution. Obviously, this is what is needed.

MICHAEL A. SLOTE

Slote examines two arguments which allegedly justify retention of personal and national wealth in the face of massive starvation. Both of these arguments, he maintains, are open to serious question. They can not justify the retention of wealth in today's world.

1. He draws an analogy between personal and national wealth. Do the arguments which apply to the former also apply to the latter?

2. Have affluent nations in fact obtained their wealth by exploiting poor ones? See O'Neill's essay for another opinion on this.

3. Pay particular attention to his analysis of Rigorism and Lenitism.

4. If there is a distinction between "life style" and overall "life plan," do arguments for wealth which rely upon pursuing a "life plan" escape Slote's criticisms?

Michael A. Slote teaches philosophy at the State University of New York at Stony Brook. The author of Reason and Skepticism *and* Metaphysics and Essence, *he has also written numerous articles on ethics, philosophy of mind, and epistomology.*

The Morality of Wealth

It is the ultimate, but not the only, aim of this paper to consider whether affluent nations have any moral right to keep their wealth when, presumably, they could alleviate poverty and starvation in other nations by giving away large parts of that wealth in the form of food, industrial products, and know-how. To approach this question, I shall first consider in some detail a parallel question about individuals, the clarification of which is helpful, perhaps even necessary, to our getting clear about the moral obligations of nations or governments. I shall present two lines of argument for the view that rich *people* are not immoral for having and keeping wealth. The arguments seem to me to have some force. But I am not convinced by either one of them, and my purpose here is to give them a thorough-going exposition in what I take to be their strongest forms, rather than to attempt to convince the reader that it is moral, not wrong, for individuals to keep wealth. On the other hand, the arguments do deserve to be answered. So I shall be spending a good deal of time pointing out what seem to me to be their major weaknesses. Then, in the last section of the paper, we shall consider whether analogous arguments can be applied with any force in the area of international morality, to defend the morality of the retention of great wealth by affluent nations in the face of the famine, poverty, and general suffering that exist in other nations, and in the affluent nations themselves. But let us proceed to the first argument about the morality of rich individuals.[1]

I

It seems to me to be reasonable to start from the assumption that men are not entirely moral islands, i.e., that we sometimes, through no choice of our own, have moral obligations to others. In particular, we are sometimes under an obligation to *prevent* great or substantial harm to or suffering by others—even if it may also be true that we are rarely, if ever, under any obligation to confer "positive" goods or benefits on others.[2] To take an obvious example, if a child is drowning and one can pull him out of the water without running any personal risk, then one ought to do so, and it would be wrong not to do so,[3] even if one is unacquainted with the child. However, it also seems probable that there are limits to our obligations to help others by preventing harms and evils. To me at least it sometimes seems mistaken to suppose that one has an obligation to go and spend one's life helping sick and starving people in India or elsewhere. Part of the reason for this may be that it can at times seem perfectly understandable, from a moral standpoint, that one should want to lead one's own life and develop one's own plans and potentialities independently of what may be going on, for better or worse, with others outside one's own family. In

---

[1]Given all that has been said for and against Utilitarianism, I hope to be forgiven for ignoring possible Utilitarian arguments for the morality of wealth.

[2]Not everyone has accepted this view—e.g., B. Gert in *The Moral Rules* (New York: Harper & Row, Publishers, Inc., 1966), p. 73. Gert's argument in this matter is based on (to my mind) unconvincing *a priori* claims about what a moral principle or rule should look like.

[3]I shall not distinguish among what one ought to do, what is obligatory, and what it is wrong, or immoral, not to do.

other words, it can sometimes seem somewhat unfair or morally arbitrary that one's moral freedom to choose one's own special kind of fulfillment in life should be abrogated by the existence of states of affairs for which one was in no way responsible and which would tend not to enter into one's life plans.

Of course, a parallel thought might occur to one about the case of the drowning child. One could say that it was unfair or arbitrary that something independent of one, like a child accidentally getting into trouble in the water, should abrogate one's moral freedom or permission to go about one's business, thus making one the moral "prey" of external and accidental circumstances. But one has only to try to make such a parallel case, as I have just done, in order to see how great the difference between the cases really is. It seems morally monstrous to use this kind of reasoning about the saving of a child when saving the child takes so little effort, and thus takes so little away from the person who does it. Such thinking seems much more plausible and much less monstrous when it concerns going off to save people from starvation and sickness, because doing such a thing makes a total difference to one's life, its structure, its style, the fulfillment of one's most basic hopes and plans. It is only when something like a basic life plan has to be sacrificed in order to prevent some evil that we feel any genuine hesitation to make such prevention obligatory. Perhaps what we feel in this regard can be expressed metaphorically or hyperbolically by saying that a man's life style as informed by his life plans is his essence and that his essence is inseparable from and the same as the man himself.[4] So, just as many have thought that one can never be morally obligated to give up one's life, no matter how good or important the cause to be served by one's death, it *may* be that one cannot be obligated to give up one's basic life style or life plans either, no matter what evils could be avoided by one's doing so.

What all the above suggests is that the reason why one may not be morally required to go off and spend one's life helping the sick and starving —when, in the absence of such people, one would have devoted one's life to deep-sea research, archaeology, or sculpture—has something to do with the fact that devoting one's life to the sick and starving would be destructive of one's basic life plans or life style. It may be that it is not morally wrong to omit or avoid doing things that interfere with one's basic life plans or style—unless there is something intrinsically wrong with *them,* unless, that is, they involve murder, rape, deceit, and the like. By intrinsic wrongness, I here mean something like wrongness of commission, as op-

---

[4]The idea that one is one's essence comes from Aristotle. It has been much attacked and much defended.

posed to wrongness of omission. And so I am saying that the following principle may be true:

> It is not morally wrong to omit doing an act if (it is reasonably believed that) doing it would seriously interfere with one's basic life style or with the fulfillment of one's basic life plans—as long as the life style or plans themselves involve no wrongs of commission.[5]

Now the distinction between sins or wrongs of omission and those of commission has not been defined, and would be hard to define, and this may affect the ultimate defensibility of the principle just stated.[6] On the other hand, the distinction may have enough common-sense intuitiveness to enable us to understand and make use of the principle. And anyone who accepts that principle will hold that there is a serious moral difference between pulling a drowning child from the water at no personal risk and going off to spend one's life helping the sick and destitute. Given the principle, the latter is not obligatory, but the former *may be.* And we could explain why it *is* wrong not to save the drowning child, if we were to add a *principle of positive obligation* to the effect that:

> One has an obligation to prevent serious evil or harm when one can do so without seriously interfering with one's life plans or style and without doing any wrongs of commission.[7]

What follows about the keeping of wealth is fairly straightforward. The refusal of most rich people to give (most of) their money and possessions

[5]Fairly similar ideas occur in J. J. Thomson's "A Defense of Abortion," *Philosophy and Public Affairs,* I (1971), esp. p. 64; and *inter alia* in Thoreau's *Civil Disobedience.* Note that in speaking of serious interference with *basic* life plans or styles, I do not mean just any kind of interference with one's life. Sensitive judgment and even ethical and psychological theory may be needed to separate out what is really basic or important to a way of life. And I certainly wish to leave it open that a person could overestimate the extent to which a certain event (e.g., the loss of one's valet or lady's maid) would interfere with one's basic life style. Note too that life *plans* seem worthier of moral consideration than life *styles,* so our principle might have more force if it were restricted to the former. But both plans and styles have to be mentioned if one is to produce an argument relevant to the majority of rich people.

[6]Also, the distinction requires some care in the drawing. If one fails to return a book one has promised to return, one has *committed* a wrong, even though one doesn't *do* anything *when* one breaks the promise. But one has done something "positive" through the combined act of promising and not delivering, and that is why we speak of a sin of commission in such a case and use the "active"-sounding phrase "breaking one's promise" in describing it. Thus, the omission of acts to which our principle is to apply include only omissions that do not involve one in commissive immoralities.

[7]This positive principle should probably be understood as restricted to those who already have (had time to acquire) a life style or plans. Those not covered could be covered by separate principles that would need to be carefully worked out.

away seems to be a sin or wrong, if at all, only of omission. But it is an omission whose avoidance would interfere in a serious way with the life style of those rich people, or most of them.[8] If so, then given the main moral principle introduced earlier, it is not immoral for rich people to omit giving their money away, as long as they reasonably believe, as I am sure they do, that such giving away would involve serious change in their life style or life plans, and as long as their life style or plans *per se* involve them in no immoralities of commission.[9] There are, however, a number of possible objections to the line of argument we have been considering that should at this point be examined.

II

There are two important kinds of objections to the foregoing argument, which I shall call the first argument. One kind objects to the moral point of view embodied in the main principle of that argument, the principle about when omissions are permissible; and it questions the thinking with which we earlier paved the way for that principle. The second kind of objection questions the applicability of that main principle to the issue at hand, the question of the morality of having and keeping one's wealth. For the principle can be used to justify the retention of wealth by the rich only if the typical life style of the rich and the retention of wealth itself do not involve "sins" of commission. And the second sort of objection will claim either that the present life style of (most) rich people intrinsically involves commissive immoralities, or that the "mere" retention of wealth typically involves a kind of commissive immorality.

Perhaps the best way of putting the first kind of objection to the first argument would base itself on a consideration of the kind of moral principles and moral point of view recently advocated by Peter Singer in "Famine, Affluence, and Morality" (reprinted in this volume).[10] For what Singer

---

[8]The exceptions may be certain rich "hippies," and perhaps certain misers, who do not make use of their wealth. Their retention of wealth could not be justified by the present argument; but perhaps such people are less justified in keeping their wealth than are those who *use* their wealth to maintain a rich life style. On the other hand, the second argument, to be given below, will attempt to justify the retention of wealth even by those who do not really use their wealth.

[9]Of course, even given that principle, it may still be wrong for many rich people not to spend *more* time and money helping the needy. For doing so would probably not seriously interfere with their basic life plans or styles. Also, in talking of the choice between giving away one's money and omitting to do so, I do not assume that the former has to involve giving away one's money impulsively and all at once. This would probably accomplish much less than one could by giving away one's fortune in a planful way over time (via foundations, etc). The real moral choice may be between giving away one's money in some intelligent planful way and keeping one's money for one's own personal uses.

[10]Peter Singer, "Famine, Affluence, and Morality," *Philosophy and Public Affairs*, I, no. 3 (Spring 1972), pp. 229–43.

says about the demands of morality is in conflict with the principle and point of view of the first argument, through its high standards of what counts as morally permissible. According to Singer, "If it is in our power to prevent something bad from happening, without thereby sacrificing anything of comparable moral importance, we ought, morally, to do it." He then says that "without sacrificing anything of comparable moral importance" is to be understood as meaning "without causing anything else comparably bad to happen, or doing something that is wrong in itself, or failing to promote some moral good, comparable in significance to the bad thing that we can prevent."[11] Now this is a very rigorous standard to set for morality, and Singer himself is aware how much this will seem to be so to ordinary people, once they become aware of the consequences of strict adherence to that standard. Partly for that reason, he considers a weaker principle to the effect that: "If it is in our power to prevent something very bad from happening, without thereby sacrificing anything morally significant, we ought, morally, to do it."[12] And he tries, where possible, to make his arguments depend on the weaker principle only. But he also makes it clear that he does so only for dialectical purposes, and that he is fully convinced of the truth of his stronger principle, despite its incompatibility with much ordinary thinking about morality. What can we say about Singer's Rigorism, as it is appropriate to call it? How serious a threat does it pose to the moral Lenitism, if I may call it thus, that is constituted by the principle of the first argument for the morality of wealth taken together with the principle of positive obligation that was also suggested earlier? It would appear that, given various reasonable empirical assumptions, there is a real conflict between Singer's strong principle (and perhaps even his weak principle), on the one hand, and the main principle of the first argument, on the other. For if Singer is correct, then there presumably are many great evils that rich people could use up most of their wealth to prevent without sacrificing anything of (comparable) moral importance. (And we can assume that they could not prevent these evils *without* using up most of their wealth.) So the rich are, in the main, wrong to retain their fortunes, if Singer's moral viewpoint is correct, and this is

---

[11]Ibid., p. 24 (in this volume).

[12]Ibid. It is worth noting that both Singer's weaker principle and his original principle are not stated as accurately as they should be. Even from Singer's moral standpoint there are possible counterexamples to them. If my friend and I come across two people in distress, and I know that whichever of them I try to help, my friend will try to help the other, then it will be true that it is in my power to prevent harm being done, say, to the nearer of the two people in distress without thereby sacrificing anything of (comparable) moral significance. But it will not be true that I ought (in particular) to prevent harm being done to the nearer of the two persons in distress. At most, I have an obligation to bring aid to one or the other of them, given the known attitude of my friend. I see no reason why Singer's principles should not be reformulated in such a way as to avoid this sort of counterexample.

inconsistent with the conclusion of the first argument for the morality of wealth stated above.

The problem facing us now is whether there is any fair or neutral way to decide which of these two moral points of view is more likely to be sound or correct. It is true, for example, that Singer's strong principle goes against the grain of much everyday moral thinking. And that probably stands against it. But it is not obvious that the principle goes against what Rawls has called our *considered* moral judgments. I think that in most of us there are moral levels to which and at which Singer's Rigorism greatly appeals. How many people have never found themselves in a house of worship tearfully listening to a sermon based on such rigorous principles and vowing to live up to those principles? That we later, in the cool of the secular, do not live up to those principles or find them overwhelming and plausible may simply attest to the power our self-centered motives have to undermine our best intentions and beliefs. On the other hand, considered moral judgments are supposed to be intelligent and impartial, and the atmosphere of a house of worship, together with the "rousing" quality of a sermon, may stir emotions to the point where unbiased reflection is impossible.[13] In cooler moments, one often sees the force of Lenitism, and one often sees the force of Rigorism, and it is hard to decide between them on the basis of the deliverances of cool reflection. Indeed, the controversy between Lenitism and Rigorism seems (approximately) to mark one of the deepest and most abiding divisions that can exist between moral philosophers and moral codes.

Before we give up on deciding between Singer's principle(s) of Rigorism and the principles of Lenitism, however, I would like to explore one further possible way in which this issue might be resolved. The idea I have in mind is related to the traditional view—whatever its precise meaning may be— that morality is practical in essence and/or function. Let us consider whether it may not be possible to treat, as an independent test of the validity or correctness of a moral code or set of principles, the moral results of everyone's believing that code or set of principles to be correct. If we have two moral codes and the acceptance of one of them by humans would yield morally better conduct than the acceptance of the other by humans, then perhaps that is a reason to say that the one code is more likely to be, or closer to being, correct for humans than the other. Now such a test will not be helpful in deciding between moral codes that disagree substantially in their judgments about which acts are morally better or worse than which

[13]Of course, it might be objected that the stirring of emotion in church *is* a proper way to get a considered moral judgment, because such judgments are never strictly intellectual and are most accurate when we are affectively involved in situations. In any case, this just opens up new problems and issues, and further illustrates the difficulty of deciding between Rigorism and Lenitism.

others. But I can see little reason to think that such disagreement must exist between Rigorism and Lenitism. Both could agree, for example, that murder was wrong and morally worse than uncharitableness and that giving one's wealth away to good causes was morally preferable to keeping it for one's own luxurious uses. The really clear-cut differences between them concern where to draw the line between positive moral rightness and positive moral wrongness. And if we assume, for the sake of argument and because it is not altogether implausible to do so, that the only differences between Rigorism and Lenitism that we need be concerned with are differences in positive, as opposed to comparative, moral judgments, then the test just proposed may be relevant to deciding between them. Whether Rigorism or Lenitism is more correct in its way of drawing the line between right and wrong will depend on whether people would act morally better if they believed Rigorism than if they believed Lenitism, or whether the reverse is true. Since it seems possible in principle that empirical investigation should yield results that resolved this latter issue to the satisfaction of both Rigorists and Lenitists, our proposed test opens up the possibility of an independent empirical way to decide between Rigorism and Lenitism as moral "theories."

It is important, however, to see what this test I am tentatively proposing really amounts to. I am not saying—as some Utilitarians and others have said—that it is sometimes morally best to encourage people to adopt a moral code that is not literally true, given the difficulties of applying the correct code. Such a view separates the truth of a moral idea from the value of the results of accepting it, and this seems to lie behind some of the things Singer himself says in his article.[14] What I am tentatively suggesting, on the contrary, is that the truth of moral principles is not independent of the moral value of the results of believing them.[15] I am stressing the closeness of theory and practice in morality, and thus the practical nature of morality, by saying, in effect, that the correct moral code is that by means of which the intellectual thought of the right and rightness of action are most closely connected.

It is also worth noting that the view I am suggesting contains an element of relativity to the human species, or at least to "maximal interaction groups" where this notion is understood in such a way that our species

---

[14]Singer, "Famine, Affluence, and Morality," p. 29 (in this volume).

[15]Cf. J. Rawls, *A Theory of Justice* (Cambridge, Mass.: Harvard University Press, 1971), p. 138, for the expression of what seems to be a related view about ethical truth; and also Maurice Merleau-Ponty, *Humanism and Terror* (Boston: Beacon Press, 1969), where it is suggested that "liberal" moral ideas are discredited by the fact that the bourgeois society that declares its allegiance to them is basically just using them as a means to and justification for its own oppression, violence, and exploitation. There are also more distant connections to be drawn between the theory we have suggested and such other views as Rule Utilitarianism, the Pragmatic Theory of Truth, and social contract theories generally.

counts as such a group. I am saying that the validity or correctness *for humans* of a moral principle depends on how morally good the actions of *humans* would be if they in general accepted the principle intellectually, which is to say that the correctness of a principle to the effect that humans ought morally to do thus and so depends on how morally well humans would behave if they all accepted that principle. I am ignoring problems about the specification of the circumstances in which human beings are to be thought of as accepting one or another moral principle or code, but I intend what I am saying to be inconsistent both with cultural relativism and with the idea that moral principles must hold for all possible rational beings. Clearly, to make our test of moral principles relative to the class of all possible rational beings would be to make the counterfactuals involved too wild to test. So some sort of relativity to the human species (or subgroups thereof) is necessary, if the kind of test we have proposed is to be of any use in deciding between Rigorism and Lenitism. Since there seems to be no other way to sharpen or focus the issue between Rigorism and Lenitism, we may be justified in making tentative use of the mankind-relative test I am proposing, at least in the present paper. The test certainly stands in need of more justification and motivation; but for reasons of space, this will have to be put off for another occasion.[16]

It might at first seem that the test we are proposing will favor Rigorism over Lenitism, and will in general favor stricter moral codes. But this is not obvious. Given how many things count as immoral on a Rigorist theory, one who intellectually adopted such a theory might tend to blur the distinction between acts that both Rigorists and Lenitists call wrong and acts that only Rigorists call wrong; and in that case, if he ever started doing the acts that only Rigorists call wrong, he might edge toward doing the things everyone calls wrong, because his own code lumped such things together. And so he might end up doing very bad things he would not have done if he had accepted Lenitist principles that separated such very bad things from things we are more likely to be tempted to do. Indeed, accepting a difficult morality like Rigorism makes it so difficult always to act morally by one's own lights that one might be led to think of morality as being beyond one's powers and, as a result, give up on morality altogether.[17]

---

[16]The idea that morality or certain moral principles can be valid *relative to* certain groups, species, or communities, is not new. Something like it can be found in Rousseau, Royce, and Wilfrid Sellars—and even in Rawls, who attempts to justify his principles of justice by the use of certain facts about the moral psychology of *humans*. (Cf. the previous reference in note 15 and numerous other places in *A Theory of Justice*.) In addition, I think one can produce strong arguments for thinking that moral validity should not be thought of as relative to any group *smaller* than the kind of "maximal interaction group" that the human species represents.

[17]Cf. J. O. Urmson's "Saints and Heroes," in A. I. Melden, ed., *Essays in Moral Philosophy* (Seattle: University of Washington Press, 1958), p. 214.

Furthermore, to the degree that one has a demanding moral code that is difficult to live up to, there is a real danger of falling into a kind of moral sentimentalism that becomes intoxicated and fascinated, and so paralyzed, by its own immorality. One thinks with a *frisson* more of excitement than of horror: "How terrible I and the whole world are, how far from righteousness." Part of the excitement comes from the tempting vanity of thinking one recognizes one's own immorality in a way that others do not. And part of it, no doubt, comes from a certain masochistic delight in guilt and self-depreciation. But whatever its sources and nature, this phenomenon can easily lead to moral paralysis and/or an acceptance of one's own immorality—through the thought that if one cannot be perfect, one may as well be evil and accept that fact.[18]

So, accepting Rigorism might lead to greater on-balance immorality than accepting Lenitism. (However, as Singer notes in his paper [pp. 29–30 in this volume], the degree to which one lives up to one's moral principles will partly depend on whether others are living up to the same principles. Thus, the question of the moral results of everyone's accepting Rigorism or Lenitism is complicated by interaction factors.) In the light of the above, it is not clear whether Rigorism or Lenitism would come out ahead on the test we have tentatively proposed; but, given the test, we at least know where we could start looking for an answer concerning the relative merits of these two deeply divided moral positions.

III

The moral principle of the first argument for the morality of wealth, and so Lenitism as a whole, are easily challenged; but they are not so easily refuted. Nevertheless, there certainly is serious doubt about their truth, and thus about whether the first argument works or can be made to work. In the present section, we shall consider whether the principle of the first argument, its validity assumed for the moment, can really be applied in the way we have applied it in the above argument for the morality of wealth. To do so we must consider whether there is any reason to claim that the life style of (most of) the rich and the very retention of wealth involve no significant immoralities of commission.

Let us first proceed to the question whether there are sins of commission intrinsic to living the way most rich people do, which, for short, we can call "living rich."[19] Later on, after setting out our second argument for the

---

[18]Cf. Hegel's discussion of the beautiful soul who keeps himself morally pure by inaction, in *The Phenomenology of Mind* (London: Allen and Unwin, 1955), pp. 644–79.

[19]Even if there are commissive wrongs intrinsic to living rich, one might be able to show that rich people who do not live this way would not be wrong to stay rich. But this would not, I think, be very interesting, since most rich people do, in fact, live rich.

morality of wealth, we shall have ample time to consider whether commissive immorality attaches to the very retention of wealth. I think the most
likely place to look for immoralities of commission in the lives of rich
people living rich would be in their treatment of those who work for them.
Those who work for the rich who live rich can be classed into two main
categories: those in their direct and immediate employ, their servants being
the most important among these, and those whose industrial, agricultural,
or other labor serves indirectly to maintain their wealth and their life style.
Possible sins of commission toward the latter we shall discuss below. For
the moment, I would like to concentrate on whether living rich involves
commissive immorality toward one's servants. (And by "living rich" I
mean to refer to a kind of luxurious living that involves the having of
servants.)

Rich people sometimes "lord it" over their servants, and surely this is
a form of unkindness, of gratuitously making people feel bad about themselves, and involves commissive wrongdoing. But do all master–servant
relationships involve such treatment? Surely not. Many masters or mis-
tresses are quite polite and amiable to their servants, and even treat them
as if they were friends. And there may be no "lording over" in such
circumstances. It does not so clearly follow, however, that the rich can
avoid being commissively bad through unkindness to their servants.

To be the servant of another person is to be subject to certain of his
whims, to be at his beck and call. And surely anyone has reason to feel bad
about being in this kind of position in relation to another.[20] One of the
things, after all, that democracy is all about is that people should not be
in this kind of position vis-à-vis a king or nobility. And it is a natural
extension, or development, of the spirit of democratic egalitarianism to
believe that there is something wrong with the master–servant relationship, something wrong with being subject to the (occasional) whim of
another human being. Now, superficial amiability and friendliness toward
servants may conceal depths of unkindness. For when one is amiable to a
servant, one tends to reinforce the thought, both in the servant's mind and

[20]Not all people employed in households to clean, etc., are at the beck and call of those
for whom they work. If a firm hires them out to do household clean-ups, they are hired for
a specific task, are not at the beck and call of their employers, and so are not even temporary
servants. A servant's job is more open-ended. Even if one has specific duties, these are subject
to change, and there is an element of subjection to the whim of another (which is part of the
luxury of having servants). Incidentally, I am not denying that regular employees are sometimes forced to be at the beck and call of their employers or superiors. This may be equivalent
to being, and so as degrading as being, a servant. But, typically, employees are not hired to
be at the beck and call of their superiors; both are supposed to be working toward some
"higher" corporate goal that is "bigger than both of them," whereas the servant is typically
or often hired to serve the convenience of his master, and not some greater, more impersonal
goal. And even when a superior orders an employee around in the service of some impersonal
goal, this is not being at the beck and call, subject to the personal whim, of the superior, and
so is not degrading in quite the way that being a servant is.

in one's own, that being a servant is the most natural, understandable thing in the world, that there is nothing wrong with being a servant. This has the effect of obscuring some of the lack of human dignity involved in being at someone's beck and call. It is not surprising, then, that so many rich people are so amiable with their servants; it is in their interest that their servants not see their degradation or humiliation but, rather, accept their position as reasonable and natural. Indeed, it is in their interest not to see the degradation, etc., themselves in any clear-cut way; for then they might feel guilty for having servants or even stop having servants; and neither of these alternatives, presumably, would serve their interests. Thus, I am not saying that the rich deliberately, consciously mislead their servants into ignorance of their degraded or undignified status. I think, rather, that by a kind of evolutionary logic, amiability and superficial friendliness toward servants tend to create more willing servants, and thus tend to survive and be reinforced across generations as an unwitting or unconscious habit among the rich. So perhaps on some unconscious level the rich do intend to deceive their servants about their status and do act in accordance with such an intention; and in that case, even in being amiable with their servants, rich people may on some level or in some way be acting unkindly towards them. If so, then it may be impossible for rich people to avoid commissive immoralities toward their servants, and we have yet another reason to wonder whether the first argument for the morality of individual wealth really works or can be made to work.

IV

The second argument for the morality of wealth that I would like to explore rests on a rather pessimistic view of human nature. Almost everyone with a great deal of money, or other wealth convertible into money, is unwilling to give any great proportion of it away to others. It is also true, however, that most of those who are poor and could use some of the money possessed by the rich would have been unwilling to part with their money, had they been in the position of the rich. And this fact, if it is one, can form the basis of an interesting argument for the morality of keeping one's wealth.

Consider the following principle:

> It is not wrong to omit doing for others what others would have omitted doing for you, if your positions had been appropriately reversed.

Roughly speaking, this principle counsels doing unto others as they *in fact* would have done unto you, rather than doing unto others as one would *ideally* have them do unto you. And given its status as a "tough" deidealized version of the Golden Rule, it is not inappropriate to call the principle just introduced the Brazen Rule. The Brazen Rule has, I think, a certain intuitive appeal and force. And it is not hard to believe that if those who are poor had from the start been rich, ànd in other appropriate ways like the rich, they would in almost every case have held onto their money the way most actual rich people do, the way it is "human nature" to do. But then it would seem, in the light of the Brazen Rule, that those who are rich are not acting immorally in omitting to spread the bulk of their wealth around among the poor, and so we have a second argument for the morality of wealth.[21]

Let us look more closely at the argument just given, and in particular at the Brazen Rule, which forms its basis. As we have formulated it, the Rule treats only of omissions. It does not claim that you are permitted to kill those who would have killed you if, for example, they had had the gun that you in fact possess. Clearly, the Brazen Rule is more plausible when restricted to the permissibility of omissions.[22] Note further that the Rule does not say: It is permissible to avoid doing something for others, if those others would have acted just as immorally to you, if positions had been appropriately reversed. This is incoherent or indefensible, given any plausible form of ethical universalizability principle, since it implies that others in the same position as I would be wrong to do what it is all right for me to do.

It is obvious, however, that the Brazen Rule is somewhat vague because of its talk of positions having been "appropriately reversed." The expression is used to place limits on how much reversal or exchange of features is to be imagined in the hypothetical situations about which the Brazen Rule talks. For the roles and features of rich and poor could not have been *completely reversed.* That would entail people's having had different parents, for example, and parentage is likely to be an *essential* feature of individuals. There are, of course, also difficult or insuperable problems in imagining interchange of intelligence, genes, physique, and other such important human features. Furthermore, there are special problems about how children, and animals, fit into the scheme of role and feature reversal. What does it even mean to say that a rich man is not wrong to omit giving away money to a poor child, because the child would have done the same if their

---

[21]Note that the present Brazen Rule argument for the morality of wealth does not require us to establish that there are no commissive immoralities involved in living rich, the way it is necessary to do in order to maintain the first argument for the morality of wealth. Because of the particular nature of the moral principles involved, the Brazen Rule argument might allow us to show that those who live rich are justified in keeping their wealth, but not in having servants; whereas the soundness of the first argument precludes this possibility.

[22]Some people might attack the arguments presented here on the grounds that the commission/omission distinction is *irrelevant* to morality. But this sort of view stands in need of a better defense than I have ever seen it given.

positions had been appropriately reversed? Does this involve imagining the child born earlier and the rich man later, and is such a thing really possible? Perhaps it does not make much sense to speak even of *appropriate* reversal of the positions of adults and children (or animals), and in any case, as we have noted, total reversal of positions is never possible even in principle. But if we restrict ourselves to beings in the same society and of nearly the same age, it may well make real, if somewhat vague, sense to talk of positions being appropriately reversed. I think we all share a fairly similar conception of what features are the appropriate ones to think of as reversed, in the context of Brazen Rule arguments. So even if we cannot define or specify what this appropriateness is or what appropriate reversal comes to, I think we can legitimately make use of such notions in arguments via the Brazen Rule. (Indeed, such notions are also implicit in the Golden Rule, but people do not seem to think that that is sufficient to undermine *it*.) Moreover, I believe that the fact that we can safely talk of appropriate reversal only with respect to beings of approximately the same age does not undermine the above-introduced Brazen Rule argument for the morality of wealth.

The Brazen Rule has, as I have already said, a certain intuitive appeal, but more than this can be said in its behalf. We typically assume that if someone refuses to help us by giving us some good he possesses and does not really need, then it is not wrong for us to do the same to him if positions are ever reversed. But what if that person never had the chance to give us the good he possesses, but would have refused to do so if the occasion had arisen? If we know this, do we have any more duty to give him some equivalent good when positions are reversed than we had in the first case? Most of us, I think, would say that we do not. But then consider, finally, the case where the person in question does not possess the kind of good we are talking about, but we know that he would never have given it to us if he had possessed it but not really needed it (as much as we do). Such a case seems not so different, morally, from the first two; and, of course, to the extent that we find that this is so, we will be inclined to accept the Brazen Rule, which deals with just this last sort of case.

Whatever the plausibility of the Brazen Rule, however, the above Brazen Rule argument for the morality of wealth is open to the objection that some, even if not many, poor people probably *would* have parted with their wealth for charitable reasons, if they had been rich. After all, some *actual* rich people have given all their money away to charitable causes. But then perhaps those who are rich should try to give their money away to the "deserving" poor who would have done the same if positions had been reversed, and so are wrong to retain their wealth. Of course, there would be incredible problems with identifying the poor people who would have given their wealth away if things had been reversed, and it is not clear that any amount of money held by a private individual would be sufficient, in present circumstances, to solve the problem of identification. So perhaps, given the small number of poor who would have given money away, actual rich people are not wrong to keep their money. But, on the other hand, perhaps the rich should spread their money around equally among the poor in order to ensure that those who would have parted with their wealth in reversed circumstances at least get *something*. In any case, the fact —or even the possibility—of such poor people, however few in number, raises difficult problems for the Brazen Rule argument for the morality of wealth, and it is not easy to see how they should or could be solved.

It is also important to distinguish arguments using the Brazen Rule in defense of the morality of retaining wealth from related arguments for the same conclusion based on the vague principle that "ought" implies "can." Someone might, for example, argue that since he, because of his given nature, is so selfish that he cannot bring himself to give away his money, he has no obligation to do so. Whatever its force, this argument seems self-serving and hypocritical. Of course, the argument based on the Brazen Rule also has its air of self-servingness. But whatever the relative self-servingness of the two arguments, the "ought"-implies-"can" argument for the morality of wealth seems to be a less good example of a *moral* argument. For it claims the right to be as one oneself is because of one's nature, whereas the Brazen Rule argument claims only the right to be as other people are.[23]

It should be noted that although the two arguments we have been focusing on in this paper are consistent with each other, the second argument based on the Brazen Rule is in conflict with the earlier-mentioned principle of positive obligation, according to which it is wrong not to prevent serious harm or evil when one can do so without seriously interfering with one's life plans or committing any sins of commission. For the Brazen Rule says that one has no obligation to help others, and prevent certain great evils or harms from happening to them, if in fact those others would have omitted helping one; and this is assumed to be so even if helping those others would not interfere with one's life plans or style. The issue between the two principles hinges, in effect, on such questions as whether it would be wrong not to feed a vicious starving man, who would never have aided one if positions had been reversed, in a situation where one can give him food without seriously affecting one's life plans. To

---

[23]Consider the principle: If certain poor people would never have given their wealth away if they had been rich, then they deserve their poverty and deserve not to get any money from the rich. This principle could be used to argue that poor people get what they deserve, and that it is not unjust that they remain poor. But the original principle does not follow from, and seems less plausible than, the Brazen Rule. And I think we should resist it and the above argument that makes use of it.

decide such a question affirmatively is to side with the earlier principle of positive obligation; to decide it negatively is to side with the Brazen Rule. Since I am unsure myself about how to answer such questions, I am inclined to play it safe and weaken the Brazen Rule in such a way as to render it compatible with the earlier principle of positive obligation. This can be done by changing it to read:

> It is not wrong to omit doing something for others that others would have omitted doing for you, if your positions had been appropriately reversed, as long as doing the thing in question would seriously interfere with your life plans and those plans do not involve any commissive immoralities.

Such a principle might then be used to argue for the morality of wealth, and the resultant argument might be stronger than either of the main arguments for the morality of wealth that we have been discussing.

V

Unfortunately, however, all the arguments for the morality of wealth that we have considered are open to an objection that it seemed best to delay mentioning until all our arguments had been stated, an objection that is, I believe, more forceful than any of those we have already explored. There is some reason to think that the retention of wealth by the rich typically is commissively immoral, independently of whether the rich live rich or keep servants. And this supposed commissive immorality derives from the way wealth is normally acquired and grows once it is acquired.

Rich people almost never simply keep money or wealth; their riches often are in the form of investments that automatically work for them and produce new wealth. And it is possible for one's wealth thus to accumulate through investment in and support of business enterprises that wrongfully hurt people or do them injustices. For example, investment in a company with unfair hiring and promotion practices is in some degree supportive of those practices. And holding bonds in a company that makes napalm is in some way supportive of the production, and probably also the use, of napalm. Now if one makes profit from unjust or harmful uses of one's money, there may be an element of commissive immorality in what one does. And this may be true even if one has only inherited one's investments and not made them oneself. For even though one may only "let" one's money be used for immoral purposes, so that from a certain standpoint it seems that one is only omitting certain actions, still it is one's own money that is being used to do injustices or harm people. And we are sometimes reluctant to distinguish what a person does from what he intentionally or knowingly lets be done by something he owns or controls. Thus, if a man watches his neighbor's sheep destroy the neighbor's garden, he may be guilty only of an omission. But if it is his own sheep he lets destroy the neighbor's garden, we have some inclination to accuse him of destroying the garden, and thus to use a commissive type of word to describe what he did. And even if the commissive word does not literally apply, the very fact that we are thus inclined to use it indicates our reluctance to make any *moral* distinction between such supposed omissions and genuine commissions.[24] Letting one's money stay invested in immoral business enterprises may count as commissively wrong, because it is one's own money that is involved. But even if it does not, letting one's money be used for immoral purposes does not seem significantly different from actively using or investing one's money for such purposes. Thus, either letting one's money be used in this way is commissively immoral or, because the moral importance of the commission/omission distinction breaks down in this kind of case, it is not morally different from commissive immorality. So, for a rich person to be morally permitted to let his money make money in large corporations and the like, it would have to be the case that his investments, together with other such investments, were not supporting corporations that a reasonable person could see were seriously involved in wrongful enterprises. To make out a good case for the morality of keeping wealth and the accumulations of wealth, on the part of actual rich people, it would be necessary to show that the wealth of such people was not invested in immoral business enterprises or that their failure to know that this *was* the case was somehow excusable. And I think this would be difficult to do. Of course, it may also need to be shown that the companies in which rich people are invested really do perpetrate injustices and harm, but I have the strong feeling that one could readily construct arguments to that effect.

On the other hand, some rich people may horde their money, and it seems possible that someone could have and spend money without ever investing it or could invest it only in companies with "social conscience." Would such a person be able to escape the charge of immorality in the retention of wealth? This will in part depend on how the wealth was acquired.[25] Obviously, many fortunes have been acquired by unscrupulous means; the metaphor "robber barons" indicates the literal truth that

---

[24]In certain areas, the *law* uses a commissive-sounding word in condemning what seems to be a culpable failure to do or a wrongful inaction. "Failure to blow a whistle or to shut off steam, although in itself inaction, is readily treated as negligent operation of a train, which is affirmative misconduct." W. Prosser, *The Law of Torts,* 3rd ed. (St. Paul, Minn.: West Publishing Co., 1964), p. 335.

[25]It will also partially depend on how it is spent. For to buy the goods of a miscreant company may be as bad as investing in it, except, perhaps, when one has to buy such goods simply to maintain a decent standard of living.

many famous entrepreneurs committed serious wrongdoings in acquiring their fortunes. Such people would presumably have no more right to retain their money than a thief has. But what about those who have simply inherited great wealth? Their mere inheriting may not involve any commissive act or any wrongdoing. But if the wealth they inherit came from a robber baron who cheated the public, they may have no more right to retain that wealth than the robber baron had. If he in effect cheated people out of money to make his empire, then one who inherits and keeps his money perpetuates his crimes. The money should, instead, be returned to those who have been harmed or their descendants, if at all possible, and to keep the money without making any efforts in that direction seems clearly to be wrong. The wrongdoing involved is not perhaps quite tantamount to being a kind of accessory after the fact to the robber barons' crimes; but it does seem tantamount to being a kind of receiver of stolen goods. And it clearly is wrong to receive and keep what one should realize has been stolen from its rightful owners, even if the immorality involved is not exactly one of commission. As in the case described just above, the moral importance of the commission/omission distinction seems to break down here. Those who inherit tainted fortunes are morally tainted by keeping them, whether or not this involves them in any immorality of commission. Or so at least it seems to me.

Now there may, of course, be people with money who have made fortunes without investing in unjust businesses or mulcting or hurting people. And perhaps these people and their heirs are morally permitted to retain their wealth, as long as they do not keep it invested in immoral enterprises. But I have serious doubts whether many rich people, even in this "land of opportunity," fall into this category. Perhaps some doctors or lawyers deserve their fees and have accumulated wealth just from their fees. Perhaps there are others. It depends, in part, on what one thinks determines desert.[26] But in any event, the considerations we have mentioned cast grave doubt on whether many actual rich people are moral in retaining their wealth, much less in letting more wealth accumulate.

The problems just raised call into question all our earlier principles about the permissibility of ommissions, including the Brazen Rule. Omissions may not be permissible—even if they protect life plans and would have been indulged in by appropriately reversed others—if they in some sense preserve or perpetuate commissive wrongdoings. One may have a duty not to profit in certain ways from the wrongdoing of others. But perhaps an important kernel of those earlier principles can be preserved. If the principles are restricted to the omission of *benefactions* or *beneficence,* they avoid

---

[26]For various views on what determines desert, see Michael Slote, "Desert, Consent, and Justice," in *Philosophy and Public Affairs,* II (1973), pp. 323–47.

the problems of perpetuating other people's misdoings and are perhaps correct. The chief mistake of our arguments for the morality of wealth would then be that of thinking of the retention of wealth as the omission of beneficence rather than as the perpetuation of, or failure to make reparation for, commissive immoralities, which is what it is in most actual cases. Omission-of-beneficence-permitting principles could, perhaps, be used to justify the retention of wealth in those instances where such retention is merely the omission of beneficence, but such cases seem to be relatively rare.[27]

VI

It is high time to consider the bearing of our previous discussion on the obligations of rich nations to poor ones. One can construct arguments for the permissibility of national affluence in our kind of world along lines parallel to the above arguments for the morality of individual wealth. For we can think up analogues of the main principles of our two earlier arguments which apply directly to nations, governments, and the like. It might be held, for example, that it is not wrong for a nation to omit actions toward poor nations which would seriously interfere with its national "way of life" or standard of living—as long as these involved no commissive wrongdoings. Using this principle, one might argue that the United States in particular has no moral obligation to help the poorer nations of the world in any way that involves the loss of its affluence—even if it does have an obligation to give *some* help to these nations. A natural moral boundary would then be set as to what a nation like ours is obligated to give to nations faced with famine and misery, a boundary that could not be passed no matter how much starvation the rest of the world faced and how much good a rich nation could do by parting with enough of its material wealth to become nonaffluent.

In a similar way, one might try to defend the morality of national affluence by use of an analogue of the Brazen Rule which applied to nations and their interactions. It could be claimed that a nation may permissibly omit doing for other nations what those other nations would have omitted doing in its behalf, if positions had been appropriately reversed; and then it could be argued that since the poorer nations would not have used up their affluence to alleviate famine and suffering, if they had been the affluent ones, nations or countries like the United States have no obligation to relieve famine and misery in other countries at the expense of their own affluence.

[27]I understand the term "beneficence" in such a way that it is not ruled out, by its very meaning, that there should be duties or obligations of beneficence.

Of course, there are problems with both the arguments just sketched. Some of these parallel problems we noted in our earlier arguments for the morality of personal wealth. Some are particular to these new arguments. Let us consider the latter first. There is some problem, I think, about any analogues of our earlier principles which apply to collectivities. It has sometimes been said that the United States Government or the American people as a whole were guilty of war crimes, or of a war of aggression, in Indochina. I can well understand the desire of morally outraged people to say such things, but I have no clear idea myself of what they mean, nor any confidence that they even make coherent sense. It is not that I am suspicious in general of reifying nations. I believe I know what it means to say that the United States declared war on Japan. But I somehow have the feeling that only individuals, not nations or governments, can be guilty or blameworthy. Some of this unsurety affects my notions of national or governmental obligation; there may be something odd about or wrong with the idea that a collectivity can have moral obligations. And perhaps we should talk only about the moral obligations individuals have to try to affect governmental or national policies. But since I cannot articulate these doubts further, and can only draw attention to them, we should let them pass and go on to other matters.

Another problem about the principles to be introduced on analogy with the individual-oriented principles of our earlier arguments concerns which collective entities they should mention. Should we be talking about the obligations of states, nations, governments, multinational corporations, countries, or peoples? Perhaps it makes a difference; perhaps it does not; but I shall usually talk of nations or countries in what follows. Note further that even if some argument using a collective analogue of our earlier principles should succeed in morally justifying various rich nations in their retention of wealth and their refusal to give massive food or other assistance to poor nations, one would not automatically be able to draw parallel conclusions about individuals in rich nations. There is no easy correlation between obligations of nations and of their citizens, as far as I can tell, and I think one could describe a situation in which a nation acted wrongly but no individual in it did; or vice versa. It is in part just such supposed possibilities that make some people wonder about the meaning of talk about national obligations in the first place.

With these caveats in mind, let us now consider whether and how arguments for the morality of national wealth based on collective analogues of our earlier principles are open to objections similar to the ones that confronted our earlier arguments for the morality of individual wealth. The first argument for the morality of national wealth that we considered assumed that nations have a certain moral permission or right to omit things that might interfere with their national ways of life. And

though there *are* problems about understanding what an *individual's* basic
life plans are or knowing when they are seriously interfered with, I think
there are even *greater* problems with the idea of a *national* way of life and
of interference with one. The American way of life can perhaps in part be
specified by reference to certain basic American institutions. But the idea
of the American way of life is also tied to the idea of what America or
Americans most basically want, and how does one find out what a nation
basically wants? For example, would it really interfere with the American
way of life, or with what Americans most basically want, if we all had to
forgo meat forever? I have less idea how to deal with this question than
I do about similar questions concerning individuals; is this perhaps because
I think psychology is more advanced than sociology? I am not sure.

Even if we had a firm grip on the notion of a national way of life, our
first argument for the morality of national wealth could be challenged by
a collective analogue of Peter Singer's Rigorism. And I am no clearer about
how to decide the issue between collective Rigorism and collective Lenitism, than I was earlier about how to decide the issue between individual
Rigorism and individual Lenitism. In addition, the argument we are considering depends heavily on the implausible assumption that the so-called
American way of life intrinsically involves no commissive wrongdoings.
Even if individual rapes and murders should not, perhaps, count as commissive wrongdoings attributable to the American way of life per se—
whatever that means—surely the activities of American corporations at
home and abroad are part of the American way of life; and many people
think that American business has always been involved in commissive
wrongdoings: stripping poorer nations of their resources, polluting their
environments, employing their inhabitants at slave wages, selling back
finished goods to them at exorbitant prices, and, in the process of such
economic colonialism, destroying their self-respect in something like the
way a master can help destroy the self-respect of a servant. And it seems
ridiculous to suppose that we have a right to omit helping the poorer
nations because that would interfere with our way of life, if that way of
life involves commissive business wrongdoings to many of those very
nations. (There probably are poor nations we have not affected in this way,
and we *may* have the right to refuse them food for their starving; but this
would, I think, need to be shown in each particular case, and it also
depends on the assumption of collective Lenitism, whose dubitability we
have already much emphasized.) In any event, I believe that our first
argument for the morality of national affluence is, if anything, less forceful
and plausible than the parallel argument about individuals that we examined earlier.

On the other hand, an argument for the morality of national affluence
based on an analogue of the Brazen Rule may avoid at least some of the

problems of the earlier parallel argument for the morality of individual wealth. One of the biggest problems about the Brazen Rule argument we applied to individuals is that there probably are many poor people who would have given their wealth away in some intelligently helpful way if they had been rich. A rich person might well have obligations to give his wealth away to such people, even if the individual-oriented Brazen Rule is correct. With nations, however, the argument seems less problematic. It is not so obvious that there is any nation which, had it been wealthy, would have impoverished itself to prevent starvation or suffering in general. Moral differences between individuals tend to balance out within a nation, and the virtuous or benevolent few rarely have great influence on major national foreign policies. On the other hand, there are problems with any collectivity-oriented Brazen Rule that parallel earlier-mentioned problems about the Brazen Rule as applied to individuals. The nation-oriented Brazen Rule permits a rich nation to let a nation of scoundrels starve, even if it could help them without serious interference with its own national lifestyle. Some will find this morally acceptable; others will not; and I am not sure what I think.

However, the most important criticism of our arguments for the morality of national wealth runs parallel to the most important criticism of our earlier arguments for the morality of individual wealth. The distinction between omissions and commissions seems to be inapplicable or to lose its moral force in situations where the failure to do something perpetuates or fails to make reparation for certain commissive misdoings. Thus, if our national standard of living or way of life has in significant part been created by the depredations of American businessmen, we may have no right to retain the rich fruits of our business enterprise, especially if many people who need our help are among those most wrongly dealt with by American business. Even our affluence in food is in great part due to our industrial capacity and so derives in part from wrongdoings in and to other nations; so don't we have an obligation to give food produced here to those who are impoverished, hungry, or suffering from malnutrition in those other nations? I think, moreover, that this would probably be true even if it were only our ancestors who had committed wrongs in business dealings. One has a duty not to profit from the crimes of others (at the expense of those who have been harmed) and one has a duty not to receive stolen goods, and to varying degrees much of our national affluence may be seen as directly or indirectly involved in such questionable dealings.

Just as we earlier were forced to modify our moral principles about individuals, there seems to be reason to change our principles about collectivities. Once the latter are restricted to permitting the omission of collective *beneficence*, they seem more plausible. Then the mistake of our arguments for the morality of national wealth can be seen to be that of thinking of the retention of national wealth as a failure of beneficence, rather than as the perpetuation of and failure to make reparation for wrongdoings that it is in most actual cases. Arguments for the morality of national affluence of the kind we have presented would not then go through. The modified collectivity-oriented omission-of-beneficence principles could perhaps be used to justify national wealth in those cases where not to give away wealth is merely to omit a beneficence, but such cases do not often arise in the actual world. If each nation had developed independently of others and some had become rich while others were impoverished, with no international injustices or harms being committed in the process, then arguments with modified principles permitting the omission of beneficence might show that rich nations were not wrong to keep their wealth on grounds that this was necessary to their way of life or that other nations would do the same in reversed circumstances. The retention of wealth might in that case really just be the omission of beneficence.

That is not, however, to say that in such a situation there would be no injustices. A world in which some nations have rich land while others have to eke out an agricultural way of life on barren soil seems a world in which by accident of circumstances some people have "got the short end of the stick," a world in which, as we say, there is no justice, or less than ideal justice. It seems unfair that such a situation should exist, just as it seems unfair that some people should be born without talents or with physical defects, but the kind of unfairness or injustice involved here is not social, but cosmic or universal.[28] Our principles permit individuals or nations to retain wealth in some possible cases where such retention allows certain cosmic injustices to persist, and this may be a problem for us. But it is important to distinguish allowing unjust situations to continue from bringing such situations about. Perhaps most rich nations or people should not retain their wealth because of its origin in injustices that they or others have brought about. But it may be permissible to remain rich if this only requires *allowing* (cosmic) injustices to *remain*. There may be fewer or less stringent obligations to do away with injustices than to refrain from perpetuating them.

On the other hand, if there are situations of cosmic injustice in which certain rich nations or individuals have no obligation to do away with that injustice and part with their wealth, it does not necessarily follow that poor

[28]Incidentally, in "Distributive Justice" (*Philosophy and Public Affairs,* III [1973], pp. 81 ff.) and, later, in *Anarchy, State, and Utopia* (New York: Basic Books, 1974), Robert Nozick has claimed that in situations of social noncooperation, each individual deserves and justly retains what he gets through his own unaided efforts. He uses this assumption to argue against Rawls's view that *different* principles of justice govern situations where there *is* social cooperation. But if there is anything to the notion of cosmic justice, Nozick's original assumption is questionable. For more on cosmic justice and its relation to social justice, see Slote, "Desert, Consent, and Justice" and the references contained therein.

nations or people have no moral right to try to take that wealth away by conquest, taxation, exappropriation, or other means—precisely in the name of universal or cosmic justice. After all, there are circumstances in which two soldiers are locked in combat and each is morally permitted to defend himself, even though the other is morally permitted to prevent him from doing so. In other words, in certain circumstances the taking away of the wealth of the wealthy may be morally justified as the rectifying of an unjust or simply bad situation, rather than as the righting of a moral wrong that rich nations or individuals themselves have done by possessing wealth and trying to keep it. Arguments of the kind we have presented here have some tendency to show that *in the abstract* a rich individual or nation might have the moral right not to give his or its wealth away to the poor, even though it was cosmically unfair for such a situation to exist and even though the poor had some sort of moral right to attempt to take that wealth away. But if one considers the *actual ways* in which wealth is acquired, invested, and used, such justifications may, in most particular cases, simply fall to pieces.[29]

[29]I am indebted, for helpful comments and criticisms, to A. C. Bienstock, P. Bienstock, P. Brown, M. Cohen, E. Erwin, V. Held, D. K. Lewis, P. Singer, J. J. Thomson, G. Watson, and, especially, J. Rachels and T. Scanlon.

ONORA O'NEILL

O'Neill assumes that persons have a right not to be killed unjustifiably. Since many famine deaths are unjustifiable, we have a duty to try to prevent and postpone them.

    1. *She compares the earth to a lifeboat. Is it a lifeboat? If it is, is it well-equipped or underequipped? How important is this difference to moral debate?*

    2. *What is the importance of property rights in lifeboat situations? Can my exercise of my property rights override your right not to be killed?*

    3. *She claims that a person's right not to be killed may sometimes be violated when the killing is indirect and not intended (for example, deaths resulting from foreign investment policies). Is she correct?*

    4. *Is there a clear distinction between killing and letting die? If so, how important is it?*

    5. *Compare her right not to be killed unjustifiably with Aiken's right to be saved from preventable death due to deprivation. How are they similar? How do they differ?*

Onora O'Neill teaches philosophy at Barnard College, Columbia University. She has written a book on Kant's ethics, Acting on Principle, *as well as a number of articles in social and political philosophy.*

"Lifeboat Earth," by Onora O'Neill, *Philosophy and Public Affairs,* IV, no. 3 (1975): pp. 273–92. Reprinted by permission of Princeton University Press.

Lifeboat Earth

If in the fairly near future millions of people die of starvation, will those who survive be in any way to blame for those deaths? Is there anything which people ought to do now, and from now on, if they are to be able to avoid responsibility for unjustifiable deaths in famine years? I shall argue from the assumption that persons have a right not to be killed unjustifiably to the claim that we have a duty to try to prevent and postpone famine deaths. A corollary of this claim is that if we do nothing we shall bear some blame for some deaths.

JUSTIFIABLE KILLING

I shall assume that persons have a right not to be killed and a corresponding duty not to kill. I shall make no assumptions about the other rights persons may have. In particular, I shall not assume that persons have a right not to be allowed to die by those who could prevent it or a duty to prevent others' deaths whenever they could do so. Nor will I assume that persons lack this right.

Even if persons have no rights other than a right not to be killed, this right can justifiably be overridden in certain circumstances. Not all killings are unjustifiable. I shall be particularly concerned with two sorts of circumstances in which the right not to be killed is justifiably overridden. The first of these is the case of unavoidable killings; the second is the case of self-defense.

Unavoidable killings occur in situations where a person doing some act causes some death or deaths which he could not avoid. Often such deaths will be unavoidable because of the killer's ignorance of some relevant circumstance at the time of his decision to act. If B is driving a train, and A blunders onto the track and is either unnoticed by B or noticed too late for B to stop the train, and B kills A, then B could not have avoided killing A, given his decision to drive the train. Another sort of case of unavoidable killing occurs when B could avoid killing A or could avoid killing C, but cannot avoid killing one of the two. For example, if B is the carrier of a highly contagious and invariably fatal illness, he might find himself so placed that he cannot avoid meeting and so killing either A or C, though he can choose which of them to meet. In this case the unavoidability of B's killing someone is not relative to some prior decision B made. The cases of unavoidable killings with which I want to deal here are of the latter sort, and I shall argue that in such cases B kills justifiably if certain further conditions are met.

149

A killing may also be justifiable if it is undertaken in self-defense. I shall not argue here that persons have a right of self-defense which is independent of their right not to be killed, but rather that a minimal right of self-defense is a corollary of a right not to be killed. Hence the notion of self-defense on which I shall rely is in some ways different from, and narrower than, other interpretations of the right of self-defense. I shall also assume that if A has a right to defend himself against B, then third parties ought to defend A's right. If we take seriously the right not to be killed and its corollaries, then we ought to enforce others' rights not to be killed.

The right of self-defense which is a corollary of the right not to be killed is a right to take action to prevent killings. If I have a right not to be killed then I have a right to prevent others from endangering my life, though I may endanger their lives in so doing only if that is the only available way to prevent the danger to my own life. Similarly if another has the right not to be killed then I should, if possible, do something to prevent others from endangering his life, but I may endanger their lives in so doing only if that is the only available way to prevent the danger to his life. This duty to defend others is *not* a general duty of beneficence but a very restricted duty to enforce others' rights not to be killed.

The right to self-defense so construed is quite narrow. It includes no right of action against those who, though they cause or are likely to cause us harm, clearly do not endanger our lives. (However, specific cases are often unclear. The shopkeeper who shoots a person who holds him up with a toy gun was not endangered, but it may have been very reasonable of him to suppose that he was endangered.) And it includes no right to greater than minimal preventive action against a person who endangers one's life. If B is chasing A with a gun, and A could save his life either by closing a bullet-proof door or by shooting B, then if people have only a right not to be killed and a minimal corollary right of self-defense, A would have no right to shoot B. (Again, such cases are often unclear—A may not know that the door is bullet-proof or not think of it or may simply reason that shooting B is a better guarantee of prevention.) A right of proportionate self-defense which might justify A in shooting B, even were it clear that closing the door would have been enough to prevent B, is not a corollary of the right not to be killed. Perhaps a right of proportionate retaliation might be justified by some claim such as that aggressors lose certain rights, but I shall take no position on this issue.

In one respect the narrow right of self-defense, which is the corollary of a right not to be killed, is more extensive than some other interpretations of the right of self-defense. For it is a right to take action against others who endanger our lives whether or not they do so intentionally. A's right not to be killed entitles him to take action not only against aggressors but also against those "innocent threats"[1] who endanger lives without being aggressors. If B is likely to cause A's death inadvertently or involuntarily, then A has, if he has a right not to be killed, a right to take whatever steps are necessary to prevent B from doing so, provided that these do not infringe B's right not to be killed unnecessarily. If B approaches A with a highly contagious and invariably lethal illness, then A may try to prevent B from getting near him even if B knows nothing about the danger he brings. If other means fail, A may kill B in self-defense, even though B was no aggressor.

This construal of the right of self-defense severs the link between aggression and self-defense. When we defend ourselves against innocent threats, there is no aggressor, only somebody who endangers life. But it would be misleading to call this right a right of self-preservation. For self-preservation is commonly construed (as by Locke) as including a right to subsistence, and so a right to engage in a large variety of activities whether or not anybody endangers us. But the right which is the corollary of the right not to be killed is a right only to prevent others from endangering our lives, whether or not they intend to do so, and to do so with minimal danger to their lives. Only if one takes a Hobbesian view of human nature and sees others' acts as always completely threatening will the rights of self-defense and self-preservation tend to merge and everything done to maintain life be done to prevent its destruction. Without Hobbesian assumptions the contexts where the minimal right of self-defense can be invoked are fairly special, yet not, I shall argue, rare.

There may be various other circumstances in which persons' rights not to be killed may be overridden. Perhaps, for example, we may justifiably kill those who consent to us doing so. I shall take no position on whether persons can waive their rights not to be killed or on any further situations in which killings might be justifiable.

JUSTIFIABLE KILLINGS ON LIFEBOATS

The time has come to start imagining lurid situations, which is the standard operating procedure for this type of discussion. I shall begin by looking at some sorts of killings which might occur on a lifeboat and shall consider the sorts of justifications which they might be given.

Let us imagine six survivors on a lifeboat. There are two possible levels of provisions:

[1]Cf. Robert Nozick, *Anarchy State and Utopia* (New York: Basic Books, Inc., 1974), p. 34. Nozick defines an innocent threat as "someone who is innocently a causal agent in a process such that he would be an aggressor had he chosen to become such an agent."

1.   Provisions are on all reasonable calculations sufficient to last until rescue. Either the boat is near land, or it is amply provisioned or it has gear for distilling water, catching fish, etc.

2.   Provisions are on all reasonable calculations unlikely to be sufficient for all six to survive until rescue.

We can call situation (1) *the well-equipped lifeboat situation;* situation (2) *the under-equipped lifeboat situation.* There may, of course, be cases where the six survivors are unsure which situation they are in, but for simplicity I shall disregard those here.

On a well-equipped lifeboat it is possible for all to survive until rescue. No killing could be justified as unavoidable, and if someone is killed, then the justification could only be self-defense in special situations. Consider the following examples:

1A.   On a well-equipped lifeboat with six persons, A threatens to jettison the fresh water, without which some or all would not survive till rescue. A may be either hostile or deranged. B reasons with A, but when this fails, shoots him. B can appeal to his own and the others' right of self-defense to justify the killing. "It was him or us," he may reasonably say, "for he would have placed us in an under-equipped lifeboat situation." He may say this both when A acts to harm the others and when A acts as an innocent threat.

1B.   On a well-equipped lifeboat with six persons, $B, C, D, E,$ and F decide to withhold food from A, who consequently dies. In this case they cannot appeal to self-defense—for all could have survived. Nor can they claim that they merely let A die—"We didn't *do* anything"—for A would not otherwise have died. This was not a case of violating the problematic right not to be allowed to die but of violating the right not to be killed, and the violation is without justification of self-defense or of unavoidability.

On an under-equipped lifeboat it is not possible for all to survive until rescue. Some deaths are unavoidable, but sometimes there is no particular person whose death is unavoidable. Consider the following examples:

2A.   On an under-equipped lifeboat with six persons, A is very ill and needs extra water, which is already scarce. The others decide not to let him have any water, and A dies of thirst. If A drinks, then not all will survive. On the other hand it is clear that A was killed rather than allowed to die. If he had received water he might have survived. Though some death was unavoidable, A's was not and selecting him as the victim requires justification.

2B.   On an under-equipped lifeboat with six persons, water is so scarce that only four can survive (perhaps the distillation unit is designed for supplying four people). But who should go without? Suppose two are chosen to go without, either by lot or by some other method, and consequently die. The others cannot claim that all they did was to allow the two who were deprived of water to die—for these two might otherwise have been among the survivors. Nobody had a greater right to be a survivor, but given that not all could survive, those who did not survive were killed justifiably if the method by which they were chosen was fair. (Of course, a lot needs to be said about what would make a selection procedure fair.)

2C.   The same situation as in (2B) holds, but the two who are not to drink ask to be shot to ease their deaths. Again the survivors cannot claim that they did not kill but at most that they killed justifiably. Whether they did so is not affected by their shooting rather than dehydrating the victims, but only by the unavoidability of some deaths and the fairness of procedures for selecting victims.

2D.   Again the basic situation is as in (2B). But the two who are not to drink rebel. The others shoot them and so keep control of the water. Here it is all too clear that those who died were killed, but they too may have been justifiably killed. Whether the survivors kill justifiably depends neither on the method of killing nor on the victims' cooperation, except insofar as cooperation is relevant to the fairness of selection procedures.

Lifeboat situations do not occur very frequently. We are not often confronted starkly with the choice between killing or being killed by the application of a decision to distribute scarce rations in a certain way. Yet this is becoming the situation of the human species on this globe. The current metaphor "spaceship Earth" suggests more drama and less danger; if we are feeling sober about the situation, "lifeboat Earth" may be more suggestive.

Some may object to the metaphor "lifeboat Earth." A lifeboat is small; all aboard have equal claims to be there and to share equally in the provisions. Whereas the earth is vast and while all may have equal rights to be there, some also have property rights which give them special rights to consume, while others do not. The starving millions are far away and have no right to what is owned by affluent individuals or nations, even if it could prevent their deaths. If they die, it will be said, this is a violation at most of their right not to be allowed to die. And this I have not established or assumed.

I think that this could reasonably have been said in times past. The poverty and consequent deaths of far-off persons was something which the affluent might perhaps have done something to prevent, but which they had (often) done nothing to bring about. Hence they had not violated the right not to be killed of those living far off. But the economic and technological interdependence of today alters this situation.[2] Sometimes deaths are produced by some persons or groups of persons in distant, usually affluent, nations. Sometimes such persons and groups of persons violate not only some persons' alleged right not to be allowed to die but also their more fundamental right not to be killed.

We tend to imagine violations of the right not to be killed in terms of the killings so frequently discussed in the United States today: confrontations between individuals where one directly, violently, and intentionally brings about the other's death. As the lifeboat situations have shown, there are other ways in which we can kill one another. In any case, we do not restrict our vision to the typical mugger or murderer context. B may violate A's right not to be killed even when

    a. B does not act alone.

    b. A's death is not immediate.

    c.   It is not certain whether A or another will die in consequence of B's action.

    d. B does not intend A's death.

The following set of examples illustrates these points about killings:

    aa. A is beaten by a gang consisting of B, C, D, etc. No one assailant single-handedly killed him, yet his right not to be killed was violated by all who took part.

    bb. A is poisoned slowly by daily doses. The final dose, like earlier ones, was not, by itself, lethal. But the poisoner still violated A's right not to be killed.

---

[2]Cf. Peter Singer, "Famine, Affluence, and Morality," *Philosophy & Public Affairs*, I, no. 3 (Spring 1972): 229–243, 232. (Included in this volume.) I am in agreement with many of the points which Singer makes, but am interested in arguing that we must have some famine policy from a much weaker set of premises. Singer uses some consequentialist premises: starvation is bad; we ought to prevent bad things when we can do so without worse consequences; hence we ought to prevent starvation whether it is nearby or far off and whether others are doing so or not. The argument of this article does not depend on a particular theory about the grounds of obligation, but should be a corollary of any nonbizarre ethical theory which has any room for a notion of rights.

cc.   *B* plays Russian roulette with *A, C, D, E, F,* and *G,* firing a revolver at each once, when he knows that one firing in six will be lethal. If *A* is shot and dies, then *B* has violated his right not to be killed.

dd.   Henry II asks who will rid him of the turbulent priest, and his supporters kill Becket. It is reasonably clear that Henry did not intend Becket's death, even though he in part brought it about, as he later admitted.

These explications of the right not to be killed are not too controversial taken individually, and I would suggest that their conjunction is also uncontroversial. Even when *A*'s death is the result of the acts of many persons and is not an immediate consequence of their deeds, nor even a certain consequence, and is not intended by them, *A*'s right not to be killed may be violated.

FIRST CLASS VERSUS STEERAGE
ON LIFEBOAT EARTH

If we imagine a lifeboat in which special quarters are provided for the (recently) first-class passengers, and on which the food and water for all passengers are stowed in those quarters, then we have a fair, if crude, model of the present human situation on lifeboat Earth. For even on the assumption that there is at present sufficient for all to survive, some have control over the means of survival and so, indirectly, over others' survival. Sometimes the exercise of control can lead, even on a well-equipped lifeboat, to the starvation and death of some of those who lack control. On an ill-equipped lifeboat some must die in any case and, as we have already seen, though some of these deaths may be killings, some of them may be justifiable killings. Corresponding situations can, do, and will arise on lifeboat Earth, and it is to these that we should turn our attention, covering both the presumed present situation of global sufficiency of the means of survival and the expected future situation of global insufficiency.

Sufficiency Situations

Aboard a well-equipped lifeboat any distribution of food and water which leads to a death is a killing and not just a case of permitting a death. For the acts of those who distribute the food and water are the causes of a death which would not have occurred had those agents either had no causal influence or done other acts. By contrast, a person whom they leave in the water to drown is merely allowed to die, for his death would have taken place (other things being equal) had those agents had no causal influence, though it could have been prevented had they rescued him.[3] The distinction between killing and allowing to die, as here construed, does not depend on any claims about the other rights of persons who are killed. The death of the shortchanged passenger of example (1B) violated his property rights as well as his right not to be killed, but the reason the death was classifiable as a killing depended on the part which the acts of the other passengers had in causing it. If we suppose that a stowaway on a lifeboat has no right to food and water and is denied them, then clearly his property rights have not been violated. Even so, by the above definitions he is killed rather than allowed to die. For if the other passengers had either had no causal influence or done otherwise, his death would not have occurred. Their actions—in this case distributing food only to those entitled to it— caused the stowaway's death. Their acts would be justifiable only if property rights can sometimes override the right not to be killed.

Many would claim that the situation on lifeboat Earth is not analogous to that on ordinary lifeboats, since it is not evident that we all have a claim, let alone an equal claim, on the earth's resources. Perhaps some of us are stowaways. I shall not here assume that we do all have some claim on the earth's resources, even though I think it plausible to suppose that we do. I shall assume that even if persons have unequal property rights and some people own nothing, it does not follow that B's exercise of his property rights can override A's right not to be killed.[4] Where our activities lead to others' deaths which would not have occurred had we either done something else or had no causal influence, no claim that the activities were within our economic rights would suffice to show that we did not kill.

It is not far-fetched to think that at present the economic activity of some groups of persons leads to others' deaths. I shall choose a couple of examples of the sort of activity which can do so, but I do not think that these examples do more than begin a list of cases of killing by economic activities. Neither of these examples depends on questioning the existence of unequal property rights; they assume only that such rights do not

[3]This way of distinguishing killing from allowing to die does not rely on distinguishing "negative" from "positive" acts. Such attempts seem unpromising since any act has multiple descriptions of which some will be negative and others positive. If a clear distinction is to be made between killing and letting die, it must hint on the *difference* which an act makes for a person's survival, rather than on the description under which the agent acts.

[4]The point may appear rather arbitrary, given that I have not rested my case on one theory of the grounds of obligation. But I believe that almost any such theory will show a right not to be killed to override a property right. Perhaps this is why Locke's theory can seem so odd —in moving from a right of self-preservation to a justification of unequal property rights, he finds himself gradually having to reinterpret all rights as property rights, thus coming to see us as the owners of our persons.

override a right not to be killed. Neither example is one for which it is plausible to think that the killing could be justified as undertaken in self-defense.

Case one might be called the *foreign investment* situation. A group of investors may form a company which invests abroad—perhaps in a plantation or in a mine—and so manage their affairs that a high level of profits is repatriated, while the wages for the laborers are so minimal that their survival rate is lowered, that is, their expectation of life is lower than it might have been had the company not invested there. In such a case the investors and company management do not act alone, do not cause immediate deaths, and do not know in advance who will die; it is also likely that they intend no deaths. But by their involvement in the economy of an underdeveloped area they cannot claim, as can another company which has no investments there, that they are "doing nothing." On the contrary, they are setting the policies which determine the living standards which determine the survival rate. When persons die because of the lowered standard of living established by a firm or a number of firms which dominate a local economy and either limit persons to employment on their terms or lower the other prospects for employment by damaging traditional economic structures, and these firms could either pay higher wages or stay out of the area altogether, then those who establish these policies are violating some persons' rights not to be killed. Foreign investment which *raises* living standards, even to a still abysmal level, could not be held to kill, for it causes no additional deaths, unless there are special circumstances, as in the following example.

Even when a company investing in an underdeveloped country establishes high wages and benefits and raises the expectation of life for its workers, it often manages to combine these payments with high profitability only by having achieved a tax-exempt status. In such cases the company is being subsidized by the general tax revenue of the underdeveloped economy. It makes no contribution to the infrastructure—e.g., roads and harbors and airports—from which it benefits. In this way many underdeveloped economies have come to include developed enclaves whose development is achieved in part at the expense of the poorer majority.[5] In such cases, government and company policy combine to produce a high wage sector at the expense of a low wage sector; in consequence, some of the persons in the low wage sector, who would not otherwise have died, may die; these persons, whoever they may be, are killed and not merely allowed to die. Such killings may sometimes be justifiable—perhaps, if

[5]Cf. P. A. Baron, *The Political Economy of Growth* (New York: Monthly Review Press, 1957), especially chap. 5, "On the Roots of Backwardness"; or A. G. Frank, *Capitalism and Underdevelopment in Latin America* (New York: Monthly Review Press, 1967). Both works argue that underdeveloped economies are among the products of developed ones.

they are outnumbered by lives saved through having a developed sector —but they are killings nonetheless, since the victims might have survived if not burdened by transfer payments to the developed sector.

But, one may say, the management of such a corporation and its investors should be distinguished more sharply. Even if the management may choose a level of wages, and consequently of survival, the investors usually know nothing of this. But the investors, even if ignorant, are responsible for company policy. They may often fail to exercise control, but by law they have control. They choose to invest in a company with certain foreign investments; they profit from it; they can, and others cannot, affect company policy in fundamental ways. To be sure the investors are not murderers—they do not intend to bring about the deaths of any persons; nor do the company managers usually intend any of the deaths company policies cause. Even so, investors and management acting together with the sorts of results just described do violate some persons' rights not to be killed and usually cannot justify such killings either as required for self-defense or as unavoidable.

Case two, where even under sufficiency conditions some persons' economic activities result in the deaths of other persons, might be called the *commodity pricing* case. Underdeveloped countries often depend heavily on the price level of a few commodities. So a sharp drop in the world price of coffee or sugar or cocoa may spell ruin and lowered survival rates for whole regions. Yet such drops in price levels are not in all cases due to factors beyond human control. Where they are the result of action by investors, brokers, or government agencies, these persons and bodies are choosing policies which will kill some people. Once again, to be sure, the killing is not single-handed, it is not instantaneous, the killers cannot foresee exactly who will die, and they may not intend anybody to die.

Because of the economic interdependence of different countries, deaths can also be caused by rises in the prices of various commodities. For example, the present near-famine in the Sahelian region of Africa and in the Indian subcontinent is attributed by agronomists partly to climatic shifts and partly to the increased prices of oil and hence of fertilizer, wheat, and other grains.

> The recent doubling in international prices of essential foodstuffs will, of necessity, be reflected in higher death rates among the world's lowest income groups, who lack the income to increase their food expenditures proportionately, but live on diets near the subsistence level to begin with.[6]

[6]Lester R. Brown and Erik P. Eckholm, "The Empty Breadbasket," *Ceres* (F.A.O. Review on Development), March–April 1974, p. 59. See also N. Borlaug and R. Ewell, "The Shrinking Margin," in the same issue.

Of course, not all of those who die will be killed. Those who die of drought will merely be allowed to die, and some of those who die because less has been grown with less fertilizer will also die because of forces beyond the control of any human agency. But to the extent that the raising of oil prices is an achievement of Arab diplomacy and oil company management rather than a windfall, the consequent deaths are killings. Some of them may perhaps be justifiable killings (perhaps if outnumbered by lives saved within the Arab world by industrialization), but killings nonetheless.

Even on a sufficiently equipped earth some persons are killed by others' distribution decisions. The causal chains leading to death-producing distributions are often extremely complex. Where they can be perceived with reasonable clarity we ought, if we take seriously the right not to be killed and seek not merely to avoid killing others but to prevent third parties from doing so, to support policies which reduce deaths. For example—and these are only examples—we should support certain sorts of aid policies rather than others; we should oppose certain sorts of foreign investment; we should oppose certain sorts of commodity speculation, and perhaps support certain sorts of price support agreements for some commodities (e.g., those which try to maintain high prices for products on whose sale poverty stricken economies depend).

If we take the view that we have no duty to enforce the rights of others, then we cannot draw so general a conclusion about our duty to support various economic policies which might avoid some unjustifiable killings. But we might still find that we should take action of certain sorts either because our own lives are threatened by certain economic activities of others or because our own economic activities threaten others' lives. Only if we knew that we were not part of any system of activities causing unjustifiable deaths could we have no duties to support policies which seek to avoid such deaths. Modern economic causal chains are so complex that it is likely that only those who are economically isolated and self-sufficient could know that they are part of no such systems of activities. Persons who believe that they are involved in some death-producing activities will have some of the same duties as those who think they have a duty to enforce others' rights not to be killed.

Scarcity Situations

The last section showed that sometimes, even in sufficiency situations, some might be killed by the way in which others arranged the distribution of the means of subsistence. Of far more importance in the long run is the true lifeboat situation—the situation of scarcity. We face a situation in which not everyone who is born can live out the normal span of human life and, further, in which we must expect today's normal life-span to be shortened. The date at which serious scarcity will begin is not generally agreed upon, but even the more optimistic prophets place it no more than decades away.[7] Its arrival will depend on factors such as the rate of technological invention and innovation, especially in agriculture and pollution control, and the success of programs to limit human fertility.

Such predictions may be viewed as exonerating us from complicity in famine deaths. If famine is inevitable, then—while we may have to choose whom to save—the deaths of those whom we do not or cannot save cannot be seen as killings for which we bear any responsibility. For these deaths would have occurred even if we had no causal influence. The decisions to be made may be excruciatingly difficult, but at least we can comfort ourselves that we did not produce or contribute to the famine.

However, this comforting view of famine predictions neglects the fact that these predictions are contingent upon certain assumptions about what people will do in the prefamine period. Famine is said to be inevitable *if* people do not curb their fertility, alter their consumption patterns, and avoid pollution and consequent ecological catastrophes. It is the policies of the present which will produce, defer, or avoid famine. Hence if famine comes, the deaths that occur will be results of decisions made earlier. Only if we take no part in systems of activities which lead to famine situations can we view ourselves as choosing whom to save rather than whom to kill when famine comes. In an economically interdependent world there are few people who can look on the approach of famine as a natural disaster from which they may kindly rescue some, but for whose arrival they bear no responsibility. We cannot stoically regard particular famine deaths as unavoidable if we have contributed to the emergence and extent of famine.

If we bear some responsibility for the advent of famine, then any decision on distributing the risk of famine is a decision whom to kill. Even a decision to rely on natural selection as a famine policy is choosing a policy for killing—for under a different famine policy different persons might have survived, and under different prefamine policies there might have been no famine or a less severe famine. The choice of a particular famine policy may be justifiable on the grounds that once we have let it get to that point there is not enough to go around, and somebody must go, as on an ill-equipped lifeboat. Even so, the famine policy chosen will not be a policy of saving some but not all persons from an unavoidable predicament.

Persons cannot, of course, make famine policies individually. Famine

[7]For discussions of the time and extent of famine see, for example, P. R. Ehrlich, *The Population Bomb,* rev. ed. (New York: Ballantine, 1971); R. L. Heilbroner, *An Inquiry into the Human Prospect* (New York: Norton, 1974); *Scientific American,* September 1974, especially R. Freedman and R. Berelson, "The Human Population"; P. Demeny, "The Populations of the Underdeveloped Countries"; R. Revelle, "Food and Population."

and prefamine policies are and will be made by governments individually and collectively and perhaps also by some voluntary organizations. It may even prove politically impossible to have a coherent famine or prefamine policy for the whole world; if so, we shall have to settle for partial and piecemeal policies. But each person who is in a position to support or oppose such policies, whether global or local, has to decide which to support and which to oppose. Even for individual persons, inaction and inattention are often a decision a decision to support the famine and prefamine policies, which are the status quo whether or not they are "hands off" policies. There are large numbers of ways in which private citizens may affect such policies. They do so in supporting or opposing legislation affecting aid and foreign investment, in supporting or opposing certain sorts of charities or groups such as Zero Population Growth, in promoting or opposing ecologically conservative technology and lifestyles. Hence we have individually the onus of avoiding killing. For even though we

a.   do not kill single-handedly those who die of famine

b.   do not kill instantaneously those who die of famine

c.   do not know which individuals will die as the result of the prefamine and famine policies we support (unless we support something like a genocidal famine policy)

d.   do not intend any famine deaths

we nonetheless kill and do not merely allow to die. For as the result of our actions in concert with others, some will die who might have survived had we either acted otherwise or had no causal influence.

FAMINE POLICIES AND PREFAMINE POLICIES

Various principles can be suggested on which famine and prefamine policies might reasonably be based. I shall list some of these, more with the aim of setting out the range of possible decisions than with the aim of stating a justification for selecting some people for survival. One very general policy might be that of adopting whichever more specific policies will lead to the fewest deaths. An example would be going along with the consequences of natural selection in the way in which the allocation of medical care in situations of great shortage does, that is, the criteria for relief would be a high chance of survival if relief is given and a low chance otherwise—the worst risks would be abandoned. (This decision is analogous to picking the ill man as the victim on the lifeboat in 2A.) However, the policy of minimizing deaths is indeterminate, unless a certain time horizon is specified. For the policies which maximize survival in the short run—e.g., preventive medicine and minimal living standards—may also maximize population increase and lead to greater ultimate catastrophe.[8]

Another general policy would be to try to find further grounds which can justify overriding a person's right not to be killed. Famine policies adopted on these grounds might permit others to kill those who will forgo their right not to be killed (voluntary euthanasia, including healthy would-be suicides) or to kill those whom others find dependent and exceptionally burdensome, e.g. the unwanted sick or aged or unborn or newborn (involuntary euthanasia, abortion, and infanticide). Such policies might be justified by claims that the right not to be killed may be overridden in famine situations if the owner of the right consents or if securing the right is exceptionally burdensome.

Any combination of such policies is a policy of killing some and protecting others. Those who are killed may not have their right not to be killed violated without reason; those who set and support famine policies and prefamine policies will not be able to claim that they do not kill, but if they reason carefully they may be able to claim that they do not do so without justification.

From this vantage point it can be seen why it is not relevant to restrict the right of self-defense to a right to defend oneself against those who threaten one's life but do not do so innocently. Such a restriction may make a great difference to one's view of abortion in cases where the mother's life is threatened, but it does not make much difference when famine is the issue. Those who might be chosen as likely victims of any famine policy will probably be innocent of contributing to the famine, or at least no more guilty than others; hence the innocence of the victims is an insufficient ground for rejecting a policy. Indeed it is hard to point a finger at the guilty in famine situations. Are they the hoarders of grain? The parents of large families? Inefficient farmers? Our own generation?

In a sense we are all innocent threats to one another's safety in scarcity situations, for the bread one person eats might save another's life. If there were fewer people competing for resources, commodity prices would fall and starvation deaths be reduced. Hence famine deaths in scarcity situations might be justified on grounds of the minimal right of self-defense as well as on grounds of the unavoidability of some deaths and the reasonableness of the policies for selecting victims. For each famine death leaves fewer survivors competing for whatever resources there are, and the most endangered among the survivors might have died—had not others done so.

---

[8]See *Scientific American*, September 1974, especially A. J. Coale, "The History of the Human Population."

So a policy which kills some may be justified on the grounds that the most endangered survivors could have been defended in no other way.

Global scarcity is not here yet. But its imminence has certain implications for today. If all persons have a right not to be killed and a corollary duty not to kill others, then we are bound to adopt prefamine policies which ensure that famine is postponed as long as possible and is minimized. And a duty to try to postpone the advent and minimize the severity of famine is a duty on the one hand to minimize the number of persons there will be and on the other to maximize the means of subsistence.[9] For if we do not adopt prefamine policies with these aims we shall have to adopt more drastic famine policies sooner.

So if we take the right not to be killed seriously, we should consider and support not only some famine policy for future use but also a population and resources policy for present use. There has been a certain amount of philosophical discussion of population policies.[10] From the point of view of the present argument it has two defects. First, it is for the most part conducted within a utilitarian framework and focuses on problems such as the different population policies required by maximizing the total and the average utility of a population. Secondly this literature tends to look at a scarcity of resources as affecting the quality of lives but not their very possibility. It is more concerned with the question, How many people should we add? than with the question, How few people could we lose? There are, of course, many interesting questions about population policies which are not relevant to famine. But here I shall consider only population and resource policies determined on the principle of postponing and minimizing famine, for these are policies which might be based on the claim that persons have a right not to be killed, so that we have a duty to avoid or postpone situations in which we shall have to override this right.

Such population policies might, depending upon judgments about the likely degree of scarcity, range from the mild to the draconian. I list some examples. A mild population policy might emphasize family planning, perhaps moving in the direction of fiscal incentives or measures which stress not people's rights but their duties to control their bodies. Even a mild policy would require a lot both in terms of invention (e.g. the development of contraceptives suitable for use in poverty-stricken conditions) and innovation (e.g., social policies which reduce the incentives and pres-

[9]The failure of "right to life" groups to pursue these goals seriously casts doubt upon their commitment to the preservation of human lives. Why are they active in so few of the contexts where human lives are endangered?

[10]For example, J. C. C. Smart, *An Outline of a System of Utilitarian Ethics* (Melbourne: Melbourne University Press, 1961), pp. 18, 44ff.; Jan Narveson, "Moral Problems of Population," *Monist* 57 (1973): 62–86; "Utilitarianism and New Generations," *Mind* 76 (1967): 62–72.

sures to have a large family).[11] More draconian policies would enforce population limitation—for example, by mandatory sterilization after a certain number of children were born or by reducing public health expenditures in places with high net reproduction rates to prevent death rates from declining until birth rates do so. A policy of completely eliminating all further births (e.g., by universal sterilization) is also one which would meet the requirement of postponing famine, since extinct species do not suffer famine. I have not in this argument used any premises which show that a complete elimination of births would be wrong, but other premises might give reasons for thinking that it is wrong to enforce sterilization or better to have some persons rather than no persons. In any case the political aspects of introducing famine policies make it likely that this most austere of population policies would not be considered.

There is a corresponding range of resource policies. At the milder end are the various conservation and pollution control measures now being practiced or discussed. At the tougher end of the spectrum are complete rationing of energy and materials consumption. If the aim of a resources policy is to avoid killing those who are born, and adequate policy may require both invention (e.g., solar energy technology and better waste retrieval techniques) and innovation (e.g., introducing new technology in such a way that its benefits are not quickly absorbed by increasing population, as has happened with the green revolution in some places).

At all events, if we think that people have a right not to be killed, we cannot fail to face up to its long range implications. This one right by itself provides ground for activism on many fronts. In scarcity situations which we help produce, the defeasibility of the right not to be killed is important, for there cannot be any absolute duty not to kill persons in such situations but only a commitment to kill only for reasons. Such a commitment requires consideration of the condition or quality of life which is to qualify for survival. Moral philosophers are reluctant to face up to this problem; soon it will be staring us in the face.

[11]Cf. Mahmood Mamdani, *The Myth of Population Control* (New York: Monthly Review Press, 1972), for evidence that high fertility can be based on rational choice rather than ignorance or incompetence.

HOWARD RICHARDS

Richards argues that principles of productive justice are needed as supplements to principles of distributive justice since inefficient production and underproduction may be, in themselves, unjust.

1. What effect will enacting measures of productive justice have on a nation's carrying capacity?

2. How does production relate to an individual's rights (e.g., one's right to use, or not use, his property any way he wishes)?

3. Does productive justice clash with environmental concerns like those raised by Hardin?

4. Does productive justice dictate radical population control?

Howard Richards teaches philosophy at Earlham College where he is coordinator of Peace and Conflict Studies. He also serves as a consultant to the Center for Research and Development in Education (CIDE) in Chile.

Productive Justice

There is too little food in the world, and what little there is is unjustly distributed. The latter proposition, that the distribution of food is unjust, need not posit equality of food distribution as the standard of justice, but requires only the premise that no defensible doctrine of distributive justice, be it based on the needs of persons, their work, their worth, their productivity, their rights, their effort, or any judicious combination of such personal characteristics, would yield an ideal distribution of food that would be coincident with or reasonably similar to that which obtains.

This article has not been previously published.

However, this paper will not disillusion those persons, if there are any, who find that food is justly distributed, but instead address itself to the question whether it is unjust that there is too little food.

Five considerations will be discussed, and it will be concluded that in combination they are sufficient to determine a reflective mind to believe that it is not unreasonable to hold that the present food shortage is unjust, and, moreover, that principles of productive justice are needed as supplements to principles of distributive justice. If this paper is sound, and if all, or even many, reflective minds should give due thought to the considerations brought forward in it, then moral progress will be made, since it is a feature of justice that if all who duly reflect come to hold that something is unjust, then that something will be unjust. And without taking an overly optimistic view of history, one can believe that a wrong that is recognized as an injustice is more likely to be righted than it otherwise would be.

Before discussing the considerations in question, I shall list them briefly:

1.   The practices responsible for keeping world food production at harmfully low levels are unjust, because they cause harm that could be averted, at a cost of only minor, morally insignificant, sacrifices.

2.   Indeed, unproductive practices kill people, and they are unjust because they are analogous to homicide in the morally relevant respects.

3.   The hungry of the earth have a right to a reasonably high level of agricultural production.

4.   Distributive justice cannot be achieved without production, from which it follows that justice requires production.

5.   It is misleading and mischievous to say that practices which sacrifice distributive justice in order to increase production are just (which we often do say) without also saying that production is a requirement of justice.

SOME ASSUMPTIONS

Before enlarging on these points, I shall state some assumptions and make some necessary clarifications concerning the nature of what I am trying to do in this paper.

First, with David Hume,[1] I assume that justice is mainly concerned with property. This assumption relates nicely to the classical definition of justice, *suum cuique tributare iustitia est,* which is usually rendered as "justice

[1]David Hume, *A Treatise of Human Nature* (various editions), Bk. III, pt. II, passim.

is to give to every man his due," but which is better rendered, "justice is to give to every man what is his." My main concern is with those laws and policies with the force of law that determine or affect wealth and income, including those bearing on property, inheritance, wages, prices, profits, and taxes; although the focus of the present paper is on food production and food distribution, much of it can be taken to imply similar conclusions with respect to other goods whose production and distribution are affected by property institutions.

Second, the paper bears primarily on justice as a virtue of social institutions, of what John Rawls calls practices,[2] and indeed mainly, as the previous paragraph indicates, on that subset of practices that is protected by the force of law, and only secondarily with just persons or just acts. It is pretty evident, in any case, that famine cannot be prevented by the just or generous isolated acts of individuals. The type of decision for which just criteria are sought in this paper is a social choice among sets of practices, where both distributive justice and productive justice should guide the choice. Such social choices, once made, fix general rules, pursuant to which competent authorities determine "what is his" in particular disputed cases. References to "our duties" are, unless the context indicates otherwise, about the duties of a person in his capacity as citizen.[3]

Third, the entire discussion takes place at the level of what Henry Sidgwick called ideal justice.[4] It is assumed that respect for the law is one element of justice, and respect for legitimate expectations another; the third, ideal, element consists of the principles that are used to evaluate, and, hopefully, to guide the evolution of, both the law and the moral rules that define legitimate expectations. Consequently, it is not a relevant objection to the present enterprise to say something like, "But I have a perfect right to put fertilizer on my golf course, for according to law it is my golf course and my fertilizer." The point of the ideal element of justice is not, at least not ordinarily and not in this paper, to say that existing laws do not apply, but rather to provide a basis for reform. Nor is it a relevant objection that we all understand the spokesmen of the United States De-

[2]John Rawls, "Justice as Fairness," *Philosophical Review,* LXVII (1958), 164, note 2: "I use the word 'practice' throughout as a sort of technical term meaning any form of activity specified by a system of rules which define offices, roles, mores, penalties, defenses, and so on, and which gives the activity its structure. As examples one may think of games and rituals, trials and parliaments, markets and systems of property."

[3]"Citizen" here does not mean merely "voter" and does not refer only to governmental action; what I have in mind is the office of citizen with respect to social, economic, political and cultural rules and expectations, i.e., one who not only adheres to them, but also helps to shape and to maintain them. See John Rawls, "Two Concepts of Rules," *Philosophical Review,* LXIV (1955), 3–32.

[4]Henry Sidgwick, *The Methods of Ethics* (London: Macmillan, 1930), Bk. III, Chap. V., pp. 264–94. See also Chap. VI and Bk. IV, Chap. III, Section 4.

partment of Agriculture, and recognize the legitimacy of the common expectations which they take for granted, when they assume that food is usually not shipped to famine areas because the people there have no money to pay for it. We know that in our culture it is expected that food is produced for the purpose of selling it at a profit, and it is expected that those who eat it pay for it. But this recognition does not forbid us to say, on grounds of ideal justice, that a world where people starve through no fault of their own, where that starvation is not due exclusively to natural calamities and might be averted by the reform of human institutions, is an unjust world that ought to be changed.

Fourth, for somewhat similar reasons it is of limited relevance to invoke the distinction between justice and benevolence. It is sometimes urged that the duty to aid the needy is not a duty of justice, but a duty of benevolence. But benevolence is not apposite where the basic structure of society is at issue, because before one can be benevolent with one's property one has to own it. Productive justice is a source of guidance when society is choosing among possible sets of laws, which would affect income and wealth in various ways. Benevolence provides guidance in the logically subsequent situation where a person's income has already accrued to him, and it is his office to decide what to do with it.

FIVE ARGUMENTS FOR PRODUCTIVE JUSTICE

Passing now from the task of locating the considerations to be adduced in a context of assumptions,[5] to the considerations themselves—the first

[5]The following additional assumptions may perhaps be taken to be tacitly understood, but for the sake of caution I set them forth here:

Fifth, only those insufficiencies of food attributable to human agency are in question. A drought is a calamity, but it is not an injustice.

Sixth, it is not contended that it is in every case unjust that resources are idle; for example, it may be the case that land ought not be tilled because if it were brought under cultivation the manpower, the fertilizer, the seeds, the insecticides, and the machine-power needed to farm it would be diverted from better uses. But this concession is not equivalent to agreeing that it is just that resources be unused if and only if no entrepreneur finds it profitable to use them. To agree to the latter proposition would be much too sweeping, and would be equivalent to denying that a duty to prevent famine would oblige us to evaluate and to improve an economic system.

Seventh, the term "production" includes not only on-farm activities, but also processing, storage, transport, and all that is needful to make food available.

Eighth, it is assumed that in the short run there are no insurmountable technical or psychological obstacles to overcoming famine, it being common knowledge that there are many hectares of underutilized land, much land devoted to nonfood crops such as coffee and tobacco, many unemployed people, and a great deal of capital

of them is a variant of an argument made by Peter Singer, to the effect that
we have a duty to aid the hungry, such a duty being an instance, or set
of instances, of the more general proposition that we should prevent bad
occurrences (i.e., harm) unless, to do so, we have to sacrifice something
morally significant.[6] The argument as presented by Singer supports a duty
of benevolence more than a principle of justice, seems to apply more to
private acts than to social practices, and seems to put more emphasis on
sharing what we have than on working more (and more efficiently) in order
to produce more. But if Singer's position is correct, it would seem reasonable to accept also a similar argument, *mutatis mutandis,* for a principle of
justice calling on us to amend our social practices, to produce more as well
as to share more, when we cannot without so doing prevent famine. There
may be disagreement as to the exact point where sacrifice becomes great
enough that it is morally significant, i.e., the point where the harm done
to some people by the adoption of practices that prevent the starvation of
other people becomes great enough that it deserves consideration; but
wherever this point may be located, it seems evident that we are not near
it. The part of the argument that may be found objectionable is the part
that asserts a duty to prevent bad occurrences, for it is traditionally and
commonly held that our duties dissipate "like the ripples made by throwing a stone into a pond,"[7] in proportion as the claimants are less intimately
associated with us, so that one's duty to one's starving mother is strong,
but one's duty to a starving stranger is weak. An objector might say that
no Briton has any duty to the peasants of Bangladesh. Furthermore, morality is more stringent with respect to actions than with respect to inertia;
so that, while it would be immoral for a Briton to fly to Bangladesh, and
there lock a Bengali in a cage with no food, causing, by this means, death
by starvation, it is less immoral, or not immoral at all, for the same Briton
to stay at home and do nothing while the same Bengali starves. Singer's

---

tied up in the production of such goods as cosmetics and passenger cars, which
would surely be classified as morally insignificant goods if the extension of that
concept be determined keeping in view the needs of the world's people. (The
proviso "in the short run" is added because ecological factors may in the long run
make our resources insufficient t · prevent famine. It is to be noted, however, that
some ecological factors, such as population and energy use, are partly or wholly
within our control, and therefore within the scope of our responsibility.) This
eighth assumption rules out objections premised on "ought implies can" which
would hold, falsely, that we have no duty to produce sufficient food because we
cannot do it.

Ninth, production should be subject to ecological constraints, utilizing labor and other
available resources, in order to satisfy human needs, subject to suitable restrictions
on the exploitation of the environment.

[6]Peter Singer, "Famine, Affluence, and Morality," *Philosophy and Public Affairs,* I, no. 3
(Spring 1972), pp. 229–43. See also this volume, pp. 22–36.

[7]The phrase quoted is from Sidgwick, *The Methods of Ethics,* p. 271.

position might be taken, if this objection is found to be persuasive, not as an analysis of our present moral condition—for our present rules have exceptions that have the effect of allowing more hardheartedness than Singer approves of—but rather as a direct appeal back to utilitarian premises and/or to moral sensibility, coupled with calling attention to pertinent facts about the extent and causes of suffering. One may hope that his paper will help to persuade people that the range of persons whom it is our duty to help should be extended, and the scope of permissible inertia diminished.

A second consideration which can be interpreted as a reinforcement of the first, has been advanced by Onora Nell, who holds that allowing people to starve to death is morally equivalent to killing them.[8] (Nell develops her case using criteria for "killing" drawn from the literature on the moral controversy over abortion, and relies on the assumption that persons have a right not to be killed.) If a case of homicide can be made out, the effect should be to extend the duty to strangers, since it is not ordinarily just (some hold it is never just) to kill anybody at all, and also to reduce the force of excuses that rely on the custom of excusing omissions more easily than commissions. The fact that many people cooperate to bring about the deaths in question does not weaken the case for homicide, since all of the accomplices to such a crime are guilty, no matter how numerous they may be. The fact that the number of victims is uncertain, there being many borderline cases where it is not clear that malnutrition is a necessary condition of death, is not decisive as long as we know that there are some deaths, that they are not excusable, and that even one such killing is morally prohibited. However, most persons whose actions and omissions support the practices that lead to death are not aware of the role that they play, nor aware of what they might do, it they would, in order to avert killing. Consequently, homicide fails to be a valid analogy, for lack of intent, with respect to those persons who do not perceive the effects of their conduct and viable alternatives. The argument for productive justice, on the ground that our failure to organize human institutions efficiently results in killing, will become stronger as the mass media and the schools increase public awareness of what needs to be done; since it will thereby become correct to ascribe malicious intent to those who continue to fail to take constructive steps to prevent famine.

Turning now to a third consideration, Gregory Vlastos has called attention to the rule that a trustee of property is obliged to manage it with a reasonably high degree of efficiency; if the trustee manages it badly, so that

---

[8]Onora Nell, "On Why Abortion is the Wrong Topic for Moral Philosophy to Bog Down In," (unpublished), p. 21: "If all persons have a right not to be killed and a corollary duty not to kill others, then we are bound to insure that famine is . . . minimized."

the income is, say, one-half of what it would be if it were well managed, then the beneficiaries can justly claim that they are being cheated of part of the income that is due them.[9] The case of the right of the beneficiaries of a trust to the proper management of it is, perhaps, a representative of the general principle that if all and only certain persons have a claim on the proceeds produced by a property, then they have a right to insist that it be well managed. Now, the persons who can lay claim to the earth's production are all and only the inhabitants of the earth, from which it should follow that everyone, including the hungry, has a right to an earth that is as productive as people can reasonably be expected to make it; from this latter proposition it follows that unproductive practices (at least large-scale ones) are unjust. But the general principle in question will not persuade persons who deny that producers have anything like a fiduciary duty to consumers; someone may hold, for example, that a man who owns farmland in fee simple has not only a legal but also a moral right to use it inefficiently or not to use it at all, and, further, he may hold that the institutions that define and protect such rights are just ones. For this reason, Vlastos' suggestion is likely to be accepted only by those who already believe that property rights should be morally evaluated in the light of their social functions, e.g., in the case of farmland, the function of agricultural production: Vlastos' suggestion should be especially welcome to those who hold, for religious reasons, that God is the Owner of the earth, and that mortal property owners are, and should conduct themselves as, His stewards.

The fourth consideration may be stated briefly: If distributive justice requires, for whatever reason, a minimum standard below which no one (or no one with some minimal level of merit) should fall, then distributive justice cannot be achieved without production. Production then becomes a requirement of justice. Consider, too, that distributive justice could too easily be evaded if production were not an obligation, for the employer who does not pay a just wage could discharge his obligation by closing the enterprise; there would then be no revenue, no employees, and no wages at all. But we would not always say in such cases that the man who had been unjust, because he paid unjust wages, had become just by ceasing to produce, nor that institutions that oblige him to take such a step, or reward him for doing so, are just institutions.

To introduce the fifth consideration, let us assume, quite realistically, that distributive justice calls for a more egalitarian distribution of incomes than that which now exists. Now consider the position of an Economics

---

[9] Gregory Vlastos, "Justice and Equality," in Richard B. Brandt, ed., *Social Justice* (Englewood Cliffs, N.J.: Prentice-Hall, 1962), Section III. Vlastos actually holds that men are jointly entitled to benefit from the means of well-being, at the highest level at which it may be secured (p. 59). If he is correct, then my weaker version should be correct *a fortiori*.

Minister (perhaps Ludwig Erhard, or Antonio Delfim Neto) who believes that even more inequality is needed in order to produce more goods, including more food. In such a case it would be natural to argue that although it is true that distributive justice calls for more equal incomes, there is another kind of justice, productive justice, which calls for less equal incomes. Such an argument appears to be implicit in the following statement made by President Geisel of Brazil on 19 March 1974. After citing statistics showing that there is a high degree of inequality of income in Brazil, he said: "A careful examination of the problem reveals that the improvement of the distribution of income, in order to make it compatible with the maintenance of high levels of economic growth, is a process that demands time and rationality. The easy distributivism that tries to reduce individual injustices by the prodigality of increases in nominal salaries, is condemned to failure because it generates inflationary tensions, limits opportunities for employment, and mutilates the potential for savings and development. Our experience prior to the revolution of 1964 and similar experiences in other countries definitely refute this emotional distributivism."[10]

Let us assume, as those philosophers who have recently addressed themselves to the question to what extent production increases can justify inequality appear to have assumed, that views of the type expressed by President Geisel are at least sometimes partly sound. The question at issue, given this assumption, is how the sacrifice of other values for the sake of production is to be described. The candidates for preferred description may be classed as follows: (1) to say, as I have suggested, that both distributive justice and productive justice ought to be considered; (2) or, alternatively, to say that justice should be sacrificed in order to increase production, where it is thought that increasing production is not a moral obligation. Under this second option may be included descriptions that are substantially similar to (2), but which do not happen to use the word "production," such as, "for the sake of efficiency," "to maintain growth," "to conquer export markets," "to be realistic," "to attract investment," "to stimulate savings," and so on, and I am prepared to argue that the reason "to curb inflation" can also usually be included in this group. Or, (3) to say that justice should be sacrificed in order to increase production, where it is understood that increasing production is a moral obligation, but where it is thought that "justice" is not the proper name of that obligation. Here again the value that is weighed in the balance against distributive justice, and which at least to some extent outweighs it, may be expressed in various ways, provided only that its realization be thought of as a moral obligation.

[10]Ernesto Geisel, remarks to first cabinet meeting, 19 March 1974, mimeographed (Brasilia: Ministry of Foreign Affairs, 1974).

The principal advantage of employing the phrase "productive justice" is to recognize that there are plausible reasons, at least those mentioned in the preceding considerations, for considering production to be an obligation of justice, quite apart from the need to make sense out of the fact that it is frequently given as a reason for not doing what justice would otherwise oblige us to do. By duly recognizing production as an obligation in its own right, we can avoid being misleading in a most mischievous way, by suggesting that production gives us excuses for doing what would otherwise be unjust, but that it never puts us under an obligation to do what is just. The careful philosophical work done on the use of production increases to justify inequality by Marcus Singer, John Rawls, and Nicholas Rescher[11] may tempt one not to give due weight to the fact that many, if not most, proposals for reform are advocated on the grounds that they will have favorable effects both on distribution and on production, e.g., land reform and adult education, to name just two. It appears that the philosophers just mentioned have devoted their attention mostly to incentive systems, where inequalities spur production, and have not stressed what may be called privilege systems, where inequalities brake production.[12] If, on the other hand, we choose to say that justice should be abandoned as an ideal for nonmoral economic reasons, then we are in the awkward position of saying that what is just should not be done, and what is unjust should be done. Even if we do not fully agree with Richard Brandt when he writes, "It is not clear that we ever use 'acted unjustly' correctly, when we cannot also correctly say "acted wrongly,' "[13] we must at least recognize that respect for the law and for morality is seriously undermined when injustice is praised and advocated.

The remaining option raises the issue of the relationship between principles of justice and the wider category of moral rules. John Stuart Mill expressed widely held views when he wrote on this point: "Justice is a name for certain classes of moral rules, which concern the essentials of human well-being more nearly, and are therefore of more absolute obligation, than any other rule for the guidance of life; and the notion which we have found to be of the essence of the idea of justice, that of a right residing

[11]Marcus Singer, *Generalization in Ethics* (New York: Alfred A. Knopf, Inc., 1961). Singer proposes a maximin criterion at pp. 202–203. John Rawls, *A Theory of Justice* (Cambridge, Mass.: Belknap Press, 1971). Nicholas Rescher, *Distributive Justice* (Indianapolis, Ind.: The Bobbs-Merrill Co., Inc., 1966). See Rescher's "effective average" proposal in part 2, section 4.

[12]Rawls certainly holds that inequalities are unjust where they do not benefit the worst-off representative man (*A Theory of Justice*, passim), but his work does not stress the fact that many institutions, particularly in famine-prone parts of the world, should be condemned precisely because the inequalities cause inefficiency. In such a case the institutions are, on Rawls's theory, unjust, but if one adds this additional consideration, then the injustice is compounded; one might say that the sign remains unchanged but the magnitude increases.

[13]Richard B. Brandt, *Ethical Theory* (Englewood Cliffs, N.J.: Prentice-Hall, 1959), p. 410.

in an individual, implies and testifies to this more binding obligation."[14] If the nearness of its concern with the essentials of human well-being be the criterion, then the claim of production is superior to that of distribution. If the existence of rights residing in individuals be the criterion, then the claim óf production is similar to that of distribution, for in both cases famine victims are determinable individuals, who could be named, who have a right to claim that practices are unjust. They could perhaps also, in some cases, claim that their legal or customary rights have been violated, but the more general point concerns the existence of persons with legitimate claims to production and to distribution, which make it possible for them to say, on occasion, even that laws are unjust. One can take this view and still agree with Mill that benevolence is not a duty of justice, since one might well hold, e.g., that to be just, institutions must be framed so that the flow of goods produced is roughly (within suitable limits of tolerance) distributed according to merit, and so that production is sufficient that the goods distributed are not harmfully and avoidably few; and that there resides in a rather numerous class of determinable individuals the right to object on grounds of injustice to institutions that do not meet these conditions; and yet also hold that once property rights are vested in an individual A, pursuant to law and pursuant to legitimate expectations in a given cultural context, there is no individual B who has a right to claim that A has a duty to be benevolent toward B.

It has already been suggested that the word "justice" is an appropriate one where property is in question, and where the entity in the other pan of the scale is (distributive) justice. And if it be held to be a break with tradition to believe that the need to produce food is germane to the design of just institutions, then let it be remembered that at the head of those who have so believed stands Plato.[15]

Another widely held view, less ample than those of Mill and Plato, is that rules of justice may be distinguished from moral rules in general because they are those rules that require equal treatment. If the need for principles of productive justice be admitted, then the equal treatment view must be taken to be an incomplete one, insofar as institutions might fulfill the various requirements that derive from the notion of equal treatment,

[14]John Stuart Mill, *Utilitarianism,* Chap. V. In the Everyman edition (London and New York: Dent and Dutton, 1910), the words quoted are at p. 55.

[15]In *The Republic,* Plato finds it unprofitable to continue to seek the meaning of justice in terms of interpersonal relations, and tries to find justice "writ large" in the constitution of an ideal state. The needs of agriculture, defense, and other practical concerns enter into the construction of that state; and it is not surprising that Plato finds (*Republic* 433 ab) that justice is performing the function for which one's nature is best fitted. Gregory Vlastos, however, who is impressed, as many philosophers have been, by the close connection between justice and equality, appears to hold that Plato made a mistake, a mistake which is partly explained but not (apparently) excused, by taking *dikaiosyne* in a sense wider than that of justice (Vlastos, "Justice and Equality," p. 31, note 2).

and still provide only an equal, or properly proportioned, share of avoidable misery.

ON WHETHER PRODUCTIVE JUSTICE IS
DIFFERENT FROM DISTRIBUTIVE JUSTICE

Some persons may be inclined to understand the foregoing considerations not as reasons for seeking principles of productive justice, but rather as reasons for incorporating the requirements of production into standards of distributive justice. In other words, they may wish to hold that what is needed is not a new concept (productive justice), but merely the proper application of an old concept (distributive justice). One's reasons for agreeing or disagreeing with these hypothetical persons who hold that the concept of distributive justice provides an umbrella wide enough to take account of the obligation to produce, are likely to vary according to what meaning one assigns to the phrase "distributive justice," and accordingly I shall divide my effort to show that productive justice is different from distributive justice into several parts, corresponding to each of several meanings that are commonly given to the latter.[16]

The Aristotelian and Thomist tradition has it that distributive justice is a proportion, such that goods are distributed in proportion to merit.[17] If, for example, the criterion of merit is number of hours worked, then distributive justice requires that if A works two hours and B one hour, then A should be paid twice as much as B.[18] An example of this type shows that it is frequently plausible to equate productive and distributive justice, for if people are paid according to how long they work, then it seems reasonable to say both that production will be augmented (because workmen have an incentive to work long hours) and the rewards are just (because they are proportional to how much one works).[19] In order to show, as I wish to do, that distributive justice and productive justice are not the same,

[16]Note that the question is the same whether or not one defines justice wholly or partly by reference to what persons would agree to under fair conditions. On such a (Rawlsian) view, one asks whether those principles that would be agreed to under fair conditions can properly be described as only principles of distributive justice.

[17]For Aristotle see Book V of the *Nichomachean Ethics*. For St. Thomas see, for example, *Summa Theologica,* II, II, Q. 58, article 11. Merit (κατά ἄξιον) is, for Aristotle, a flexible term, and any number of personal characteristics can be taken to constitute merit. But for something to be a criterion of merit, that thing must be a characteristic of the person whose merit it is. Productive justice sometimes requires preferential treatment that is not premised on a person's characteristics, hence *a fortiori* not on his merits.

[18]St. Thomas uses this example. See his *Commentary on the Nichomachean Ethics* (Chicago: Henry Regnery Co., 1964), Section 941.

[19]If some workmen work harder in an hour or get more done in less time, then the criterion of merit can be adjusted to count harder or better work as more meritorious, in such a way that it will remain plausible to say that distributive and productive justice are identical.

it would suffice to exhibit a case in which distributive justice requires one result and productive justice another. Superficially, at least, it appears that such cases abound, for it is common for leaders of developing countries to say that it is regrettably necessary to postpone considerations of distributive justice in order to stimulate economic growth. For purposes of analysis, however, let us assume a single case, in which the facts are stipulated. Much of the arable land of Nicaragua is devoted to natural pasture for cattle, producing 10 kilos of protein per hectare per year, protein which is consumed in the form of beef by that small portion of the population that can afford it. There is an obvious distributive injustice here, for it is not fair that some eat meat while others starve. But this is not the injustice to which I wish to draw attention. My point concerns the need to change production goals and techniques. It turns out to be the case, let us stipulate, that the only way to feed the population is to produce protein-rich legumes and grains, at a rate of 100 kilos of protein per hectare per year. And it turns out to be the case that the only feasible way to do that is to increase the rewards of cultivators, and decrease those of ranchers.

In such a case, the merits of cultivators and ranchers may be, for all we know, the same, but productive justice requires that the former be rewarded. This might be true even if (*per impossibile*) the change from 10 to 100 kilos of protein per hectare were accompanied by an egalitarian social revolution, such that everyone's material rewards were the same, for it might still be a necessary condition of feeding the population that esteem or other nonmaterial rewards be accorded to possessors of cultivating skills, to the detriment of possessors of ranching skills. Under such circumstances, distributive justice calls for equal treatment, while productive justice requires preferential treatment.[20] It follows that productive justice cannot be subsumed under the rubric of distributive justice, where the latter is defined as distribution proportional to merit.

John Rawls may be taken as representative of a class of philosophers who do not emphasize the word "distributive," but who nonetheless treat of that concept of justice which applies "whenever there is an allotment of something rationally regarded as advantageous or disadvantageous."[21] Rawls sets out to solve Aristotle's problem (namely, that of just allotment), but he does not propose to solve it in Aristotle's way (he will not conclude

[20]To make the point more sharply, one can suppose that ten years ago the people of Nicaragua could be fed by letting cattle graze on natural pastures. Population growth and climatic variations have now changed circumstances, while the relevant characteristics of the persons concerned (ranchers and cultivators) have not changed. These suppositions make it easy to focus on the point that preference for cultivators is premised on circumstances independent of their personal characteristics.

[21]Rawls, *A Theory of Justice*, p. 7.

that distribution should be according to merit). It might be further observed that Rawls follows in Aristotle's footsteps in the respect that he addresses himself to the question, under what circumstances can one justify departure from the standard of equal distribution of goods—Aristotle's answer to that question being that it is justified when merit is unequal, and Rawls's answer being that it is justified when inequality benefits everyone, including those worst off.[22] It is a noteworthy feature of Rawls's position that the best off need demonstrate no merit in order for it to be just that they receive a more-than-equal share. It suffices that their having more in fact leads through some sequence of causal relationships to benefit for the worst off. It follows that productive considerations which represent necessary conditions for benefiting the worst off (or, for that matter, for benefiting anybody at all) must enter into Rawls's criteria for the allotment of advantages. Rawls has a good reason, therefore, for not emphasizing the word "distributive," for his theory of justice in fact calls for a combination of distributive and productive justice.

One might, no doubt, decide to broaden the scope of the phrase "distributive justice" so that it is simply a name for whatever pattern of property distribution ought to obtain. On such a view, whatever might be the proper inputs to the decision-making process, the name of the output would be "distributive justice." I have already said enough to make it unnecessary to repeat my reasons for believing that to decide to use the phrase in this way would neither accord with ordinary usage, nor respect tradition, nor illuminate the issues at stake. Here I shall add that even if the unwise decision to use the phrase in this broad and somewhat amorphous way were taken, productive justice would still refer to something above and beyond distributive justice, if the duty to produce has implications not only for who should have what, but also for what people should do with property when they have it.

FURTHER IMPLICATIONS FOR THE WORLD
HUNGER PROBLEM

It is often observed that even if the population explosion could be brought under control, and even if the rich were to share their surplus with the poor, the world hunger problem would not be solved, because surpluses are not large enough to meet world needs. Such observations (sometimes abetted by the assumption that the population explosion cannot be brought under control) are used to justify apathy and inaction on the

---

[22]Rawls's theory is, of course, much more complicated than this, but a fuller account of his views here would not affect the point being made.

grounds that nothing can be done. They may even be used to claim that the rich should not share their food, on the ground that a world where some are rich and some are poor is better than a world where all are poor. But those who argue in this vein overlook productive justice completely. The point is not what would happen if we should share what we have— the point is what would happen if we should share what we can produce. It is possible production and not presently existing food supplies that sets the moral standard. And we need not think in terms of producing more artichokes, coffee, and tobacco, but rather in terms of producing more of those foods that most efficiently satisfy human nutritional requirements. Looking at the matter in this way, and taking a reasonably optimistic view of the population problem, there is every reason to believe that the world hunger problem can be solved, no reason for apathy, and no reason for inaction.[23]

Our thinking should not be limited only to what the United States could do if it should employ its agricultural potential, and in any event no one wants the poor nations to be forever dependent on the United States for their food supplies.[24] Within the poor countries themselves productive justice usually fares no better than distributive or social justice, and there is much to be done in the areas of reducing waste, inefficiency, and idleness.

These considerations suggest that the moral indignation that is expressed on food issues is frequently misplaced. It is not the starving child and the extravagant banquet that should awaken our moral sentiments, but the underutilized land, the unemployed work force, and the factories that are closed waiting for passenger car sales to pick up when they could be making tractors. We should retrain our sentiments so that we will be made indignant not by the effects, but by the causes. Our sentiments will then be more constructive, because they will be more likely to lead to actions that will solve the problem.

It is, of course, one thing to see what needs to be done on a physical level (e.g., soybeans need to be planted) and another thing to design the economic system that will organize cooperative effort so that what needs to be done will be done. As a first step, the study of economic systems should feature the evaluation of the economic performance of a society in terms of how well that society complies with the obligation to produce. To

[23]See John McHale, and Magda Cordell McHale, *Human Requirements, Supply Levels and Outer Bounds: A Framework for Thinking about the Planetary Bargain* (New York: The Aspen Institute for Humanistic Studies, 1975).

[24]On the other hand, in spite of the fact that it would be desirable for the poor countries to attain self-sufficiency in food supplies, it may be inevitable that to some extent North America and Australia will always be the granaries of the world, for the geographical reason that those locations have the most good soil.

borrow a phrase from the field of operations research, an economy should be judged according to how closely slack variables (which represent unused resources) approach zero.[25]

On a political level, the concept of productive justice throws into relief a far-reaching implication of one of the main justifications of human inequality. If inequality is justified because it augments production, then it follows that production ought to be augmented. The same argument that makes it morally plausible to say that some should have more than others, adds weight to the claim that resources ought to be mobilized in order to satisfy human needs.

[25]In recent years, social scientists have become increasingly aware of the inadequacy of indices of the volume of economic transactions, such as Gross National Product, as measures of welfare, and they are seeking more accurate means of measuring the performance of an economy as an instrument for satisfying human needs and achieving the good life. See, for example, E.B. Sheldon and R. Parke, "Social Indicators," *Science,* 16 May 1975. A comparable movement is needed to measure more accurately the extent to which a society fails to mobilize productive resources. See, however, the sixth assumption in note 5 above.

JAMES RACHELS

Meat eating, Rachels argues, is immoral. The production of meat not only causes great animal suffering, it also wastes massive quantities of edible protein. This protein, if recovered, could ease the world food shortage.

1. How substantially do the dietary habits of the affluent nations contribute to the world food shortage?

2. Is Rachels arguing that we ought to be frugal with protein or that we ought to share it?

3. What effect would a meatless diet have on the Western economy? Is this a morally relevant consideration?

James Rachels is Professor of Philosophy at the University of Miami in Coral Gables, Florida. He has contributed articles on ethics to various philosophical journals and has served as the chairman of the Society for Philosophy and Public Affairs. His article, "Active and Passive Euthanasia" in The New England Journal of Medicine *(1975), was the subject of considerable discussion among doctors as well as philosophers.*

Vegetarianism and "The Other Weight Problem"

It is now common for newspapers and magazines to carry the ultimate indictment of glutted Americans: ads for weight salons or reducing schemes next to news accounts of starvation in Africa, Latin America, or elsewhere. The pictures of big-bellied children nursing on emptied breasts tell of the other "weight problem."[1]

This article has not been previously published.

[1]Colman McCarthy, "Would We Sacrifice to Aid the Starving?" *Miami Herald,* 28 July 1974, p. 2-L.

There are moral problems about what we eat, and about what we do with the food we control. In this essay I shall discuss some of these problems. One of my conclusions will be that it is morally wrong for us to eat meat. Many readers will find this implausible and even faintly ridiculous, as I once did. After all, meat eating is a normal, well-established part of our daily routines; people have always eaten meat; and many find it difficult even to conceive of what an alternate diet would be like. So it is not easy to take seriously the possibility that it might be wrong. Moreover, vegetarianism is commonly associated with Eastern religions whose tenets we do not accept, and with extravagant, unfounded claims about health. A quick perusal of vegetarian literature might confirm the impression that it is all a crackpot business: tracts have titles like "Victory Through Vegetables" and promise that if one will only keep to a meatless diet one will have perfect health and be filled with wisdom. Of course we can ignore this kind of nonsense. However, there are other arguments for vegetarianism that must be taken seriously. One such argument, which has recently enjoyed wide support, has to do with the world food shortage. I will take up that argument after a few preliminaries.

I

According to the United Nations Food and Agriculture Organization, about 15,000 people die of malnutrition every day—10,000 of them are children. Millions more do not die but lead miserable lives constantly on the verge of starvation. Hunger is concentrated in poor, underdeveloped countries, out of sight of the 70 million Americans who are overweight from eating too much.

Of course, there is some malnutrition in the United States—a conservative estimate is that 40 million Americans are poor enough to qualify for assistance under the Federal Food Stamp Program, although fewer than half that number are actually helped. But it is easy to misinterpret this statistic: while many of these Americans don't get *enough* to eat, neither are they starving. They do not suffer the extreme deprivation that reduces one's life to nothing more than a continual desperate search for food. Moreover, even the milder degree of malnutrition is an embarrassing anomaly; we are not a poor country, especially not in food. We have an abundance of rich farmland which we use with astonishing efficiency. (Although in some important ways our use of land is very inefficient. I will come to that in a moment.) The "Foodgrain Yield" of American farms is about 3,050 pounds per acre. For comparison, we may note that only Japan does significantly better, with a yield of 4,500 pounds per acre; but in Japan 87 workers per 100 acres are needed to obtain this yield, while in the

United States only *one* worker per 100 acres is required![2] If some Americans do not get enough to eat, it is not because we lack the food.

It does not require a very sophisticated argument to show that, if we have an overabundance of food while others are starving, we should not waste our surplus but make it available to those who need it. Studies indicate that the average American family throws out with the garbage about 10 percent of the food it buys.[3] Of course, it would be impractical for us to try to package up our leftover beans and potatoes at the end of each meal and send them off to the poor. But it would not be impractical for us to buy somewhat less, and contribute the leftover money to agencies that would then purchase the food we did not buy and deliver it to those in need.

The argument may be put this way: First, suppose you are about to throw out a quantity of food which you are unable to use, when someone offers to take it down the street to a child who is starving. Clearly, it would be immoral for you to refuse this offer and insist that the food go into the garbage. Second, suppose it is proposed that you *not buy* the extra food, and instead give the money to provide for the child. Would it be any less immoral of you to refuse, and to continue to buy unneeded food to be discarded? The only important difference between the two cases is that by giving money, and not leftover food, better nourishment can be provided to the child more efficiently. Aside from some slight inconvenience—you would have to shop a bit more carefully—the change makes no difference to *your* interests at all. You end up with the same combination of food and money in each case. So, if it would be immoral to refuse to give the extra food to the child and insist on throwing it into the garbage, it is also immoral for us to buy and waste food when we could buy less and give the extra money for famine relief.

II

It is sometimes objected that famine-relief efforts are futile because the problems of overpopulation and underdevelopment in some parts of the world are insoluble. "Feed the starving millions," it is said, "and they will survive only to produce more starving millions. When the population in those poor, overcrowded countries has doubled, and then tripled, *then* there will be famine on a scale we have hardly dreamed of. What is needed in those countries is population control and the establishment of sound

[2]These figures are based on studies conducted in 1969–1971. They are from James Grant, "A New Development Strategy," *Foreign Policy,* 12 (1973).

[3]One such study is reported in *Time,* 26 January 1976, p. 8.

agricultural systems. But, unfortunately, given the religious, political, and educational situations in those countries, and the general cultural malaise produced by generations of ignorance and grinding poverty, these objectives are impossible to attain. So we have to face the fact that transfusions of food today, no matter how massive, only postpone the inevitable starvation and probably even make it worse."

It must be conceded that, *if* the situation really were this hopeless, then we would have no obligation to provide relief for those who are starving. We are not obligated to take steps that would do no good. What is wrong with this argument is that it paints too gloomy a picture of the possibilities. We have no conclusive evidence that the situation is hopeless. On the contrary, there is good reason to think that the problems can be solved. In China starvation is no longer a serious problem. That huge population is now adequately fed, whereas thirty years ago hunger was common. Apparently, Chinese agriculture is now established on a sound basis. Of course, this has been accomplished by a social regimentation and a denial of individual freedom that many of us find objectionable, and, in any case, Chinese-style regimentation cannot be expected in other countries. But this does not mean that there is no hope for other countries. In countries such as India, birth control programs can help. Contrary to what is popularly believed, such programs are not foredoomed to failure. During India's third "Five Year Plan" (1961–66) the birth rate in Bombay was reduced to only 27 per 1000 population, only a bit higher than the U.S. rate of 23 per 1000.[4] This was the best result in the country, but there were other hopeful signs as well: for example, during the same period the birth rate in a rural district of West Bengal dropped from 43 to 36 per 1000. Experts do not regard India's population problem as hopeless.

It is a disservice to the world's poor to represent the hunger problem as worse than it is; for, if the situation is made to appear hopeless, then people are liable to do nothing. Nick Eberstadt, of the Harvard Center for Population Studies, remarks that:

> Bangladesh is a case in point. The cameramen who photograph those living corpses for your evening consumption work hard to evoke a nation of unrecognizable monsters by the roadside. Unless you have been there, you would find it hard to imagine that the people of Bangladesh are friendly and energetic, and perhaps 95% of them get enough to get by. Or that Bangladesh has the richest cropland in the world, and that a well-guided aid program could help turn it from a famine center into one of the world's great breadbaskets. To most people in America the situation must look hopeless

[4]B. L. Raina, "India," in Bernard Berelson, ed., *Family Planning and Population Programs: A Review of World Developments* (Chicago: University of Chicago Press, 1966), pp. 111–22.

and our involvement, therefore, pointless. If the situation is so bad, why shouldn't we cut off our food and foreign aid to Bangladesh, and use it to save people who aren't going to die anyway?[5]

So, even if it is true that shipments of food *alone* will not solve the problems of famine, this does not mean that the problems cannot be solved. Short-term famine-relief efforts, together with longer-range population control programs and assistance to improve local agriculture, could greatly reduce, if not altogether eliminate, the tragedy of starvation.

III

I have already mentioned the waste of food thrown out with the garbage. That waste, as great as it is, is small in comparison to a different sort of waste which I want to describe now.

But first let me tell a little story. In this story, someone discovers a way of processing food so as to give it a radically new texture and taste. The processed food is no more nutritious than it was unprocessed, but people like the way it tastes, and it becomes very popular—so popular, in fact, that a great industry grows up and almost everyone comes to dine on it several times a week. There is only one catch: the conversion process is extremely wasteful. Seven-eighths of the food is destroyed by the process; so that in order to produce one pound of the processed food, eight pounds of unprocessed food are needed. This means that the new kind of food is relatively expensive and only people in the richer countries can afford to eat much of it. It also means that the process raises moral questions: Can it be right for some people to waste seven-eighths of their food resources, while millions of others are suffering from lack of food? If the waste of 10 percent of one's food is objectionable, the waste of 87.5 percent is more so.

In fact, we do use a process that is just this wasteful. The process works like this: First, we use our farmland to grow an enormous quantity of grain —many times the amount that we could consume, if we consumed it as grain or grain products. But we do not consume it in this form. Instead, we feed it to animals, and then we eat the animals. The process is staggeringly inefficient: we have to feed the animals eight pounds of protein in the form of grain to get back one pound in the form of meat, for a wastage of 87.5 percent. (This is the inefficient use of farmland that I referred to

[5]Nick Eberstadt, "Myths of the Food Crisis," *The New York Review of Books,* 19 February 1976, p. 32. Eberstadt's article contains a good survey of the problems involved in assessing the world food situation—how bad it is, or isn't. He concludes that the situation is bad, but not at all hopeless. See also various articles in Philip H. Abelson, ed., *Food: Politics, Economics, Nutrition and Research* (Washington, D.C.: American Association for the Advancement of Science, 1975).

earlier; farmland that could be producing eight pounds of "unprocessed" food produces only one pound "processed.")

Fully one-half of all the harvested agricultural land in the United States is planted with feed-crops. We feed 78 percent of all our grain to animals. This is the highest percentage of any country in the world; the Soviet Union, for example, uses only 28 percent of its grain in this way. The "conversion ratio" for beef cattle and veal calves is an astonishing *21 to 1*—that is, we feed these animals 21 pounds of protein in the form of grain to get back 1 pound in the form of meat. Other animals process protein more efficiently, so that the average conversion ratio is "only" 8 to 1. To see what this means for a single year, we may note that in 1968 we fed 20 million tons of protein to livestock (excluding dairy cattle), in return for which we got 2 million tons of protein in meat, for a net loss of 18 million tons. This loss, in the United States alone, was equal to 90 percent of the world's estimated protein deficit.[6]

If we did not waste grain in this manner, there would clearly be enough to feed everyone in the world quite comfortably. In 1972–1973, when the world food "shortage" was supposedly becoming acute, 632 pounds of grain was produced annually for every person on earth (500 pounds is enouth for adequate nourishment). This figure is actually *rising,* in spite of population growth; the comparable figure for 1960 was under 600.[7]

What reason is there to waste this incredible amount of food? Why raise and eat animals, instead of eating a portion of the grain ourselves and using the rest to relieve hunger? The meat we eat is no more nourishing than the grain the animals are fed. The only reason for preferring to eat meat is our enjoyment of its taste; but this is hardly a sufficient reason for wasting food that is desperately needed by people who are starving. It is as if one were to say to a hungry child: "I have eight times the food I need, but I can't let you have any of it, because I am going to use it all to make myself something really tasty."

This, then, is the argument for vegetarianism that I referred to at the beginning of this essay. If, in light of the world food situation, it is wrong for us to waste enormous quantities of food, then it is wrong for us to convert grain protein into meat protein as we do. And if we were to stop doing this, then most of us would have to become vegetarians of at least a qualified sort. I say "of a qualified sort" for two reasons. First, we could still eat fish. Since we do not raise fish by feeding them food that could be consumed by humans, there is no argument against eating fish comparable to this one against eating livestock. Second, there could still be a small

[6]The figures in this paragraph are from Frances Moore Lappé, *Diet for a Small Planet* (New York: Ballantine Books, Inc., 1971), part I. This book is an excellent primer on protein.

[7]Eberstadt, "Myths of the Food Crisis," p. 34.

amount of beef, pork, etc., produced without the use of feeds suitable for human consumption, and this argument would not rule out producing and eating that meat—but this would be such a small amount that it would not be available to most of us.

This argument against meat eating will be already familiar to many readers; it has been used in numerous books and in magazine and newspaper articles.[8] I am not certain, however, that it is an absolutely conclusive argument. For one thing, it may be that a mere *reduction* in the amount of meat we produce would release enough grain to feed the world's hungry. We are now wasting so much food in this way that it may not be necessary for us to stop wasting all of it, but only some of it; so we may be able to go on consuming a fair amount of meat without depriving anyone of food. If so, the argument from wasting food would not support vegetarianism, but only a simple decrease in our meat consumption, which is something entirely different. There is, however, another argument for vegetarianism which I think is conclusive. Unlike the argument from food wastage, this argument does not appeal to the interests of humans as grounds for opposition to meat eating. Instead, it appeals directly to the interests of the animals themselves. I now turn to that argument.

IV

The wrongness of cruelty to animals is often explained in terms of its effects on human beings. The idea seems to be that the animals' interests are not *themselves* morally important or worthy of protection, but, since cruelty to animals often has bad consequences for *humans,* it is wrong to make animals suffer. In legal writing, for example, cruelty to animals is included among the "victimless crimes," and the problem of justifying legal prohibitions is seen as comparable to justifying the prohibition of other behavior, such as homosexuality or the distribution of pornography, where no one (no human) is obviously hurt. Thus, Louis Schwartz says that, in prohibiting the torturing of animals:

> It is not the mistreated dog who is the ultimate object of concern ... Our concern is for the feelings of other human beings, a large proportion of whom, although accustomed to the slaughter of animals for food, readily identify themselves with a tortured dog or horse and respond with great sensitivity to its sufferings.[9]

[8] For example, in Lappé's *Diet for a Small Planet,* and in several of the articles anthologized in Catherine Lerza and Michael Jacobson, eds., *Food for People Not for Profit: A Sourcebook on the Food Crisis* (New York: Ballantine Books, Inc., 1975).

[9] Louis B. Schwartz, "Morals Offenses and the Model Penal Code," *Columbia Law Review,* 63 (1963); reprinted in Joel Feinberg and Hyman Gross, eds., *Philosophy of Law* (Encino, Calif.: Dickenson Publishing Company, Inc., 1975), p. 156.

Philosophers also adopt this attitude. Kant, for example, held that we have no direct duties to nonhuman animals. "The Categorical Imperative," the ultimate principle of morality, applies only to our dealings with humans:

> The practical imperative, therefore, is the following: Act so that you treat humanity, whether in your own person or in that of another, always as an end and never as a means only.[10]

And of other animals, Kant says:

> But so far as animals are concerned, we have no direct duties. Animals are not self-conscious, and are there merely as means to an end. That end is man.[11]

He adds that we should not be cruel to animals only because "He who is cruel to animals becomes hard also in his dealings with men."[12]

Surely this is unacceptable. Cruelty to animals ought to be opposed, not only because of the ancillary effects on humans, but because of the direct effects on the animals themselves. Animals that are tortured *suffer,* just as tortured humans suffer, and *that* is the primary reason why it is wrong. We object to torturing humans on a number of grounds, but the main one is that the victims suffer so. Insofar as nonhuman animals also suffer, we have the *same* reason to oppose torturing them, and it is indefensible to take the one suffering but not the other as grounds for objection.

Although cruelty to animals is wrong, it does not follow that we are never justified in inflicting pain on an animal. Sometimes we are justified in doing this, just as we are sometimes justified in inflicting pain on humans. It does follow, however, that there must be a *good reason* for causing the suffering, and if the suffering is great, the justifying reason must correspondingly powerful. As an example, consider the treatment of the civet cat, a highly intelligent and sociable animal. Civet cats are trapped and placed in small cages inside darkened sheds, where the temperature is kept up to 110° F by fires.[13] They are confined in this way until they finally die. What justifies this extraordinary mistreatment? These animals have the misfortune to produce a substance that is useful in the manufacture of perfume. Musk, which is scraped from their genitals once a day for as long as they can survive, makes the scent of perfume last a

[10]Immanuel Kant, *Foundations of the Metaphysics of Morals,* trans. Lewis White Beck (Indianapolis: The Bobbs-Merrill Co., Inc., 1959), p. 47.

[11]Immanuel Kant, *Lectures on Ethics,* trans. Louis Infield (New York: Harper Torchbooks, 1963), p. 239.

[12]Ibid., p. 240.

[13]Muriel the Lady Dowding, "Furs and Cosmetics: Too High a Price?" in Stanley and Roslind Godlovitch and John Harris, eds., *Animals, Men and Morals* (New York: Taplinger Publishing Co., Inc., 1972), p. 36.

bit longer after each application. (The heat increases their "production" of musk.) Here Kant's rule—"Animals are merely means to an end; that end is man"—is applied with a vengeance. To promote one of the most trivial interests we have, thousands of animals are tormented for their whole lives.

It is usually easy to persuade people that this use of animals is not justified, and that we have a moral duty not to support such cruelties by consuming their products. The argument is simple: Causing suffering is not justified unless there is a good reason; the production of perfume made with musk causes considerable suffering; our enjoyment of this product is not a good enough reason to justify causing that suffering; therefore, the use of animals in this way is wrong. At least my experience has been that, once people learn the facts about musk production, they come to regard using such products as morally objectionable. They are surprised to discover, however, that an exactly analogous argument can be given in connection with the use of animals as food. Animals that are raised and slaughtered for food also suffer, and our enjoyment of the way they taste is not a sufficient justification for mistreating them.

Most people radically underestimate the amount of suffering that is caused to animals who are raised and slaughtered for food.[14] They think, in a vague way, that slaughterhouses are cruel, and perhaps even that methods of slaughter ought to be made more humane. But after all, the visit to the slaughterhouse is a relatively brief episode in the animal's life; and beyond that, people imagine that the animals are treated well enough. Nothing could be further from the truth. Today the production of meat is Big Business, and the helpless animals are treated more as machines in a factory than as living creatures.

Veal calves, for example, spend their lives in pens too small to allow them to turn around or even to lie down comfortably—exercise toughens the muscles, which reduces the "quality" of the meat, and besides, allowing the animals adequate living space would be prohibitively expensive. In these pens the calves cannot perform such basic actions as grooming themselves, which they naturally desire to do, because there is not room for them to twist their heads around. It is clear that the calves miss their mothers, and like human infants they want something to suck: they can be seen trying vainly to suck the sides of their stalls. In order to keep their meat pale and tasty, they are fed a liquid diet deficient in both iron and roughage. Naturally they develop cravings for these things, because they need them. The calf's craving for iron is so strong that, if it is allowed to

---

[14]By far the best account of these cruelties is to be found in Chapter 3 of Peter Singer's *Animal Liberation* (New York: New York Review Books, 1975). I have drawn on Singer's work for the factual material in the following two paragraphs. *Animal Liberation* should be consulted for a thorough treatment of matters to which I can refer here only sketchily.

turn around, it will lick at its own urine, although calves normally find this repugnant. The tiny stall, which prevents the animal from turning, solves this "problem." The craving for roughage is especially strong since without it the animal cannot form a cud to chew. It cannot be given any straw for bedding, since the animal would be driven to eat it, and that would spoil the meat. For these animals the slaughterhouse is not an unpleasant end to an otherwise contented life. As terrifying as the process of slaughter is, for them it may actually be regarded as a merciful release.

Similar stories can be told about the treatment of other animals on which we dine. In order to "produce" animals by the millions, it is necessary to keep them crowded together in small spaces. Chickens are commonly kept eight or ten to a space smaller than a newspaper page. Unable to walk around or even stretch their wings—much less build a nest—the birds become vicious and attack one another. The problem is sometimes exacerbated because the birds are so crowded that, unable to move, their feet literally grow around the wire floors of the cages, anchoring them to the spot. An "anchored" bird cannot escape attack no matter how desperate it becomes. Mutilation of the animals is an efficient solution. To minimize the damage they can do to one another, the birds' beaks are cut off. The mutilation is painful, but probably not as painful as other sorts of mutilations that are routinely practiced. Cows are castrated, not to prevent the unnatural "vices" to which overcrowded chickens are prone, but because castrated cows put on more weight, and there is less danger of meat being "tainted" by male hormones.

> In Britain an anesthetic must be used, unless the animal is very young, but in America anesthetics are not in general use. The procedure is to pin the animal down, take a knife and slit the scrotum, exposing the testicles. You then grab each testicle in turn and pull on it, breaking the cord that attaches it; on older animals it may be necessary to cut the cord.[15]

It must be emphasized that the treatment I am describing—and I have hardly scratched the surface here—is not out of the ordinary. It is typical of the way that animals raised for food are treated, now that meat production is Big Business. As Peter Singer puts it, these are the sorts of things that happened to your dinner when it was still an animal.

What accounts for such cruelties? As for the meat producers, there is no reason to think they are unusually cruel men. They simply accept the common attitude expressed by Kant: "Animals are merely means to an end; that end is man." The cruel practices are adopted not because they are cruel but because they are efficient, given that one's only concern is to produce meat (and eggs) for humans as cheaply as possible. But clearly this

---

[15]Singer, *Animal Liberation,* p. 152.

use of animals is immoral if anything is. Since we can nourish ourselves very well without eating them, our *only reason* for doing all this to the animals is our enjoyment of the way they taste. And this will not even come close to justifying the cruelty.

V

Does this mean that we should stop eating meat? Such a conclusion will be hard for many people to accept. It is tempting to say: "What is objectionable is not *eating* the animals, but only making them suffer. Perhaps we ought to protest the way they are treated, and even work for better treatment of them. But it doesn't follow that we must stop eating them." This sounds plausible until you realize that it would be impossible to treat the animals decently and still produce meat in sufficient quantities to make it a normal part of our diets. As I have already remarked, cruel methods are used in the meat-production industry because such methods are economical; they enable the producers to market a product that people can afford. Humanely produced chicken, beef, and pork would be so expensive that only the very rich could afford them. (*Some* of the cruelties could be eliminated without too much expense—the cows could be given an anesthetic before castration, for example, even though this alone would mean a slight increase in the cost of beef. But others, such as overcrowding, could not be eliminated without really prohibitive cost.) So to work for better treatment for the animals would be to work for a situation in which most of us would *have* to adopt a vegetarian diet.

Still, there remains the interesting theoretical question: *If* meat could be produced humanely, without mistreating the animals prior to killing them painlessly, would there be anything wrong with it? The question is only of theoretical interest because the actual choice we face in the supermarket is whether to buy the remains of animals that are *not* treated humanely. Still, the question has some interest, and I want to make two comments about it.

First, it is a vexing issue whether animals have a "right to life" that is violated when we kill them for trivial purposes; but we should not simply assume until proven otherwise that they *don't* have such a right.[16] We assume that humans have a right to life—it would be wrong to murder a normal, healthy human even if it were done painlessly—and it is hard to think of any plausible rationale for granting this right to humans that does

[16]It is controversial among philosophers whether animals can have any rights at all. See various essays collected in Part IV of Tom Regan and Peter Singer, eds., *Animal Rights and Human Obligations* (Englewood Cliffs, N.J.: Prentice-Hall, 1976). My own defense of animal rights is given in "Do Animals Have a Right to Liberty?" pp. 205–223, and in "A Reply to VanDeVeer," pp. 230–32.

not also apply to other animals. Other animals live in communities, as do humans; they communicate with one another, and have ongoing social relationships; killing them disrupts lives that are perhaps not as complex, emotionally and intellectually, as our own, but that are nevertheless quite complicated. They suffer, and are capable of happiness as well as fear and distress, as we are. So what could be the rational basis for saying that we have a right to life, but that they don't? Or even more pointedly, what could be the rational basis for saying that a severely retarded human, who is inferior in every important respect to an intelligent animal, has a right to life but that the animal doesn't? Philosophers often treat such questions as "puzzles," assuming that there must be answers even if we are not clever enough to find them. I am suggesting that, on the contrary, there may not be any acceptable answers to these questions. If it seems, intuitively, that there *must* be some difference between us and the other animals which confers on us, but not them, a right to life, perhaps this intuition is mistaken. At the very least, the difficulty of answering such questions should make us hesitant about asserting that it is all right to kill animals, as long as we don't make them suffer, unless we are also willing to take seriously the possibility that it is all right to kill people, so long as we don't make them suffer.

Second, it is important to see the slaughter of animals for food as part of a larger pattern that characterizes our whole relationship with the nonhuman world. Animals are wrenched from their natural homes to be made objects of our entertainment in zoos, circuses, and rodeos. They are used in laboratories, not only for experiments that are themselves morally questionable,[17] but also in testing everything from shampoo to chemical weapons. They are killed so that their heads can be used as wall decorations, or their skins as ornamental clothing or rugs. Indeed, simply killing them for the fun of it is thought to be "sport."[18] This pattern of cruel exploitation flows naturally from the Kantian attitude that animals are nothing more than things to be used for our purposes. It is this whole attitude that must be opposed, and not merely its manifestation in our willingness to hurt the animals we eat. Once one rejects this attitude, and no longer regards the animals as disposable at one's whim, one ceases to think it all right to kill them, even painlessly, just for a snack.

But now let me return to the more immediate practical issue. The meat at the supermarket was not produced by humane methods. The animals whose flesh this meat once was were abused in ways similar to the ones

---

[17]See Singer, *Animal Liberation,* Chap. 2.

[18]It is sometimes said, in defense of "non-slob" hunting: "Killing for pleasure is wrong, but killing for food is all right." This won't do, since for those of us who are able to nourish ourselves without killing animals, killing them for food *is* a form of killing for pleasure, namely, the pleasures of the palate.

I have described. Millions of other animals are being treated in these ways now, and their flesh will soon appear in the markets. Should one support such practices by purchasing and consuming its products?

It is discouraging to realize that no animals will actually be helped simply by one person ceasing to eat meat. One consumer's behavior, by itself, cannot have a noticeable impact on an industry as vast as the meat business. However, it is important to see one's behavior in a wider context. There are already millions of vegetarians, and because they don't eat meat there *is* less cruelty than there otherwise would be. The question is whether one ought to side with that group, or with the carnivores whose practices cause the suffering. Compare the position of someone thinking about whether to buy slaves in the year 1820. He might reason as follows: "The whole practice of slavery is immoral, but I cannot help any of the poor slaves by keeping clear of it. If I don't buy these slaves, someone else will. One person's decision just can't by itself have any impact on such a vast business. So I may as well use slaves like everyone else." The first thing we notice is that this fellow was too pessimistic about the possibilities of a successful movement; but beyond that, there is something else wrong with his reasoning. If one really thinks that a social practice is immoral, that *in itself* is sufficient grounds for a refusal to participate. In 1848 Thoreau remarked that even if someone did not want to devote himself to the abolition movement, and actively oppose slavery, ". . . it is his duty, at least, to wash his hands of it, and, if he gives it no thought longer, not to give it practically his support."[19] In the case of slavery, this seems clear. If it seems less clear in the case of the cruel exploitation of nonhuman animals, perhaps it is because the Kantian attitude is so deeply entrenched in us.

VI

I have considered two arguments for vegetarianism: one appealing to the interests that humans have in conserving food resources, and the other appealing directly to the interests of the animals themselves. The latter, I think, is the more compelling argument, and in an important sense it is a deeper argument. Once its force is felt, any opposition to meat eating that is based only on considerations of food wastage will seem shallow in the same way that opposition to slavery is shallow if it is based only on economic considerations. Yet the second argument does in a way reinforce

[19]Henry David Thoreau, *Civil Disobedience* (1848).

the first one. In this case at least, the interests of humans and nonhumans coincide. By doing what we ought to do anyway—ceasing to exploit helpless animals—we would at the same time increase the food available for hungry people.

SELECTED READINGS

BOOKS

Brown, Lester R., with Erik P. Eckholm. *By Bread Alone.* New York: Praeger Publishers, Inc., 1974.

Brown, Peter G., and Henry Shue, eds. *Food Policy: U.S. Responsibility in the Life and Death Choices.* Forthcoming by Free Press.

Ehrlich, Paul. *The Population Bomb.* New York: Ballantine Books, Inc., 1971.

Lucas, George R., guest editor. *Soundings,* LIX, no. 1 (Spring 1976). A special issue on "World Famine and Lifeboat Ethics: Moral Dilemmas in the Formation of Public Policy."

Paddock, Paul, and William Paddock. *Famine—1975!* Boston: Little, Brown and Company, 1968.

Simon, Arthur. *Bread for the World.* New York: Paulist Press, 1975.

Simon, Arthur, and Paul Simon. *The Politics of World Hunger.* New York: Harper's Magazine Press, 1973.

ARTICLES

Brown, Lester, R. "To Avoid a Global Food Crisis." *Current* 167 (November 1974): 25–36.

Callahan, Daniel. "Doing Well by Doing Good: Garrett Hardin's 'Lifeboat Ethic'." *The Hastings Center Report* 4 (December 1974): 1–4.

Eberstadt, Nick. "Myths About Starvation." *The New York Review of Books* XXIII (19 February 1976): 32–37.

Fagley, Richard. "On Helping the Hungry." *The Christian Century* 84 (21 June 1971): 811–13.

———. "The World Is Hungry." *America* 118 (24 February 1968): 250–51.

"Food and Population: Thinking the Unthinkable." *Science News* 106 (30 November 1974): 340.

"Great American Guilt Market." *National Review* 26 (20 December 1974): 1444.

GREEN, WADE. "Triage." *New York Times Magazine,* 5 January 1975, pp. 9, 11, 44, 45, 51.

HARDIN, GARRETT. "Living on a Lifeboat." *Bioscience* 24, no. 10 (October 1974): 561–68.

———. "The Tragedy of the Commons." *Science* 162 (13 December 1968): 1243–48.

"Humane Intentions, Cruel Consequences." *Fortune* 91 (January 1975): 61–62.

LAPPE, FRANCES. "The Fat Get Fatter." *The Nation* 215 (20 October 1972): 404–405.

———. "The World Food Problem." *Commonweal* 99 (8 February 1974): 457–59.

MALLOY, MICHAEL. "Let 'Em Starve." *The National Observer,* 29 March 1975, pp. 1, 17.

McLAUGHIN, MARTIN. "Feeding the Unfed." *Commonweal* 100 (12 July 1974): 376–78.

NEUHAUS, RICHARD. "The Politics of Hunger." *Commonweal* 99 (8 February 1974): 460.

ROSENFELD, STEPHEN, "What Happened to 'America the Beneficent'?" *Saturday Review World* 1 (18 December 1973) 14, 16, 18, 19.

SHRIVER, DONALD W. JR. "Lifeboaters and Mainlanders: A Response." *Soundings* LIX (Summer 1976): 234–43.

SIMON, LAURENCE. "The Ethics of Triage." *Christian Century* 95 (8 January 1975): 12–15.

VERGHESE, PAUL. "Muddled Metaphors: An Asian Response to Garrett Hardin." *Soundings* LIX (Summer 1976): 244–49.